GRAPHIS DESIGN 98

GRAPHIS DESIGN 98

· ·

THE INTERNATIONAL ANNUAL OF DESIGN AND ILLUSTRATION

DAS INTERNATIONALE JAHRBUCH ÜBER DESIGN UND ILLUSTRATION

LE RÉPERTOIRE INTERNATIONAL DU DESIGN ET DE L'ILLUSTRATION

EDITED BY · HERAUSGEGEBEN VON · EDITÉ PAR:

B. MARTIN PEDERSEN

PUBLISHER AND CREATIVE DIRECTOR: B. MARTIN PEDERSEN

BOOK PUBLISHER: ROB DRASIN

EDITORS: CLARE HAYDEN, HEINKE JENSSEN

ASSOCIATE EDITORS: DANIEL IMAL, PEGGY CHAPMAN

ART DIRECTOR: JOHN JEHEBER

DESIGNER: JENNY FRANCIS

PHOTOGRAPHER: ALFREDO PARRAGA

GRAPHIS INC.

(OPPOSITE) ILLUSTRATOR: SANDRA HENDLER / CLIENT: USISKIN CONTEMPORARY ART

(COVER) PHOTO: CRAIG CUTLER

CONTENTS

INHALT

SOMMAIRE

REMARKS

WE EXTEND OUR HEARTFELT THANKS TO CON-TRIBUTORS THROUGHOUT THE WORLD WHO HAVE MADE IT POSSIBLE TO PUBLISH A WIDE AND INTERNATIONAL SPECTRUM OF THE BEST WORK IN THIS FIELD.

ENTRY INSTRUCTIONS FOR ALL GRAPHIS BOOKS MAY BE REQUESTED FROM:
GRAPHIS INC.
141 LEXINGTON AVENUE
NEW YORK, NY 10016-8193

ANMERKUNGEN

UNSER DANK GILT DEN EINSENDERN AUS ALLER WELT, DIE ES UNS DURCH IHRE BEI-TRÄGE ERMÖGLICHT HABEN, EIN BREITES, INTERNATIONALES SPEKTRUM DER BESTEN ARBEITEN ZU VERÖFFENTLICHEN.

TEILNAHMEBEDINGUNGEN FÜR DIE GRAPHIS-BÜCHER SIND ERHÄLTLICH BEIM:
GRAPHIS INC.
141 LEXINGTON AVENUE
NEW YORK, NY 10016-8193

ANNOTATIONS

TOUTE NOTRE RECONNAISSANCE VA AUX DE-SIGNERS DU MONDE ENTIER DONT LES ENVOIS NOUS ONT PERMIS DE CONSTITUER UN VASTE PANORAMA INTERNATIONAL DES MEILLEURES CRÉATIONS.

LES MODALITÉS D'INSCRIPTION PEUVENT ÊTRE OBTENUES AUPRÈS DE:
GRAPHIS INC.
141 LEXINGTON AVENUE
NEW YORK, NY 10016-8193

(OPPOSITE) DESIGN: VANDERSCHUIT STUDIO
(NEXT PAGE & PAGE 248) PHOTO: CRAIG CUTLER

COMMENTARIES

KOMMENTARE

COMMENTAIRES

FIN DE SIÉCLE DESIGN: AN INVENTORY AND RETROSPECTIVE TRIBUTE TO GIEDION

Once upon a time there were companies with clearly defined philosophies and designers entrusted with a mission for the welfare of the majority of people. There was an open job market, simple work tools conducive to harmony between hand and brain, and identifiable career paths, often within the same company. International forums and associations such as ICSID, ICOGRADA and IFI were created under the aegis of UNESCO to represent designers. Urbanization introduced new design specialties such as signage, environmental graphics, and corporate identity. Mechanization reigned and everyone found his niche. No one saw, or rather, no one wished to see the harbingers of the end of an era and the premises of another—the post-industrial era. Neither economists, nor politicians, nor designers saw the change coming. However, change had been brewing on the scene for a long time: the 1973 oil crisis, the decline of industrial zones in all European countries, the frightening ascendency of the computer (recall the crazy computer HAL, an "anagram" of IBM moved by one letter, in the Stanley Kubrick film "2001, Space Odyssey"), the anti-establishment protests of 1968, which extended from France to all of Europe, Japan's arrival among the major international players, and the fundamental transformations brought about by the miniaturization of components and new materials resulting in significant lifestyle changes. ● However, contrary to all expectations, the 1980s began with fanfare: financial speculation yielded far more fruitful results than manual labor, a craze for luxury signalled an economy surfing on quick profit, and a "star system" took over the field of design. The designer was no longer a missionary in service to Society; instead he became its standard, an outward sign of wealth. He became in himself a medium of communication. Every field was affected: architecture, product design, graphic design, fashion—each producing its own divas in whose shadow it was difficult for others to survive. ● This surface energy masked the absence of any analysis of these phenomena, and thus delayed development of a solution for these problems. At the end of the eighties, none of the problems had been dealt with; the nineties are the decade of the hangover and the year 2000 is rapidly approaching, with no apparent cause for optimism. ● As Ezio Manzini states in *Artefacts*, "The culture of modernity that we have known until now was born in a strong and simple world. Strong and simple were the objects that surrounded us, the space-time relationship, the hierarchy of values that explained our choices. Today, there is very little left of that world. We now live in a world that seems fluid, complex, unsettled and unpredictable." ● Giedeon died twice, mechanization lost power, and we evolved into a world both fluid and unknown, governed by a market economy whose effects could be seen, but not its outlines. The cards were shuffled and redealt, but it was still not possible to tell which hand was dealing or which hand was being played. ● Design, more than ever dependent on and in step with political economy, had to find new paths and new techniques which mirrored social forces. Designers became stewards of a new mission: that of helping to decode this new world. ● As the *Independent* stated in 1992, "Indeed it may be an aspect of the "fin de siècle" condition to discover that in our ideological vacuum, there is no refuge to be found in the past....Rather, we have to map new futures as we go, without the aid of transcendental visions." ● The new economic logic that took root in the mid- 1980s called out to the design professions. And even if accepting an ever-changing economy is not always easy, its challenging aspects should still be recognized: ● *The virtual: is a rose still a rose?* The prophetic image of Magritte's pipe, "this is not a pipe," has never been more timely. As Ezio Manzini states in *Artefacts*, "The notion of reality has always been connected to density, to weight, to material inertia. Thus, for many of us, a sense of ill-being and nostalgia for a lost world." ● One consequence of career transformations is a certain uncloistering of the creative professions that allows for greater and freer circulation in all areas of creative production. ● The evils that creative design careers suffer are well known. For far too long, designers have been trained according to the same model and in too great a quantity for a market which has shrunk. Architecture is one significant example of this phenomenon. The end of work as we know it, as dramatic as this may be in terms of economic, social and personal consequences, should lead to reflection on how to restructure work methods. An evolution in professional practices and qualifications will certainly also evolve. ● It is an understatement to say that the industrial world has changed. In most Western countries, industry, which was mostly manufactural after WWII, has become service-oriented. Yet, until now, designers have rarely looked toward "service design" and still over-concentrate on the product. Recently, however, design companies have shown the encouraging trend of diversifying into multimedia. The product-service balance will be a key element for future growth in the profession. ● *From cultural identity to cultural exception.* The issue of cultural identity is more European than American. How can a country remain itself within a union of fifteen others? France's reticence comes from a fear of Anglo-Saxon cultural colonization in French cinema, literature, language and the Internet as well as parts of its commercial market. All this has led to the very French idea of a "cultural exception." In the catalog of the London Design Museum's exhibit "National Characteristics in Design," Stephen Bayley wrote, "they [the French] couldn't really give up their own way of life. An obsession with film noir, Bogart, chewing gum and James Dean seems to be the real extent of American cultural imperialism. The French have struggled to go their own way. This struggle shows in the schizophrenia and idiosyncracy of their designs." ● The decline in associations and international design organizations has been a recurring problem over the last twenty years in most Western countries. An apparent lack of motivation on the part of young designers to invest themselves in the very associations that federate them should be analyzed in a positive light. It is time to offer new paths to solidarity. The Internet may be one of these paths, but it is not the only one. ● Contrary to what one might have expected, the big industrial firms created in the 1980s have long been perceived as an obstacle to design. Their structures and ways of operating leave little room for the special client-designer relationship. Nevertheless, these "mega-groups" are like the megalopolises in which we live: as soon as one looks past the massive scale, the space becomes fragmented into "villages." One no longer lives in London, for example, but in Chelsea, Islington or Chiswick. As Claude Braunstein, a French designer, writes, "I work in one of these companies as if I were working within the structure of a smaller company, with a small group of people working together on a project." ● *"Made in" or "Assembled in?"* It is increasingly difficult to know whether a product is made in France or merely assembled in France. Companies in the automobile industry, for example, subcontract the manufacture of their components to companies in several other countries. Only the final assembly is done locally. This creates problems in the areas of design coherence, the product's global appeal, the follow-through in the production process, and final respect for design. In the luxury goods industry, this is a fundamental issue because it is linked directly to a company's image and status. A brand name's legitimacy depends largely on the country from which it originates. ● *The imprisonment of designers.* Designers have long been wedged between their status as artists and as orchestra leaders, never knowing if they should appear before clients dressed in velvet beret and lavallière or in the gray businessman's suit. It remains to be seen whether this has changed much since the 1980s, a decade that allowed the two models to coexist. While the return of a decorative, baroque style has displeased more than one designer, it has at least lightened the atmosphere and changed client-designer relationships. The designer is neither a diva nor an engineer; he is essentially an agitator and a heckler, and if he is not, he cannot bring his client the "other perspective" expected of him. The world into which we have ventured, though often while backtracking, needs agitators to make sense out of seeing, touching and understanding. While designers are not the only people we need, they are nevertheless, major players.

FRANÇOISE JOLLANT KNEEBONE, A DESIGN HISTORIAN, HAS BEEN DIRECTOR OF THE *ECOLE CAMONDO* IN PARIS SINCE 1994. SHE HAS BEEN DIRECTOR OF DESIGN FOR LOUIS VUITTON, SERVED AS AN ARTISTIC ADVISER FOR THE MUSÉE DES ARTS DÉCORATIFS IN PARIS AND HAS BEEN RESPONSIBLE FOR NUMEROUS EXHIBITIONS AND EVENTS AT THE CENTRE GEORGES POMPIDOU.

. . . .

Es war einmal: Eine festumrissene Unternehmenslandschaft, hinsichtlich Praxis als auch Marktnische klar abgegrenzte Berufe, mit einer Mission betraute Designer zum höheren Wohl der Mehrheit, aktive und die besten Leute ihres Fachs an sich ziehende Berufsorganisationen, ein offener Arbeitsmarkt, in dem man risikolos zirkulieren konnte, einfache Werkzeuge, durch die Hand und Gehirn harmonierten und deren Handhabung dank der gewonnenen Erfahrung von einer Generation an die nächste vermittelt wurde, eine identifizierbare Berufsplanung, häufig innerhalb derselben Struktur. ● Mit Optimismus wurden das ICSID, das ICOGRADA und die IFI, Foren der Begegnung und Förderung, unter der Ägide der UNESCO gegründet, um die Stimme der Schaffenden auf internationaler Ebene zu vertreten. ● Die Urbanisation eröffnete neue Bereiche wie Beschilderung und Beschriftung, urbane Einrichtungen und Markenzeichen. ● Die Mechanisierung herrschte, und jeder fand da seinen Platz und kam auf seine Rechnung. ● Man sah oder vielmehr wollte nicht die Vorzeichen vom Ende einer Epoche und dem Beginn einer neuen sehen, der nachin dustriellen Ära. Weder die Ökonomen noch die Politiker noch die Designer sahen den Umschwung kommen. ● Dabei waren die Akteure des Wechsels schon seit langem auf der Bühne: die Ölkrise von 1973, der Zerfall riesiger Teile der Industrie in allen Ländern Europas, der gewaltige Aufstieg der Informatik, die Angst macht (man erinnert sich gewiss an den verrückten Computer aus Stanley Kubricks "2001: A Space Odyssey". Dieser Computer auf Abwegen hiess HAL, Anagramm für IBM, eine Verschiebung um jeweils einen Buchstaben), die von Frankreich aus auf ganz Europa übergreifenden Protestbewegungen der sechziger Jahre, der Eintritt Japans in den Kreis der Grossen, die grundlegenden Veränderungen im Produktdesign, welche die Miniaturisierung der Einzelteile und die neuen Materialien mit sich brachten, die tiefgreifenden Wandlungen in den Lebensstilen. ● Entgegen allen Erwartungen beginnen die achtziger Jahre mit einem Paukenschlag: die Industrie wird vom Ökonomischen überholt, die Früchte der Spekulation bringen mehr ein als jene der Arbeit, die Begeisterung für den Luxus ist Anzeichen einer Wirtschaft, die auf dem schnellen Profit surft, das "Starsystem" erfasst das Design: Der Designer ist kein Missionar im Dienste der Gesellschaft mehr, er ist deren Aushängeschild, das äussere Zeichen von Reichtum, er wird in sich selbst ein Kommunikationsmittel. Alle Richtungen sind davon betroffen: Architektur, Produktdesign, Graphik-Design, Mode bringen ihre Diven hervor, in deren Schatten es schwierig ist zu überleben. ● Diese Oberflächendynamik verdeckt in Wirklichkeit, dass es an einer Analyse der Phänomene fehlt, womit man sich der Lösung der Probleme entzieht, sie beträchtlich verzögert. ● Man hat die 80er Jahre hinter sich gelassen, ohne irgendetwas geregelt zu haben. Der Morgen nach dem Fest ist immer quälend: in den 90ern herrscht Katerstimmung. Das Jahr 2000 ist nah, aber noch immer sieht man keinen Silberstreifen am Horizont. ● «Die Kultur der Modernität, die wir bis jetzt gekannt haben, ist in einer festen und einfachen Welt entstanden, und einfach waren die Gegenstände um uns, das Raum-Zeit-Verhältnis, die Wertehierarchie, die unseren Entscheidungen zugrunde lag. Heute ist von dieser Welt kaum mehr etwas übrig. Wir leben jetzt in einer Welt, die schwer fassbar, vielschichtig, unbeständig und unvorhersehbar zu sein scheint (*Ezio Manzini, Artefacts*).» ● Giedion ist zweimal gestorben, die Mechanisierung hat ihre Herrschaft eingebüsst, und wir

befinden uns nun in einer schwer fassbaren, unbekannten Welt, bestimmt von einer Marktwirtschaft, deren Wirkungen wir erkennen, nicht aber deren Konturen. Die Karten sind gemischt und von neuem verteilt worden, wir erkennen aber noch nicht, wer gegeben hat, noch welches Spiel gespielt wird. ● Das Design, mehr denn je vom Ökonomischen und Politischen abhängig und damit verknüpft, muss neue Wege suchen, neue Formen der Praxis, die der sich abzeichnenden Gesellschaft angepasst sind. Die Designer sind von nun an Träger einer neuen Mission: Uns zu helfen, jene Welt zu entziffern. ● «Vielleicht besteht tatsächlich ein Aspekt des Fin-de-siécle-Zustandes in der Entdeckung, dass in unserem ideologischen Vakuum in der Vergangenheit keine Zuflucht zu finden ist... Wir müssen vielmehr neue Zukünfte entwerfen, ohne Hilfe von transzendentalen Wunschbildern (*The Independent, 1992*).» ● Die neue wirtschaftliche Logik, die im Verlauf des Jahrzehnts bestimmend geworden ist, fordert die Designberufe heraus. Und wenn der Wechsel unvermeidbar ist, muss man überall nach seinen positiven Aspekten Ausschau halten: ● Das Virtuelle: is a rose still a rose? Magrittes prophetisches Bild von der Pfeife, «Ceci n'est pas une pipe», ist aktueller denn je und diente vor kurzem als Werbeidee für Canada Dry. Die Wirklichkeit ist von nun an nicht mehr, was sie einmal war. «Der Begriff der Realität ist immer mit Dichte, Gewicht, materieller Trägheit verbunden worden. Daher, für viele von uns, ein Unbehagen und eine Sehnsucht nach einer verlorenen Welt (*Ezio Manzini, Artefacts*).» ● Der Wandel der Berufe, deren eine Folge die Aufhebung der Trennung zwischen den kreativen Berufen ist, erlaubt jetzt eine freiere Zirkulation auf allen Gebieten kreativen Schaffens. ● Der Untergang der Arbeit in ihrer bisherigen Form, so dramatisch er in seinen wirtschaftlichen, sozialen und persönlichen Folgen ist, muss zu einem Nachdenken über die Umgestaltung der Arbeitsweisen führen, zu einem Wandel der Qualifikationen und der Berufspraxis: Die Übel, an der die kreativen Berufe leiden, sind wohlbekannt: Zu lange hat man kreativ Tätige nach demselben Modell und in zu grosser Zahl ausgebildet, für einen Markt, der nicht nur nicht grösser, sondern im Gegenteil geschrumpft ist. Die Architektur ist in dieser Hinsicht ein bezeichnendes Beispiel. ● Zu sagen, die Welt der Industrie habe sich verändert, ist ein Euphemismus. In den meisten westlichen Ländern ist die Industrie, die nach dem zweiten Weltkrieg vor allem eine herstellende war, zu einem überwiegenden Teil zu einer Dienstleistungsindustrie geworden. Nun haben sich aber die Designer bis jetzt kaum dem Design im Bereich Dienstleistungen zugewandt und sind immer noch zu sehr auf das Produkt konzentriert. Von entscheidender Bedeutung für einen Zuwachs in diesen Berufen wird das Gleichgewicht Produkte-Dienstleistungen sein. Es lässt sich jedenfalls bei Design-Ateliers in letzter Zeit eine ermutigende Diversifikation Richtung Multimedia feststellen. ● Von der kulturellen Identität zum kulturellen Ausnahmefall. Die kulturelle Identität ist, ganz einfach aufgrund der Zusammensetzung Europas, eher eine europäische als amerikanische Frage. Wie bleibt man bei einer Hochzeit zu fünfzehnt man selbst? Frankreich ist wie Grossbritannien, aber in einer anderen Form, von dieser Verlagerung stark betroffen. Im Gegensatz zu diesem Land hat sein Zögern auch mit einer Furcht vor einer kulturellen Kolonisierung durch die angelsächsische Welt mit ihren Produkten zu tun: Kino, Literatur, Internet, aber auch Marktanteile, Verlust der Führungsrolle der französischen Sprache. Daher das sehr französische Konzept des «kulturellen

Ausnahmefalls». Über das französische Design schreibt Stephen Bayley im Katalog zur Ausstellung des Design Museum *National Characteristics in Design*: «...Sie könnten die eigene Lebensart nicht wirklich aufgeben. Der amerikanische Kulturimperialismus scheint sich in Wirklichkeit darauf zu beschränken, dass man vom Film noir, von Bogart, Kaugummi und James Dean besessen ist. Die Franzosen haben dafür gekämpft, ihren eigenen Weg zu gehen. Dieser Kampf zeigt sich in der Schizophrenie und Idiosynkrasie ihrer Designs.» ● In fast allen westlichen Ländern ist der Niedergang der Berufsverbände und der internationalen Design-Organisationen ein in den letzten zwanzig Jahren immer wiederkehrendes Problem gewesen. Auch hier muss die anscheinend nachlassende Motivation der jungen Designer, sich für die Verbände, in denen sie zusammengeschlossen sind, einzusetzen, auf positive Weise analysiert werden. Es ist Zeit, neue Wege der Solidarität vorzuschlagen. Internet kann ein solcher Weg sein, ist aber nicht der einzige. ● Die grossen Industriegruppen, die seit den achtziger Jahren entstanden sind, hat man häufig als Hemmnis für ein Vordringen des Designs betrachtet, obwohl man ja das Gegenteil denken könnte. Ihre Strukturen und ihre Arbeitsweise bieten für die ideale Beziehung zwischen Designer und Kunden in der Tat nur wenig Raum. Es verhält sich jedoch mit diesen «Megagruppen» wie mit den Riesenstädten, in denen wir leben: Sobald das menschliche Mass verloren geht, sieht man, wie der Raum in «Dörfer» aufgeteilt wird. So lebt man zum Beispiel nicht in London, sondern in Chelsea, Islington oder Chiswick. Genauso, sagt Claude Braunstein, ein französischer Designer, der diese unternehmerischen Megastrukturen gut kennt, «arbeite ich innerhalb dieser Gruppen, wie mit einem kleinen oder mittleren Unternehmen, mit einer kleinen Gruppe von Leuten an einem Projekt». ● *Made in* oder *assembled in*? Zu wissen, ob ein Produkt *made in France* oder nur *assembled in France*

ist, wird immer schwieriger. Die Unternehmen, etwa in der Automobilindustrie, geben die Fertigung der Einzelteile in verschiedenen Ländern in Auftrag, nur die Endzusammensetzung erfolgt an einem Ort. Dies stellt einen vor das Problem der Kohärenz des Designs, der Geschlossenheit des Objekts, der fortlaufenden Kontrolle der Herstellung und der endgültigen Wahrung des Designs. In der Industrie für Luxusartikel ist diese Frage von grundlegender Bedeutung, denn Image und Status der Unternehmen stehen damit in engem Zusammenhang: Die Legitimierung einer Marke hängt zu einem grossen Teil vom Land ab, in dem sie ansässig ist. ● Auch Designer werden eingesperrt. Lange haben die Designer eingezwängt gelebt zwischen ihrer Stellung als Künstler und als Dirigent, nie recht wissend, ob sie sich ihren Kunden mit Kordsamtmütze und locker gebundenem Schal oder im grauen Anzug des seriösen leitenden Angestellten präsentieren sollen. Es ist nicht sicher, ob sie das jetzt hinter sich haben, aber die achtziger Jahre haben es möglich gemacht, dass beides nebeneinander besteht. Wohl hat die Wiederkehr des Dekorativen, des Stils, des Barocken nicht wenige in Wehklage ausbrechen lassen, es kommt ihr aber zumindest das Verdienst zu, dass die Atmosphäre lockerer geworden ist und sich die Beziehungen zwischen Kunde und Designer gewandelt haben. Der Designer ist weder eine Diva noch ein Ingenieur; er ist wesensgemäss ein Aufrührer, ein Unruhestifter, und wenn er das nicht ist, wird er nicht den «anderen Blick» mitbringen können, den der Kunde von ihm erwartet. Die Welt, die wir nun, häufig rückwärtsgewandt, betreten haben, braucht positive Unruhestifter, damit Sinn entsteht, den man erkennen, berühren und verstehen kann. Die Designer sind nicht die einzigen, die wir brauchen, aber Hauptakteure sind sie in jedem Fall. ● Red. Anmerkung: Siegfried Giedion (1888-1968) verfasste u.a. das viel beachtete Werk *Die Herrschaft der Mechanisierung*.

···

FRANÇOISE JOLLANT KNEEBONE, 1939 IN PARIS GEBOREN, IST SEIT 1994 DIREKTORIN DER ECOLE CAMONDO IN PARIS. SIE WAR UNTER ANDEREM BERATERIN FÜR DIE ABTEILUNG DES 20. JAHRHUNDERTS DES MUSÉE DES ARTS DÉCORATIFS IN PARIS SOWIE DESIGN-DIREKTORIN BEI LOUIS VUITTON UND HAT ZAHLREICHE AUSSTELLUNGEN UND VERANSTALTUNGEN FÜR DAS CENTRE GEORGES POMPIDOU IN PARIS ORGANISIERT. HEUTE BEFASST SICH FRANÇOISE JOLLANT KNEEBONE VOR ALLEM MIT DESIGN-THEORIE UND GESCHICHTE. SIE IST CHEVALIER DE L'ORDRE DES ARTS ET LETTRES UND FELLOW OF THE ROYAL SOCIETY OF ARTS.

···

Il était une fois un paysage d'entreprises aux contours définis, des professions bien cernées dans leurs pratiques comme dans leur niche de marché, des designers investis d'une mission pour le mieux-être du plus grand nombre, des organisations professionnelles actives et attirant le meilleur de la profession, un marché du travail ouvert, dans lequel on pouvait circuler sans risque, des outils de travail simples, qui conjuguaient harmonieusement la main et le cerveau, dont on transmettait la pratique par le fruit de l'expérience acquise d'une génération à la suivante, des plans de carrière indentifiables, souvent dans la même structure, dans l'optimisme, l'ICSID, l'ICOGRADA et l'IFI, forums de rencontres et de promotion, étaient créés sous l'égide de l'UNESCO pour porter internationalement la voix des créateurs, l'urbanisation ouvrait la voie à de nouveaux domaines comme la signalétique, le mobilier urbain, l'image de marque. La mécanisation était au pouvoir et chacun y trouvait sa place et son compte. ▲ On ne vit pas, ou plutôt on ne voulut pas voir les signes avant-coureurs de la fin d'une époque et les prémices d'une autre, l'ère postindustrielle. Ni les économistes, ni les politiques, ni les designers ne virent venir la mutation. ▲ Pourtant, les acteurs du changement étaient déjà en scène depuis longtemps: la crise pétrolière de 1973, la chute de pans entiers de l'industrie dans tous les pays d'Europe, la montée en puis-

sance de l'informatique, qui effraie – on se souvient de l'ordinateur fou du film de Stanley Kubrick «2001, odyssée de l'espace». Cet ordinateur déviant s'appelait HAL, anagramme d'IBM, à une lettre près –, les mouvements contestataires des années 68, qui, de France, s'étendent à l'Europe, l'arrivée du Japon dans la cour des grands, les mutations fondamentales que la miniaturisation des composants et les nouveaux matériaux allaient entraîner dans le design des produits, les mutations profondes des styles de vie. ▲ Or, contre toute attente, les années 80 commencent en fanfare: l'économique prend le pas sur l'industriel, le fruit de la spéculation rapporte plus que celui du travail, l'engouement pour le luxe est le signe d'une économie qui surfe sur le profit rapide, le «star-système» envahit le design: le designer n'est plus un missionnaire au service de la Société, il en est l'étendard, le signe extérieur de richesse, il devient un média de communication en lui-même. Toutes les disciplines sont touchées: l'architecture, le design de produits, le design graphique, la mode, produisent leurs divas, à l'ombre desquelles il est difficile de survivre. ▲ Ce dynamisme de surface masque en fait l'absence d'analyse des phénomènes, donc élude, retarde le plus possible la solution des problèmes. ▲ On sort des années 80 sans avoir rien réglé: les lendemains de fête sont toujours douloureux et les années 90 sont la décennie de la gueule de bois. A l'aube de l'an 2000, il n'y a toujours pas d'embellie en vue. ▲ «The culture of modernity that we have known until now was born in a strong and simple world. Strong and simple were the objects that surrounded us, the space-time relationship, the hierarchy of values that explained our choices. Today, there is very little left of that world. We now live in a world that seems fluid, complex, unsettled and unpredictable». Ezio Manzini, Artefacts. ▲ Giedion est mort deux fois, la mécanisation a perdu le pouvoir, et nous sommes désormais dans un monde fluide, inconnu, régi par une économie de marché dont nous voyons les effets, mais pas les contours. Les cartes ont été battues et redistribuées, mais nous ne voyons pas encore qui a la main ni quel jeu on joue. ▲ Le design, plus que jamais dépendant et solidaire de l'économique et du politique, doit trouver de nouvelles voies, de nouvelles pratiques adaptées à la Société qui se profile. Les designers sont désormais porteurs d'une nouvelle mission: celle de nous aider à déchiffrer ce monde-là. ▲ «Indeed it may be an aspect of the «fin de siècle» condition to discover that in our ideological vacuum, there is no refuge to be found in the past... Rather, we have to map new futures as we go, without the aid of transcendental visions». The Independent, 1992. ▲ La nouvelle logique économique qui s'est mise en place au cours de la décennie interpelle les professions du design. Et si on ne peut faire l'économie du changement, il faut en rechercher partout les aspects positifs: ▲ Le virtuel: is a rose still as rose? L'image prophétique de la pipe de Magritte, «ceci n'est pas une pipe» n'a jamais été plus d'actualité et, plus récemment, le slogan publicitaire du Canada dry. La réalité n'est désormais plus ce qu'elle était: «The notion of reality has always been connected to density, to weight, to material inertia. Thus, for many of us, an ill-being and nostalgia for a lost world». Ezio Manzini, Artefacts. ▲ La mutation des métiers, dont l'une des conséquences est le décloisonnement des métiers de la création, permet désormais de circuler plus librement dans tous les domaines de la création. ▲ La disparition du travail dans sa forme actuelle, pour dramatique qu'elle soit dans ses conséquences économiques, sociales et personnelles, doit pousser à une réflexion sur le repositionnement des modes de travail, et à une évolution des qualifications et de pratique professionnelle: les maux dont souffrent les métiers de la création sont bien connus: on a trop longtemps formé des créateurs sur le même modèle et en trop grand nombre, pour un marché qui non seulement ne s'est pas agrandi, mais s'est au contraire rétréci. L'architecture en est à cet égard un exemple significatif. ▲ C'est un euphémisme de dire que le monde industriel a changé. Dans la plupart des pays occidentaux, l'industrie, majoritairement manufacturière après la Seconde Guerre mondiale, est largement devenue une industrie de service. Or les designers se sont jusqu'à présent très peu tournés vers le design de services et sont encore trop concentrés sur le produit. L'équilibre produits-services sera un élément-clé de croissance de ces métiers. Toutefois, on constate une diversification encourageante récente de cabinets de design vers la création dans le domaine du multi-média. ▲ De l'identité culturelle à l'exception culturelle. La question de l'identité culturelle est plutôt européenne qu'américaine pour des raisons évidentes de constitution de l'Europe. Comment rester soi-même au sein d'un mariage à quinze? La France est, comme la Grande-Bretagne mais sous une forme différente, très affectée par ce glissement. Contrairement à celle-ci, ses réticences englobent la crainte d'une colonisation culturelle du monde anglo-saxon à travers ses productions: cinéma, littérature, Internet, mais aussi parts de marché, perte du leadership de la langue française. D'oĴ le concept très français de «l'exception culturelle». Du design français, Stephen Bayley écrit, dans le catalogue de l'exposition du Design museum «National Characteristics in Design»: «...They couldn't really give up their own way of life. An obsession with film noir, Bogart, chewing-gum and James Dean seems to be the real extent of American cultural imperialism. The French have struggled to go their own way. This struggle shows in the schizophrenia and idiosyncracy of their designs». ▲ Le déclin des associations professionnelles et des organisations internationales de design a été un problème récurrent des vingt dernières années dans la plupart des pays occidentaux. Là aussi, l'apparente démotivation des jeunes designers pour s'investir dans les associations qui les fédèrent doit être analysée de manière positive. Il est temps de proposer des voies nouvelles de solidarité. Internet peut être l'une d'elles, mais non la seule. ▲ Les grands groupes industriels qui se sont constitués depuis les années 80 ont souvent été perçus comme un obstacle à la pénétration du design, contrairement à ce que l'on pourrait penser. Leurs structures et leur mode de fonctionnement laissent en effet peu de place à la relation privilégiée client-designer. Toutefois, il en est de ces «méga-groupes» comme des mégalopoles dans lesquelles nous vivons: dès que se perd l'échelle humaine, on voit se fragmenter l'espace en «villages». Par exemple, on n'habite pas Londres, mais Chelsea, Islington ou Chiswick. De même, dit Claude Braunstein, designer français qui conna"t bien ces méga-structures d'entreprises, «je travaille au sein de ces groupes comme avec une PMI, avec un petit groupe de gens autour d'un projet». ▲ *Made in* ou *assembled in*»? Il est de plus en plus difficile de savoir si un produit est 'made in France' ou seulement 'assembled in France'. Les entreprises, comme l'industrie automobile, sous-traitent la fabrication de leurs composants dans plusieurs pays, seul l'assemblage final étant localisé. Cela pose le problème de la cohérence du design, de la globalité de l'objet, du suivi de fabrication et du respect final du design. Dans l'industrie du luxe, cette question est fondamentale, car liée à l'image et au statut des entreprises: la légitimité d'une marque tient en grande partie au pays dans lequel elle est assise. ▲ On emprisonne bien les designers. Les designers ont longtemps vécu coincés entre leur statut d'artiste et celui d'homme orchestre, ne sachant jamais s'ils devaient se présenter chez leurs clients avec le béret de velours et la lavallière, ou en costume gris du cadre sérieux. Il n'est pas sûr qu'ils en soient sortis, mais les années 80 ont permis de faire coexister les deux. Le retour du décoratif, du style, du baroque, s'il a fait hurler plus d'un, a au moins le mérite d'avoir allégé l'atmosphère et modifié les relations client-designer. Le designer n'est ni une diva, ni un ingénieur; il est par essence un agitateur, un perturbateur, et s'il ne l'est pas, il ne peut apporter à son client «l'autre regard» qu'on attend de lui. Le monde dans lequel nous sommes entrés, souvent à reculons, a besoin de perturbateurs positifs pour donner du sens à voir, à toucher et à comprendre. Si les designers ne sont pas les seuls dont nous avons besoin, ils sont, en tout cas, des acteurs majeurs.

FRANÇOISE JOLLANT KNEEBONE DIRIGE L'ÉCOLE CAMONDO DEPUIS 1994. DE SA MISSION EN TANT QUE CONSEILLER ARTISTIQUE POUR LE DÉPARTEMENT DU XXe SIÈCLE DU MUSÉE DES ARTS DÉCORATIFS À PARIS, EN PASSANT PAR CELLE DE DIRECTEUR DU DESIGN CHEZ LOUIS VUITTON, OU ENCORE RESPONSABLE DES NOMBREUSES EXPOSITIONS ET ÉVÉNEMENTS AU SEIN DU CENTRE GEORGES POMPIDOU, F. JOLLANT KNEEBONE SE POSE AUJOURD'HUI COMME UN DES THÉORICIENS ET HISTORIENS DU DESIGN.

Hideki Nakajima

Toshihiro Onimaru

Steve Sandstorm

Dale Frommelt

Jennifer Sterling

Neal Zimmermann

Olaf Stein

Jeff Larson

Glenn Tutssel

Jaimie Alexander

Ted Leonhardt

Yoshimaru Takahashi

BY RYNN WILLIAMS

The Best in Design

A multitude of choices fuels the creative process. Many of these are subtle, driven by little more than intuition–a certain texture, shape, or typeface just "works," while others seem dated, bland, or derivative. Other larger decisions–those concerning distribution perhaps, or positioning–can be more difficult, part of a more strategic evolution. But ultimately all these choices are crucial in the arduous task of creating a design which will stand head and shoulders above the rest. ●For GRAPHIS DESIGN 98, Graphis has tackled its own set of difficult decisions. From the hundreds of entries selected to represent the best in international design, we've chosen to highlight 13 projects from the various design categories including environmental design, exhibits, promotion, billboards, editorial, and brochures, as paragons of smart, practical, and innovative work. In talking to the people behind the scenes, we've tried to provide a glimmer of insight into the elusive creative process–into what kind of thinking takes a good idea, and makes it great.

Hideki Nakajima, *Cut* magazine

In his editorial work for the Japanese pop culture magazine *Cut* (pages 84-87), the Tokyo based designer Hideki Nakajima takes a firm stand against what he sees as the inundation of computer-based imagery. "I always make my typography letter by letter, and then take a photo of it," Nakajima says. "For editorial works, the budget is usually very limited, so I do not get some company to make them. The shooting is done at my office, which is very small. This usually lasts until midnight or very early morning. I try to cut costs that way and give my best effort to make something very special. I hope all these works will somehow express my opposition to the flooding of instant computer designs in the world now." The cover featuring the rock star Bjork, for instance, was typically simple: "The shooting took place in a hotel in Tokyo," Nakajima says. "We put a cloth on a wall, and it was done in 15 minutes. I brought strawberries for the shooting, since I heard that she liked them." For the Patricia Arquette cover Nakajima says he took a mirrored sphere, 40cm in diameter, to the roof, placed the letter 'A' on it, and shot it. "The color of blue is the reflection of the color of the sky," he says, adding, "since the sphere reflected all the surroundings, we had to find a very open space."

Dale Frommelt, Dale Frommelt Design

The similarity between cathedrals and art galleries wasn't lost on Dale Frommelt—both are spaces devoted to quiet contemplation. So when the Kansas City, Missouri-based designer was commissioned to create furniture (pages 192, 193) for an artist's penthouse that sits atop the Grand Arts gallery in Kansas City, he decided to fill the high ceilinged, gallery-white space with a bedroom suite that was gothic in feel. "It's all about looking up to the heavens," Frommelt says. Each of the four maple bedposts is a nod to the cathedral spire, he says, and in an effort to continue the airy, spire-like feeling "each is a form on its own that is cinched down on the mattress." On the other hand, the tables and chairs that Frommelt designed for the gallery itself are firmly rooted in practical considerations. "This is my first attempt to design a product that would be primarily made from recycled materials," Frommelt says, "and that could be broken down into basic elements and stored flat." These elements can also be recombined to create expanded sizes and shapes—"like Lego furniture." The chair is also equipped with a set of wheels that works like a fulcrum when tipped backwards, and retracts when placed in sitting position.

Olaf Stein, Factor Design

"Our goal is to convince the client that progressive and risky solutions can be successful," says Olaf Stein of Factor Design, the Hamburg-based design firm, "because they attract the attention of target groups. Without attracting the target groups in our crazy world, the money spent on design is wasted." And surely Römerturm Feinstpapier, a leading German paper manufacturer, feels its own investment well spent. Factor Design's swatch book system for Römerturm (page 173), *Die Kollectionen*, is an elegant but efficient system that holds 17 swatch books containing all the different paper lines, and one "overview" book with all the different colors and textures in chip form. "We developed one image, a printed sample that shows different printing techniques like four-color offset printing, hot foil stamping and blind embossing," Stein says. "It gives the user the opportunity to compare the same image on all the different papers." *Die Kollectionen* was either mailed out to prospective clients or presented by Römerturm consultants in ad agencies or design studios, Stein says, and for that reason the package can be carried using an integrated handle. "We, the people at Factor Design, are the target group of Römerturm too. So we developed something that we would like to have for our own."

Jaimie Alexander, Fitch Inc.

While trying to revamp the Hush Puppies image for the 1990s (page 169), there was a question as to whether to keep the cute little dog. "But we found that the dog was the most positive association the consumer had," says Jaime Alexander, art director at Fitch Inc., the Worthington-Ohio based firm that redesigned the packaging for Hush Puppies footwear. "So our goal was, just from an identity standpoint, to hold on to the dog and update the interpretation of it." The update included a whole new approach to children's packaging, "because we found that very little kids, even as young as four, influence what their parents buy for them," Alexander says. While the peekaboo hole in the end of the box came as a result of research that said it makes them more durable when taken on and off the shelves, "What we did was integrate it into the design so it kind of became a distinctive attribute of the brand." Sure, the new look was targeted to kids," but it's a little sophisticated to appeal to the parent too," Alexander says. "This is a case where often the packaging does get onto the retail floor—it was really designed to be a combination of functional packaging and display at the point-of-sale."

RYNN WILLIAMS IS A FREELANCE WRITER AND FORMER ASSOCIATE EDITOR OF GRAPHIS MAGAZINE

Toshihiro Onimaru, Graphics and Designing Inc.

Quiches and tarts are probably not the first thing that comes to mind when one thinks of Japanese cuisine. And while this may have been a stumbling block for Toshihiro Onimaru, art director of Graphics and Designing, Inc., in Tokyo, it also left him a wide open field when it came to creating letterhead (pages 97, 137) for G&D Management, Inc., an affiliate of the design company which manages the first "Quiche & Tart" cafe and restaurant in Japan. "Quiche and tart dishes by themselves have had low popularity in Japan, and in order to raise interest in them, I decided that illustration, rather than a photographic design would be most effective," Onimaru says. "Some people may say that this logo seems too classic, or even out-of-date. But the restaurant's concept is to serve a contemporary interpretation of homemade taste, and it seems necessary to express such a concept in a clearly visualized form." Onimaru shuns nostalgia, he says, and "decided to use lettering and a color palette that made sense to today's Japanese." With one restaurant now open in Tokyo and another one slated to open by the fall, Onimaru says G & D Management "gives us a good opportunity to manage and experiment with everything we design and produce."

Mark Crawford, Intralink Film Graphic Design

With billboard upon billboard lining the glitzy expanse of Hollywood's Sunset Strip, Mark Crawford and Anthony Goldschmidt, creative directors of Intralink Film Graphic Design, knew they needed something extra if their billboard for the high-action film "Twister" (page 155) was to grab the attention of the jaded passersby. "We thought it would be interesting to think along the lines of the damages," Crawford says, "and of what sort of force would have done that kind of damage." So instead of taking the expected route— a billboard, for instance, with an image of a tornado from the movie— Intralink constructed a structure with pieces of wood, tires, and metal sticking out of it, "as if a twister itself had come down Sunset Boulevard, as if it had picked up and thrown these objects through an existing billboard." Erected before the release of the movie, the three dimensional aspect of the billboard made it stand out, literally, from all the competition, Crawford says, and it also "evoked an emotion." The billboard is huge to start with, Crawford says, "but by showing the destruction, rather than the actual tornado, it made the viewer imagine something much larger than the billboard itself."

Jennifer Sterling, Jennifer Sterling Design

"Organization eliminates tedium," says Jennifer Sterling. So when the principal of San Francisco's Sterling Design set out to produce a self-promotion piece (pages 194, 195) two years ago, she modeled it on the binders that she puts together for each of her clients at the start of a job. "I wanted something that was typical of what I do for clients—a piece that would last awhile, that was modular and inexpensive, and that can be updated," she says. "This book separates into five sections, and I can arrange it in any order I want depending on the client I'm going after. If someone calls for annual reports, I'll put them all up front. A year from now I can take out pieces that no longer work for me." The flexible aluminum binder and accompanying metal business cards fit into a soft mesh carrying case. "I wanted to symbolize hard goods and soft goods," says Sterling, who recently started her own products company, featuring such items as aluminum Post-It notes ("I hated the all those yellow things sticking out of my books, she says.) Sterling's name and address, which run, subtly, along the edge of her stationery, are blind debossed.

This, she says, "is kind of indicative of my work. My work is rather quiet."

Jeff Larson, The Larson Group

The Larson Group is based in Rockford, Illinois, just west of Chicago, in an area that is heavily industrial. So while the opportunity was always there, says Jeff Larson, his design firm had tried to stay away from doing brochures for companies like Pearson Fastener, who specializes in screws (page 59). "They all look the same," Larson says, "heavy-handed and uninteresting." But this time the client called and said they knew what all the competition was doing, and they wanted to do something different. "It was a chance to show the product in its raw form and make it visually exciting." Larson concentrated on the graphically intriguing forms of the fasteners themselves, using very little copy." We went back to showing the end product and that really tells the story," he says. Also, since all parts are made in the US, the brochure featured photographs of the workers in the shop, which conveyed the message without having to spell it out with unnecessary verbiage. Larson also secured the embossed mat board cover to the fourteen pages of the brochure with Pearson Fasteners, which are raised to enhance their visual impact.

Ted Leonhardt, The Leonhardt Group

It makes sense that, when hired to design signage and way-finding systems for the outdoor goods retailer REI, The Leonhardt group came up with a system that looked like the trail markers one might find while out hiking in the woods (page 99). It makes even more sense when you learn that the newly opened REI flagship store in downtown Seattle measures over 80,000 square feet. "Considering the sheer size of the store, when we were doing the graphics, we had to make sure people knew where they were going," says Ted Leonhardt, president of the Seattle-based design firm. And rather than look like just another superstore, the new flagship "had to reflect the REI culture—especially concern with the environment," Leonhardt says. "So we tried to use materials that were either recycled or natural, things like wood, oxidized metal, and stone. The main sign is a big boulder with REI's logo sandblasted into it," Leonhardt says. Another Leonhardt-designed sign that got a lot of attention was, interestingly enough, the one for the women's restroom. "Instead of a woman's figure, skirted and just standing there, we had an active woman who was climbing — one leg up, arms swinging. But obviously there are state and federal regulations about this kind of thing, so we really had to push it through," Leonhardt says.

Steve Sandstrom, Sandstrom Design

Pavlov Productions, a division of the Sony Entertainment conglomerate that produces mostly television commercials, not only lacked a visual identity when Steve Sandstrom of Sandstrom Design signed on, it also lacked a name. "The folks at Sony, because of the motion picture studio, have tremendous special effects capabilities for their commercials, and what our client didn't want to do is come up with an identity that would only deliver technology as a look or feeling—'Oh, those are the effects guys'— because that's a pretty limiting place to be," says Sandstrom, creative director of the Portland, Oregon design firm. "Science was a way we could allude to it, but it's done in such a way that it's all kind of a joke." Not only is the scientific aspect of the company's new visual identity (pages 70, 71) rather tongue-in-cheek; a sense of naiveté pervades everything Pavlov, from business cards (which are perforated), to videotape labels (which were inspired by parking tickets). "All this is aimed at art directors, creative directors, copywriters, broadcast directors, and if our design is a little rough around the edges they know we did it on purpose. It's actually anti-graphic design. We've created forms that look like they might have been created in a laboratory, more in the world of government issue than in the world of style."

Yoshimaru Takahashi, *Ti* magazine

The visually arresting Japanese magazine *Ti* (pages 90, 91) is not just another commercial enterprise, according to Yoshimaru Takahashi, one of the five art directors that make up its editorial board. A project of the Japan Typographers Association, *Ti* is a non-profit, voluntary effort on the part of JTA members and supporters, whose monthly aim is to "communicate design excellence and thus spread enlightenment about what good design means," Takahashi says. From April 1995 to March 1996, the magazine focused "on the concept of literate culture. The underlying philosophy was that every element of literate culture is structured by the urban experience and communication design," Takahashi says. "Each month featured a special issue, which were stepping stones along the road to understanding. We viewed these editions as explorations into typography and communication design." Of course, too many cooks can sometimes make for a hectic kitchen, and even Takahashi will admit that "the individuality of the members presented a problem when it came to reaching a consensus in time to meet editorial deadlines. We got around this by rotating responsibility for separate issues of the magazine among each of the five members," which include Takahashi, Akio Okumura, Shinnosuke Sugisaki, Toshiyasu Nanbu, and Ken Miki.

Glenn Tutssel, Tutssels

To commemorate the 150th anniversary of Dewar's—makers of the world-renowned Scotch Whisky—Glenn Tutssel, creative director of the London-based design firm Tutssels, decided to mine some of Scotland's own nascent resources. Students at a number of the country's best design colleges took part in a competition to revamp the Dewar's decanter; the winning design was produced by art student Fiona Burnett (page 59). "The Dewar's anniversary decanter has been produced in a strictly limited edition of 1846 individually numbered pieces," Tutssel says. Burnett's design "is based on a traditional Scottish brooch and pin and mixes stylish cosmopolitan modernity with traditional Celtic motifs," says Tutssel. The commemorative decanter "uses high quality pewter metalwork for the brooch motif, which has been adapted to work as the casing at the top of the bottle. The pewter was dripped into enamel and the bottle shaped so that the curved tension of the bottle holds the clip tightly across the surface. Underneath there is a screw top," Tutssel says. Burnett's original drawing was slightly more decorative than the finished project, says Tutssel, and featured a hole in its center. The hole was unfeasible, he says, as the bottle wouldn't have been able to stand up. Instead, an opaque sandblasting effect was used to give the impression of a hole.

Neal Zimmermann, Zimmermann Crowe Design

"ZCD has worked with Levi's for years" says Neal Zimmermann, of the San Francisco-based design firm Zimmermann Crowe Design. Lately, they've been concentrating on the three-dimensional realm—retail shop concept designs, fixtures, and displays. Levi's Traditional and Western retail fixture program (page 115) was designed for "small town retailers and western retailers who respond to a traditional image of Levi's, not the racier, more urban image," Zimmermann says. The idea behind Levi's Heritage Shop was to promote Levi's as the originator of blue jeans and highlight the company's history. Because the stores are in Denver "We worked with an industrial WPA look," rather than with cowboy imagery "which is more associated with the Western consumer, not a jeans consumer" Zimmermann says. "The fun and uniqueness was in the personal distress of each sign, some were taken home by a guy from the sign shop and shot with a .38." Levi's Wide Leg fixture "incorporates imagery and a triangular element inspired by the logo, with hanging jeans to show the massiveness of the leg," Zimmermann says, and the earth-tones of the Americana display, designed for retailers during the summer Olympics in Atlanta, "were created to contrast to the red, white, and blue product offering."

EINE AUSWAHL DES BESTEN DESIGNS DES JAHRES VON RYNN WILLIAMS. RYNN WILLIAMS IST FREIE AUTORIN UND EHEMALIGE REDACTEURIN VON GRAPHIS.

Der kreative Prozess hat viele Facetten. Eine ganze Anzahl davon sind unauffällig und intuitiver Natur – eine bestimmte Oberflächenbeschaffenheit, Form oder Schrift «funktioniert» einfach, während andere Lösungen veraltet, fade oder abgenutzt wirken. Grössere Entscheidungen – z.B. hinsichtlich der Verteilung oder Positionierung – sind manchmal schwieriger und eher strategischer Natur. Im Endeffekt sind aber alle Aspekte wichtig, wenn ein Design unter anderen herausragen soll. ● Für *Graphis Design 98* hatte Graphis seine eigenen schwierigen Entscheidungen zu treffen. Aus Hunderten von Arbeiten, die als Beispiele des besten internationalen Designs ausgewählt wurden, haben wir 13 Projekte aus den verschiedenen Kategorien ausgesucht – Umweltdesign, Displays, Promotionen, Billboards, Editorial Design und Broschüren. Es sind kluge, praktische und innovative Designlösungen. In Gesprächen mit den Kreativen, die dahinter stehen, haben wir versucht, eine Vorstellung des kreativen Prozesses zu bekommen und herauszufinden, wie aus einer guten Idee ein grossartiges Endprodukt wurde.

Hideki Nakajima, Magazin *Cut*

In der Gestaltung der Seiten der japanischen Pop-Zeitschrift Cut (S. 84-87) manifestiert sich Hideki Nakajimas Abneigung gegen Computerdesign und die damit verbundene Überladung der Seiten. Nakajima ist Graphik-Designer und lebt und arbeitet in Tokio: «Das Budget für die Gestaltung von Zeitschriften ist gewöhnlich sehr klein, deshalb vergebe ich den Auftrag nicht ausser Haus. Die Aufnahmen werden in meinem Studio gemacht, und das ist winzig. Meistens dauert es bis Mitternacht oder bis in den frühen Morgen. Ich versuche, auf diese Weise Kosten zu sparen und trotzdem etwas Aussergewöhnliches zu machen. Ausserdem ist das mein Protest gegen die Flut von Computer Design, und ich hoffe, das kommt irgendwie zum Ausdruck.» Die Produktion des Umschlags, der den Rockstar Bjork zeigt, ist typisch für die unkomplizierte Arbeitsweise. «Die Aufnahmen wurden in einem Hotel in Tokio gemacht», sagt Nakajima. «Wir bedeckten eine Wand mit einem Tuch, und in 15 Minuten war alles vorbei. Ich hatte Erdbeeren mitgebracht, weil ich gehört hatte, dass sie sie gern mag.» Für den Umschlag mit Patricia Arquette platzierte Nakajima eine Kugel mit Spiegelglas (Durchmesser 40cm) auf dem Dach, setzte den Buchstaben A darauf und machte dann Aufnahmen. «Das Blau ist eine Reflexion der Farbe des Himmels», sagt er und fügt hinzu, «wir mussten einen freien Raum finden, weil sich natürlich alles in der Kugel spiegelt.»

Dale Frommelt, Dale Frommelt Design

Die Verwandtschaft zwischen Kathedralen und Galerien ist Dale Frommelt nicht entgangen - beides sind Orte stiller Kontemplation. Als der Designer aus Kansas City in Missouri den Auftrag erhielt, Möbel (S. 192, 193) für das über der Grand-Arts-Galerie in Kansas City gelegene Penthouse eines Künstlers zu entwerfen, beschloss er, in den hohen weissen Räumen ein Schlafzimmer im gothischen Stil einzurichten. «Alles, worauf es ankommt, ist der Blick hinauf in den Himmel. Jeder der vier Bettpfosten aus Marmor ist eine Anspielung auf den Turm einer Kathedrale», sagt Frommelt, und um das luftige Gefühl eines Turms noch zu verstärken, hat jeder «eine eigene Form und ist an der Matratze befestigt.» Andererseits sind die Tische und Stühle, die Frommelt für die Galerie selbst entworfen hat, das Ergebnis äusserst praktischer Überlegungen. «Es ist mein erster Versuch, ein Produkt zu entwerfen, das zum grössten Teil aus wiederverwertetem Material besteht und das man in einzele Grundteile zerlegen und flach lagern kann.» Diese Teile lassen sich auch neu zu grösseren Möbelstücken zusammensetzen – «es sind eine Art Lego-Möbel.» Der Stuhl ist mit Rädern ausgestattet, die wie ein Gelenk funktionieren, wenn man den Stuhl nach hinten kippt – in normaler Sitzposition verschwinden sie wieder.

Olaf Stein, Factor Design

«Unser Ziel ist es, den Kunden zu überzeugen, dass fortschrittliche, riskante Lösungen sehr erfolgreich sein können, weil sie Aufmerksamkeit bei den Zielgruppen erzeugen», sagt Olaf Stein von Factor Design in Hamburg. «Wenn man in unserer verrückten Welt die Zielgruppen nicht erreicht, ist das für Design ausgegebene Geld verschwendet.» Römertum Feinstpapier, ein führender Papierhersteller in Deutschland, findet, dass ihr Geld gut investiert ist. Das Musterbuch-System, «Die Kollektionen», das Factor Design für Römertum (S. 173) entworfen hat, ist ein elegantes und gleichzeitig sehr effizientes System, das 17 Musterbücher mit den verschiedenen Papiersorten enthält sowie ein Buch, das in Form kleiner Karten einen Überblick über die verschiedenen Farben und Qualitäten bietet. «Wir haben ein Bild eingesetzt, ein gedrucktes Beispiel, das die verschiedenen Drucktechniken wie Vierfarbendruck, Foliendruck und Blindprägung demonstriert», sagt Stein. «Es gibt dem Benutzer die Möglichkeit, das Bild auf den verschiedenen Papierqualitäten zu vergleichen.» Die Kollektion wurde gemäss Stein an potentielle Kunden verschickt und vom Aussendienst der Firma Werbeagenturen und Design-Studios präsentiert, weshalb die Kollektion mit einem integrierten Griff versehen wurde. «Factor Design gehört auch zur Zielgruppe von Römerturm, und wir haben deshalb etwas entwickelt, das ganz unseren eigenen Vorstellungen entspricht.»

Jaimie Alexander, Fitch Inc.

Als die Überarbeitung ihres Images für die 90er Jahre zur Debatte stand (S. 169), fragte man sich, ob man an dem niedlichen kleinen Hund festhalten solle. «Wir kamen zu dem Schluss, dass die mit dem Hund verbundenen Assoziationen der Konsumenten ausgesprochen positiv sind», sagt Jaime Alexander, Art Director von Fitch Inc, der Designfirma aus Worthington, Ohio, die die Verpackung für Hush Puppies (Schuhe) überarbeitete. «Was den Firmenauftritt anging, so wollten wir nur die Umsetzung des Hundes etwas auffrischen.» Die Verpackung der Kinderartikel wurde zum Beispiel völlig neu überarbeitet, weil «wir festgestellt hatten, dass Kinder, selbst wenn sie erst vier Jahre alt sind, mitbestimmen, was ihre Eltern für sie einkaufen», sagt Alexander. Während das Guckloch hinten an der Schachtel angebracht wurde, weil Untersuchungen gezeigt hatten, dass sie dadurch stabiler sind und dem ständigen Herausziehen und Zurückstellen besser standhält, «integrierten wir

es auf eine Weise in das Design, dass es zu einer Art Erkennungszeichen für die Marke wurde». Natürlich war der neue Look auf Kinder ausgerichtet, «aber er ist gleichzeitig anspruchsvoll, so dass er auch die Eltern anspricht», sagt Alexander. «Hier haben wir ein Produkt, dessen Verpackung oft in den Verkaufsräumen zu sehen ist – sie sollte deshalb eine Kombination einer funktionnellen Verpackung und eines Ladendisplays sein.»

Toshihiro Onimaru, Graphics and Designing Inc.

Man denkt nicht unbedingt an Quiches und Obsttorten, wenn von der japanischen Küche die Rede ist. Das mag die Aufgabe von Toshihiro Onimaru, Art Director von Graphics and Designing, Inc. in Tokio, nicht gerade erleichtert haben, aber es bot gleichzeitig grossen Spielraum, als er das Briefpapier (S. 97, 137) für G&D Management, Inc. entwarf. Es handelt sich dabei um eine Filiale der Designfirma, die das erste «Quiche & Tart»-Café und Restaurant in Japan führt. «Quiches und Torten ansich sind bei den Japanern nicht gerade populär, und um ihr Interesse zu wecken, beschloss ich, statt Photographie eine Illustration zu verwenden, von der ich mir eine grössere Wirkung versprach.», sagt Onimaru. «Einige Leute finden das Logo vielleicht zu klassisch oder sogar altmodisch. Aber das Konzept des Restaurants besteht darin, eine zeitgemässe Version hausgemachter Kuchen anzubieten, und es erschien mir unerlässlich, ein solches Konzept im Bild ganz klar auszudrücken.» Onimaru mag, wie er sagt, Nostalgisches nicht und «beschloss, eine Schrift und Farbpalette zu wählen, die den modernen Japanern entsprechen». Bisher gibt es ein Restaurant in Tokio und ein weiteres soll im Herbst eröffnet werden. G&D Management «gibt uns eine gute Gelegenheit, mit allem, was wir entwerfen und produzieren, zu experimentieren und Erfahrungen zu sammeln», sagt Onimaru in diesem Zusammenhang.

Mark Crawford, Intralink Film Graphic Design

Da sich an Hollywoods glitzerndem Sunset Strip Billboard an Billboard reiht, wussten Mark Crawford und Anthony Goldschmidt, Kreativ Direktoren von Intralink Film Graphic Design, dass sie etwas Besonderes brauchten, wenn ihr Billboard für den Action Film *Twister* (S. 155) die Aufmerksamkeit der übersättigten Passanten auf sich ziehen sollte. «Wir dachten, es sei vielleicht interessant, in Richtung der Verwüstungen zu denken», sagt Crawford, «und daran, welche Kräfte notwendig sind, um derartige Schäden anzurichten.» Statt also den üblichen Weg zu wählen – zum Beispiel ein Billboard mit einem Standbild aus dem Film, das einen Tornado zeigt –, konstruierte Intralink ein Gebilde, aus dem Holzstücke, Reifen und Metall herausragen, «als wenn ein Tornado auf dem Sunset Boulevard gewütet und diese Objekte in ein vorhandenes Billboard geschleudert hätte.» Das Billboard wurde noch vor dem Start des Films in den Kinos aufgestellt, und es ragte im wahrsten Sinne des Wortes aus den anderen Billboards heraus. «Und es wirkte auch emotional», sagt Crawford. Das Billboard an sich ist riesig, aber indem «die Zerstörung statt des Tornados selbst gezeigt wurde, wirkte das Billboard auf den Betrachter viel mächtiger als es eigentlich war.»

Jennifer Sterling, Jennifer Sterling Design

«Organisation verhindert Langeweile», sagt Jennifer Sterling. Als die Leiterin von Sterling Design in San Francisco sich vor zwei Jahren daran machte, eine Eigenwerbung zu konzipieren (S. 194, 195), dienten die Mappen, die sie bei jedem Auftrag für die Kunden zusammenstellt, als Vorbild. «Ich wollte etwas, dass typisch für das ist, was ich für die Kunden tue – etwas, das über längere Zeit brauchbar und preiswert ist und sich jederzeit anpassen lässt», sagt sie. «Der Katalog besteht aus fünf Kapiteln, und ich kann ihn zusammensetzen, wie ich will, je nach Art des Kunden, den ich anspreche *(auf Seite 210 fortgesetzt)*

GRAPHIS

DESIGN

NINETY-EIGHT

National Audubon Society 1995 Annual Report

1 2

Birds Wild life & Habitat

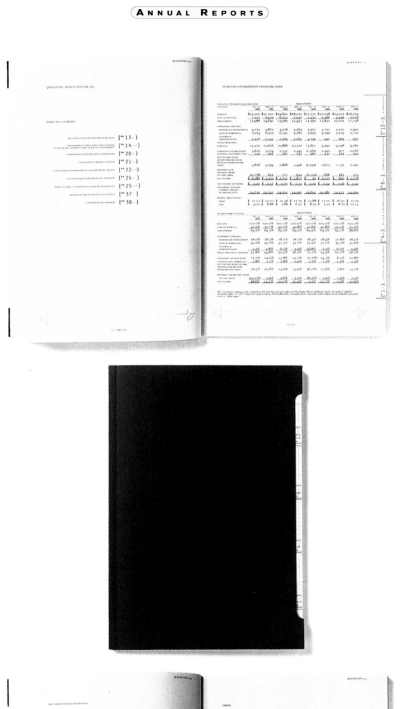

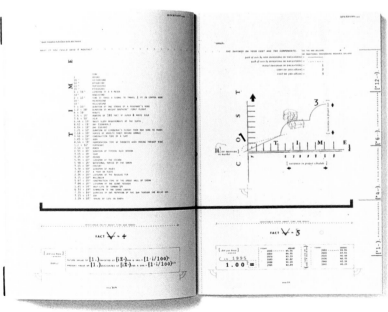

■ *3-5* **JENNIFER STERLING DESIGN** *Quickturn Design Systems Inc.*

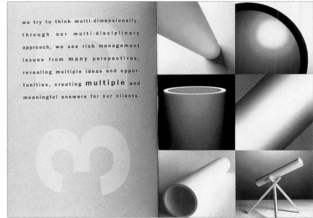

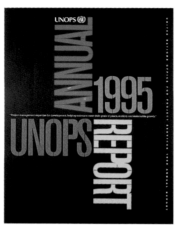

do not open

Experience + capacity = finding the best people

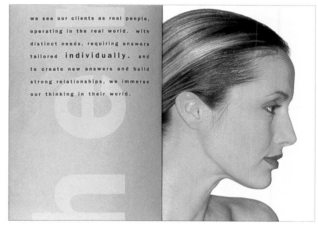

tapping a world of suppliers for quality and price

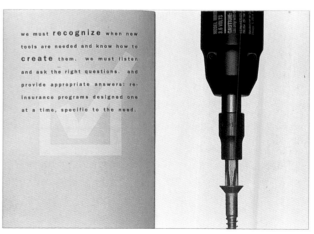

■ 6-9 **EMERSON, WAJDOWICZ STUDIOS** *United Nations Office for Project Services* ■ 10-13 **LEIMER CROSS DESIGN** *Zurich Reinsurance Centre, Inc.*

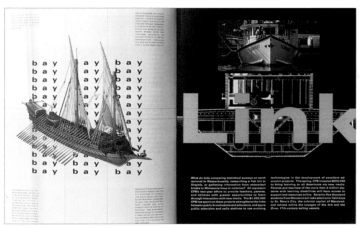

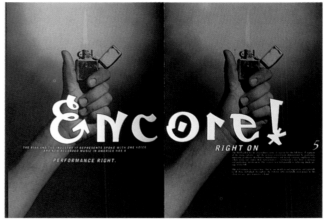

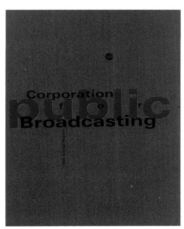

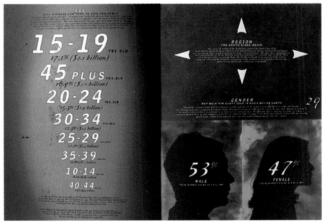

The radio station conducts a month-long series of weekly interviews on its magazine show, "Midweek," as part of *Beyond Survival*. It airs several interviews as local inserts in *Morning Edition* before their television broadcast. Producers repackage the television forum for radio broadcast. • The station develops a resource guide filled with information about **community programs** and names of those willing to serve as mentors. The station provides discussion and information about this project on television, radio, and online. • **Fish Kill** – "When students access data themselves they have ownership and a greater sense of accomplishment," says Susan Walton, a teacher at Peasley Middle School in Gloucester. WHRO provides Internet access to students in Ms. Walton's summer science class to help them study a fish kill in the York River. • The students collect water, test it, and compare it to information in *Bay Link*, an online database developed by The Virginia Institute of Marine Science, the College of William and Mary, Old Dominion University, and other educational institutions. The **children measure salinity**, change the water temperature, monitor fish mouth movements, and conclude that the fish die from lack of oxygen. • "This experiment was compelling to the children because we worked with real data on the Internet, thanks to the access WHRO provided," says Ms. Walton. "Their enthusiasm grew by leaps and bounds; they made hundreds of associations between this project and their own environment; they became natural investigators." • **You Sank My Battleship!** Simulating the Civil War naval battle between the *USS Monitor* and the *CSS Virginia* may seem like a new age video game, but it will soon be a part of *Bay Link*'s online museum of exhibits and instructive lessons. WHRO helps Mark Friedman, manager of information systems for the Mariners' Museum in Newport News, create an interactive web site for the museum on which visitors can

replay the historic battle between the turreted ironclads. "If we let a person steer the *Virginia*, he's going to be a little shocked at being checked at every turn by the *Monitor*," says Friedman. • Why? Friedman's simulation will show how the *Virginia*'s engine makes steering difficult, and how the amount of water the vessel draws slows the ship down and prevents it from going into the shallows like the *Monitor*. • Users will also see how the *Virginia*'s eight-cannon arsenal fares against the *Monitor*'s more limited firepower, and how the *Monitor*'s faster turret, and the fact that the *Virginia*'s cannons can only be fired one at a time, evens out the balance of power. • The mock battle ends in a draw as it does in history. But the real lesson isn't about who wins or loses, it's about understanding the "why" behind the battle. • **Middlesex Globetrotters** – You might easily imagine that students e-mailing messages to worldwide contacts and researching complex topics on the Internet would be in a media-savvy urban classroom. But the children at St. Clare Walker Middle School in Middlesex County, Virginia, involved in these technological tasks, are in an isolated location surrounded by nothing more than the rivers, tributaries, and creeks that flow into the Chesapeake Bay. • In Middlesex County, comprising 9,000 people, only three students out of a class of 30 might have a computer at home. WHRO and CPB are helping Karen Richardson, the seventh grade reading teacher at the school, teach these children about people and places far beyond their rural setting through Internet access in their classroom. • Her students will soon correspond with archaeologists working on Mayan ruins, unearthing information about artifacts and culture they've been studying. They will soon down load Civil War photos from the Library of Congress for a social studies unit. • Thanks to a CPB grant, Ms. Richardson's students will learn to create their own web pages and publish their work. "Their reading and writing skills improve as they are learning about geography or history," says Ms. Richardson. • She hopes to have students test and analyze water conditions to determine their effect on local oyster platforms, and record the findings online to help those in the community who fish the waterways.

■ *14-17* **MICHAEL GUNSELMAN INC.** *Corporation for Public Broadcasting* ■ *18-21* **RECORDING INDUSTRY ASSOCIATION OF AMERICA** *(in-house)*

|2   3|

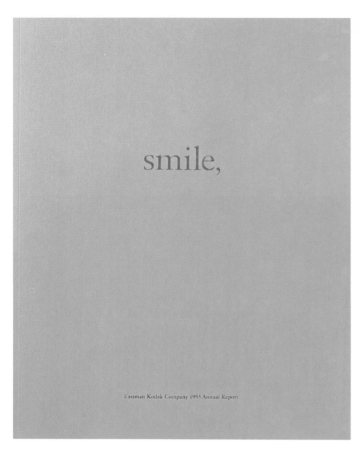

22 23

24 25

■ *22* **VSA PARTNERS, INC.** *Eastman Kodak Company* ■ *23* **EMERSON, WAJDOWICZ STUDIOS** *The Rockefeller Foundation*
■ *24* **ORIGIN DESIGN COMPANY LTD.** *Trans/Power New Zealand Ltd.* ■ *25* **URBAN OUTFITTERS** *(in-house)*

■ 26 JOHN BRODY DESIGN CONSULTANTS, INC. *Greater Pittsburgh Council, Boy Scouts of America*

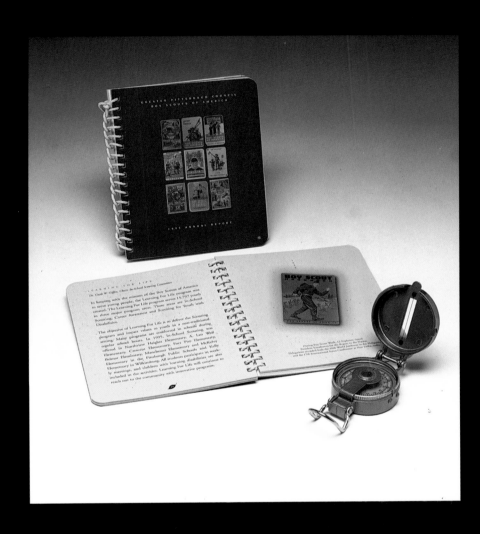

26

■ *27-30* **LEIMER CROSS DESIGN** *Expeditors International of Washington, Inc.*

31

32

■ *32* **DYE, VAN MOL AND LAWRENCE** *Middle Tennessee Council, Boy Scouts of America*

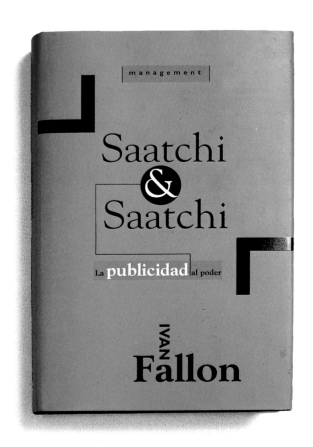

33 34

35 36

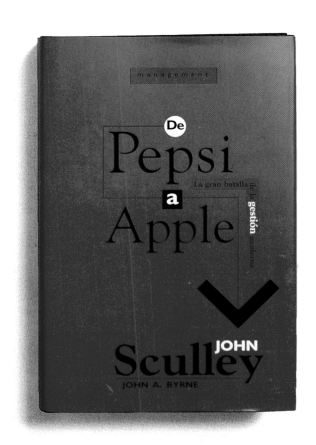

37   38

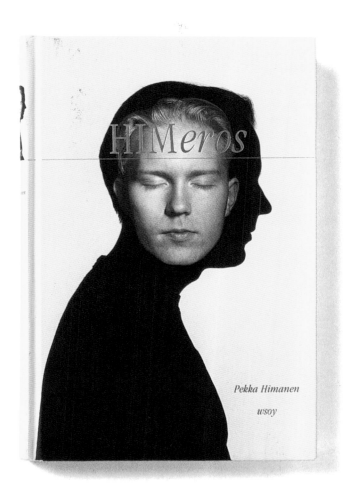

■ *39-42* **PENTAGRAM DESIGN INC.** *Monacelli Press*

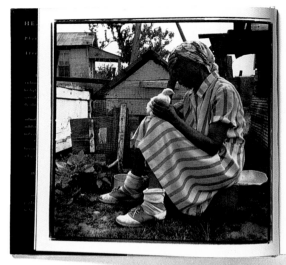

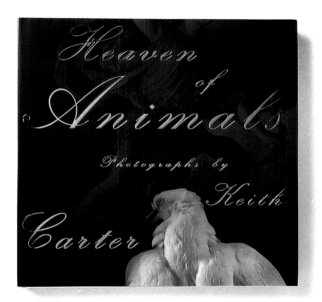

Sleeping Swan 1995

■ 43-48 **D. J. STOUT** *Rice University Press*

Parrot and Girl 1994

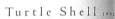

Turtle Shell 1992

46

47

48

Afterword

What's living, and what's dead? A string of lit, draped lamps hung on a line looks like a coven of Klansmen gathered for their own mass lynching ("Ghosts"). A party dress is hung on a wall, yet askew, as if there's an invisible inhabitant inside it, caught in the middle of a dance, right leg kicking high ("Jessamine's Gown"). His head turned to one side and out of focus in the background, a young boy holds a tortoise, shot from below in sharp focus, as if for sacrifice ("Turtle Shell"). A man and a boy stand before a fire; the man's expression conveys the knowledge of the adept (he may not like what he sees, but he knows he can do nothing about it), while the little boy, framed by the man's outstretched arms as a presumptive initiate, looks suspicious: What am I getting into ("Open Arms")? Shot from above, a bandanna is wrapped around a head, but a small tear looks like a bullet hole ("Star Bandanna").

Yet there is little menace in these pictures, and no hint of an artist seeking the weird, the damaged, the damned. Rather there is a sense of some grand, age-old ritual underway, with each figure in these pages—the living often looking toward death, the inanimate as likely caught in the postures of the animate—positioned to assume an appointed role. When the sun goes down (in some pictures), or when the sun comes up (in others), at some point well past the last page in the book, there will be resolution. Everyone and everything will remove masks, reclaim faces and bodies, and go back to ordinary life. You kind of hope so, at any rate.

49 50

■ 49 **DUFFY DESIGN** *Children's Defense Fund* ■ 50 **DUFFY DESIGN** *Heritage Press*

51

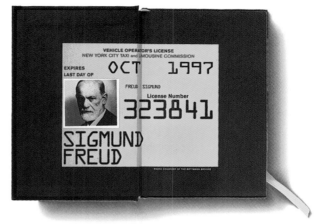

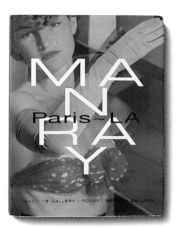

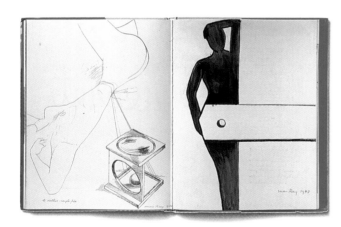

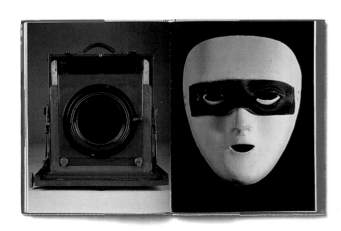

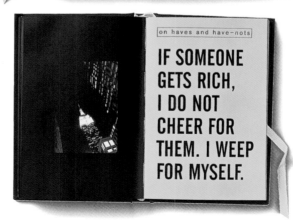

■ *52-55* **DESIGN & DIRECTION INC.** *Smart Art Press* ■ *56-59* **CHRONICLE BOOKS** *(in-house)*

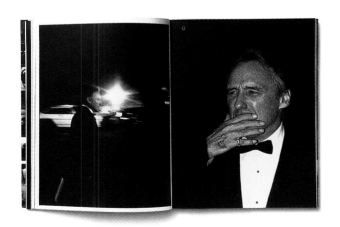

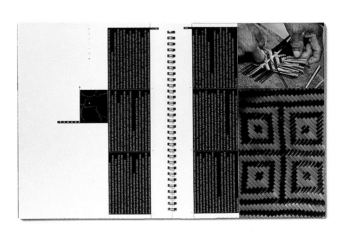

■ *60-63* **ARNELL GROUP** *Rapoport Printing* ■ *64-67* **EDUARDO CHUMACEIRO** *Casa Alejo Zuloaga, Fundación Polar*

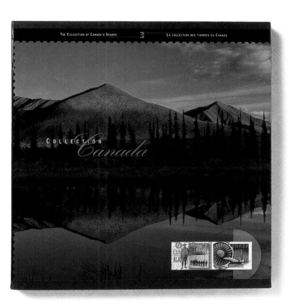

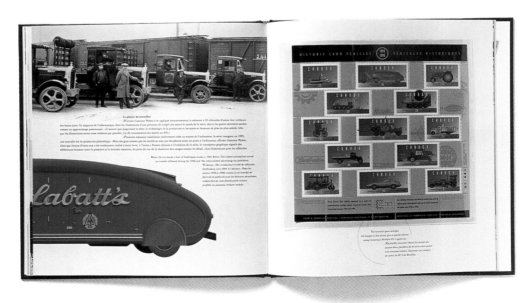

■ *68-70* **ESKIND WADDELL** *Canada Post Corporation*

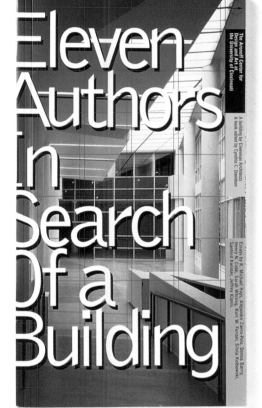

Eleven Authors In Search Of a Building

The Arnoff Center for Design and Art at the University of Cincinnati

A building by Eisenman Architects
A book edited by Cynthia C. Davidson

Essays by K. Michael Hays, Alejandro Zaera-Polo, Donna Barry, Henry N. Cobb, Sarah Whiting, Kurt W. Forster, Silvia Kolbowski, Sanford Kwinter, Jeffrey Kipnis.

71 72

YOU WORE THEM: IN THE CALIFORNIA GOLD MINES, DURING THE BOOM YEARS, DURING THE DEPRESSION, ON ASSEMBLY LINES, IN THE FIELDS, IN SMALL TOWN AMERICA, IN THE VAST URBAN SPRAWL, TO SCHOOL, TO GRADUATION, TO PROTEST, TO VOTE, TO WOODSTOCK, TO WOODSTOCK II, ON YOUR FIRST DATE, WHEN YOU BROKE UP, TO YOUR WEDDING, TO THE OFFICE, TO SURF THE INTERNET, WITH A CHANEL BLAZER, WITH A PLAIN WHITE T-SHIRT, IN THE WHITE HOUSE, TO FIT IN, TO STAND OUT, TO BE YOURSELF.

73

74

75

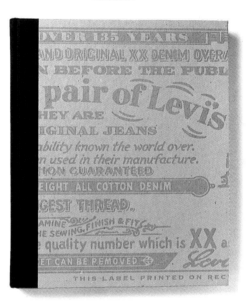

■ 73-78 **TURNER DUCKWORTH** *Levi Strauss & Co.*

Even,today, the Levi's brand finds itself in the most remote places on earth. This spread from Details Magazine, shows one such consumer in his preferred daily garb and his tribal raiment for visiting photographers.

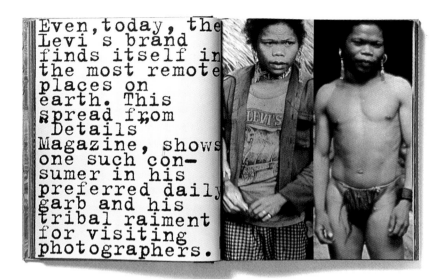

THE SIMPLE ACT OF PLACING A METAL RIVET IN THE CORNERS OF PANTS POCKETS REVOLUTIONIZED THE WAY WE WEAR CLOTHES. IT HAS BEEN MADE OF COPPER, OF NONDESCRIPT METAL WITH A COPPER WASH, AND EVEN IN BLUE AND HOT PINK. IT HAS BEEN HAND-POUNDED INTO DENIM AS TOUGH AS STEEL AND MACHINE APPLIED AT THE SPEED OF SOUND. IT'S EVEN BEEN REMOVED AND SUBSTITUTED WITH STITCHING. BUT NO MATTER WHAT IT HAS LOOKED LIKE, SINCE 1873, THE HUMBLE RIVET HAS ALWAYS PROUDLY PROCLAIMED ITSELF TO BE FROM "LS&CO. S.F."

79

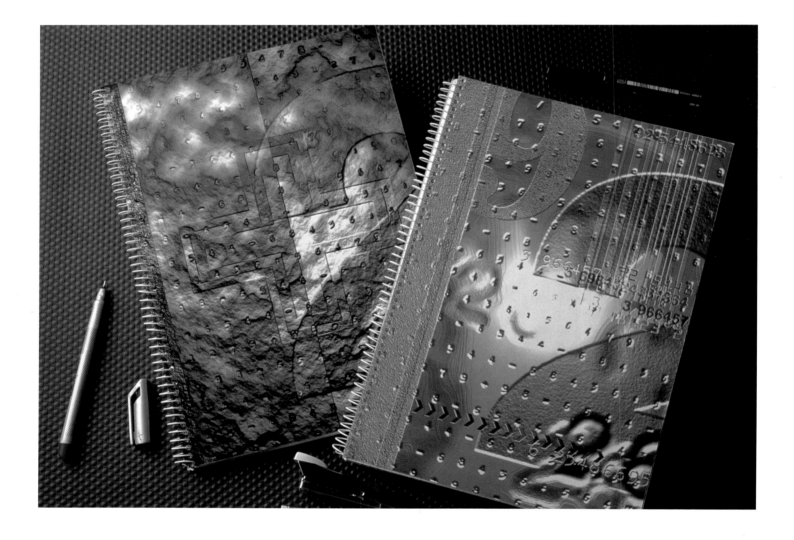

■ *79* **ART FORCE STUDIO** *Füzföi Papir Ltd.*

■ *80, 81* **LE PETIT DIDIER** *Arsenal/Yan Zoritchak*

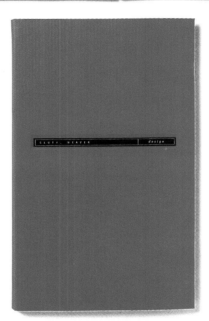

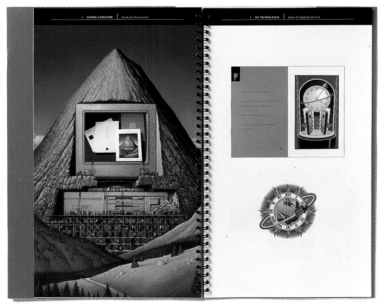

■ *82-84* **GLUTH WEAVER DESIGN** *(in-house)*

82

83

84

■ *85* EMERY VINCENT DESIGN *(in-house)*

■ *85* **EMERY VINCENT DESIGN** *(in-house)*

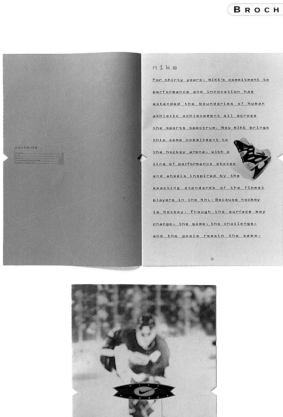

nike

For thirty years, NIKE's commitment to performance and innovation has extended the boundaries of human athletic achievement all across the sports spectrum. Now NIKE brings this same commitment to the hockey arena, with a line of performance skates and wheels inspired by the exacting standards of the finest players in the NHL. Because hockey is hockey. Though the surface may change, the game, the challenge, and the goals remain the same.

contents

MAYBE GREAT PRODUCTS AREN'T ABOUT BEAUTIFUL DESIGN

MAYBE GOOD DESIGN ISN'T PRETTY

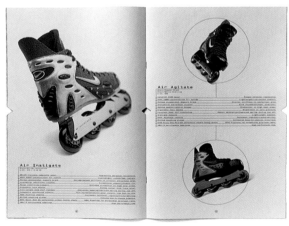

Air Agitate

Air Instigate

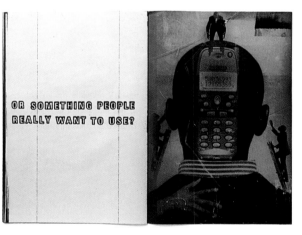

OR SOMETHING PEOPLE REALLY WANT TO USE?

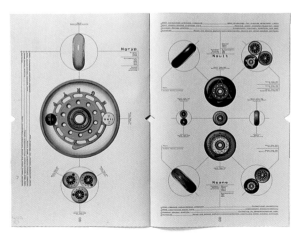

Ngryp

Nault

Nsane

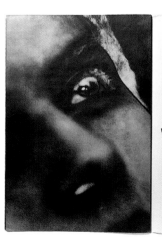

IS IT GOING TO BE SOMEBODY'S IDEA OF WHAT'S BEAUTIFUL?

■ 86-89 **NIKE IMAGE DESIGN** *Nike, Inc.* ■ 90-93 **CAHAN & ASSOCIATES** *GVO*

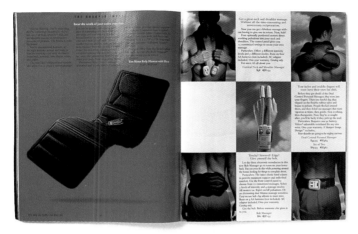 

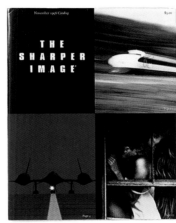 

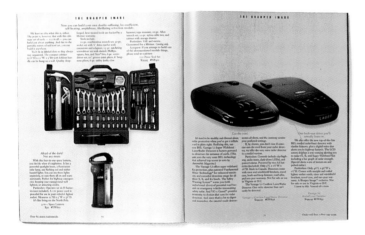 

■ *94-97* **GOODBY, SILVERSTEIN & PARTNERS** *The Sharper Image* ■ *98-101* **HEBE: WERBUNG & DESIGN** *(in-house)*

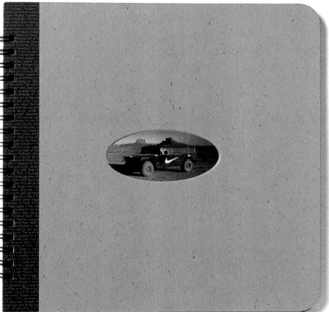

■ *102* **CIPRIANI KREMER DESIGN** *Lotus Corporation* ■ *103* **NIKE IMAGE DESIGN** *Nike, Inc.*

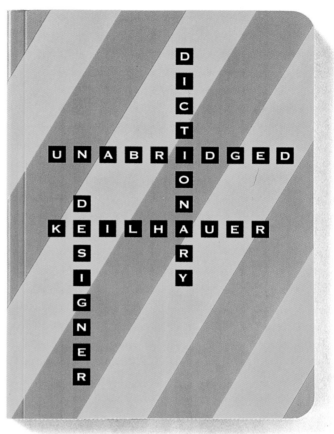

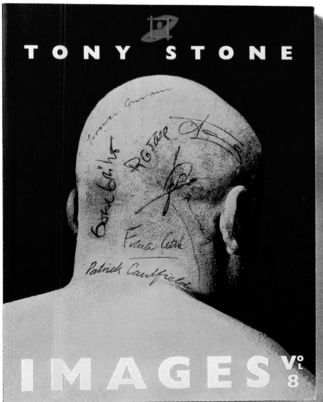

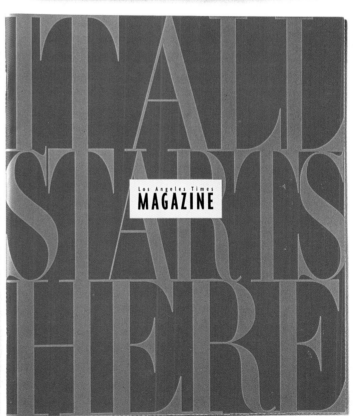

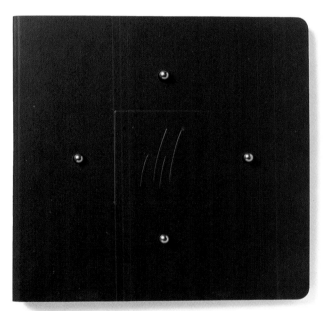

■ *108-110* **JØRN MOESGÅRD A/S** *Bent Krogh A/S*

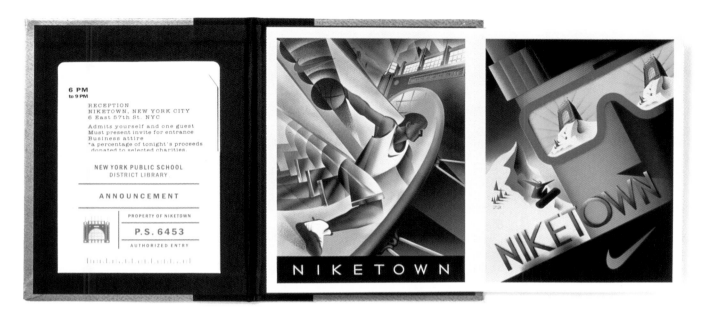

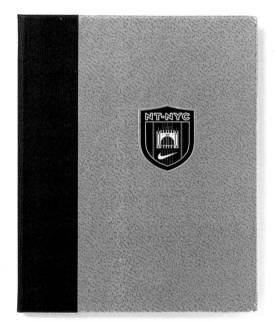

■ *111-113* **NIKE IMAGE DESIGN** *Nike, Inc.*

114 115

SOMETHING OLD

WILLIAMS-SONOMA
The Wedding Registry
COMPUTER-NETWORKED TO 140 STORES IN 115 CITIES NATIONWIDE

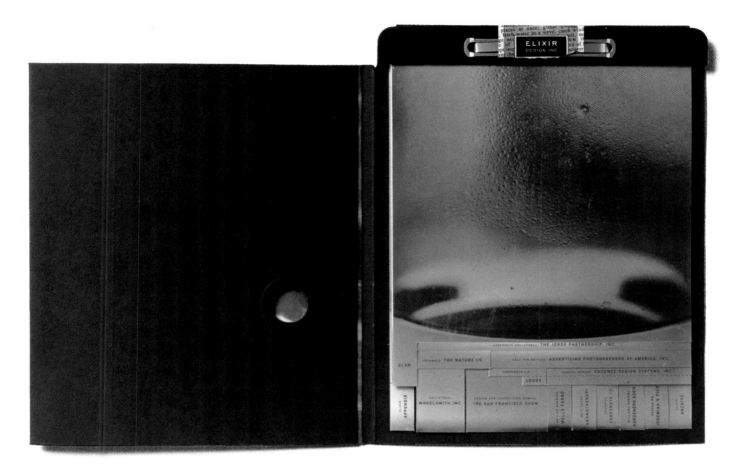

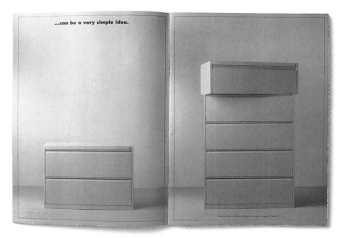

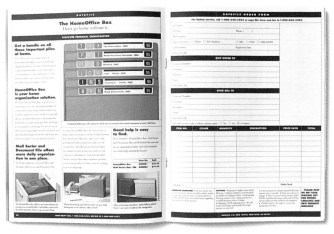

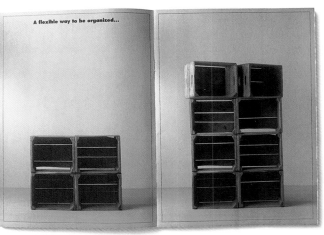

■ *118-121* **FAN ON DESIGN COMMUNICATION** *Benetton Sport System* ■ *122-125* **BARNES DESIGN OFFICE** *Datafile, Inc.*

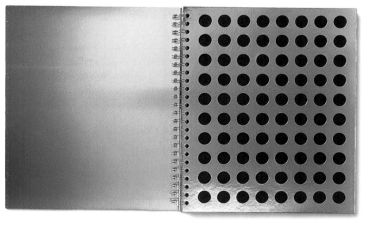

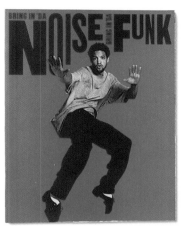

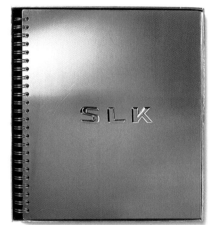

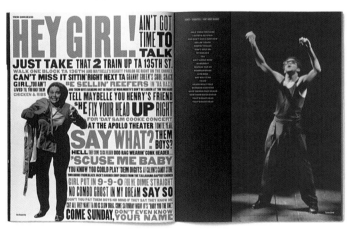

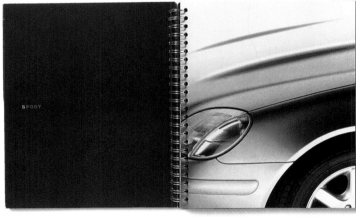

■ *126-129* **PENTAGRAM DESIGN INC.** *Public Theater NYC* ■ *130-133* **SPRINGER & JACOBY** *Mercedes-Benz AG*

■ *134* **TOSI ASSOCIATI** *Tipolito* ■ *135* **NIKE IMAGE DESIGN** *Nike, Inc.*

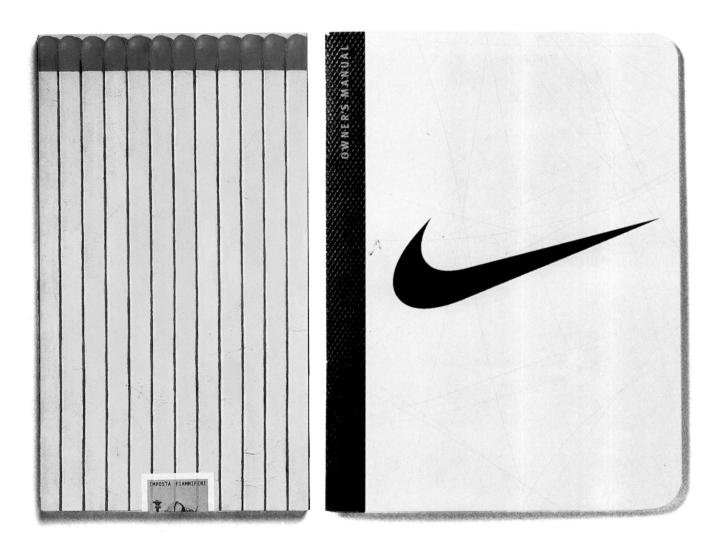

■ *134* **TOSI ASSOCIATI** *Tipolito* ■ *135* **NIKE IMAGE DESIGN** *Nike, Inc.*

136

137

138

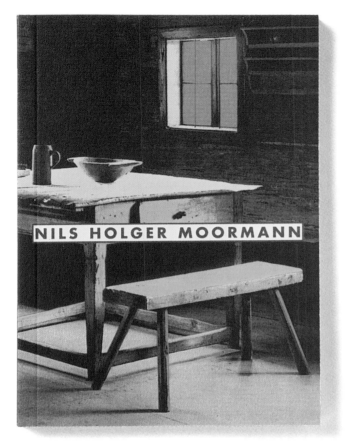

139 140

141 142

■ *139* **WERK 3, GRAPHIC DESIGN** *Nils Holger Moormann GmbH* ■ *140* **MILTON GLASER INC.** *Windows on the World*
■ *141, 142* **SAATCHI & SAATCHI/PACIFIC** *Toyota Motor Sales USA, Inc.*

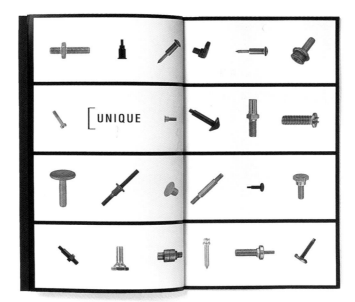

143

144

145

■ *143-145* **THE LARSON GROUP** *Pearson Fastener*

■ *146* **JENNIFER STERLING DESIGN** *(in-house)* ■ *147* **TREY SPEEGLE DESIGNS** *Hedy Klineman*

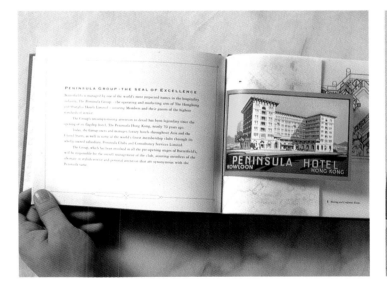

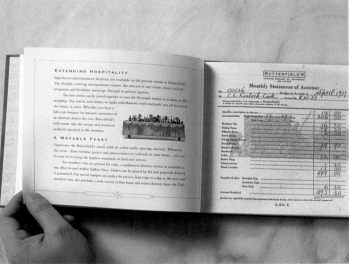

■ *148-153* **PPA DESIGN LTD.** *Swire Properties*

154

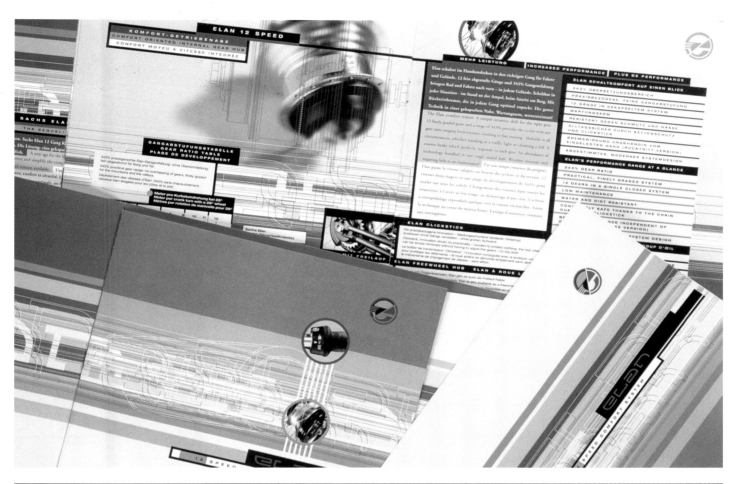

■ *155, 156* **SIMON & GOETZ** *Fichtel & Sachs GmbH*

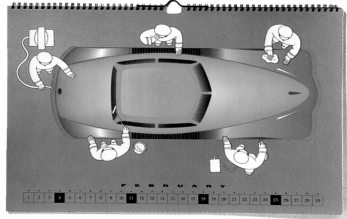

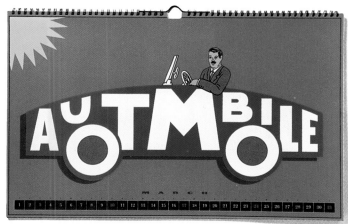

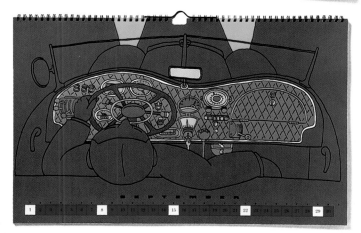

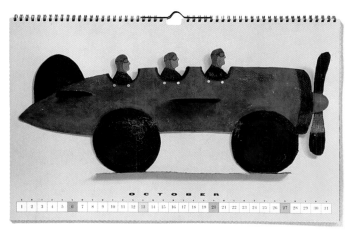

■ *158-165* **THE PUSHPIN GROUP** *The Pushpin Group, Mohawk Paper, Berman Printing*

A.D.IIIIIOOIIOI

A.D.1997

IOII

january february march april may june july august september october november december

11

IOOOO

january february march april may june july august september october november december

16

■ *166-168* **AHN GRAPHICS** *Self-promotion*

169 TURNER DUCKWORTH Levi Strauss & Co.

169

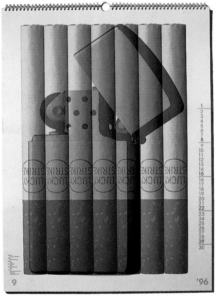

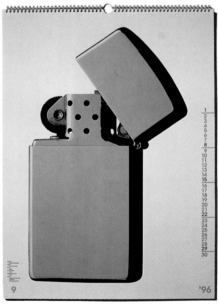

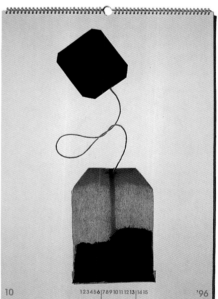

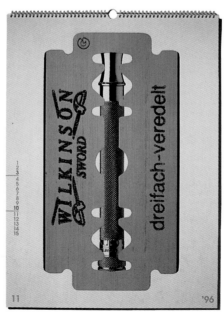

■ *170-178* **FALKENTHAL, ADAM, TV DRUCK** *(in-house)*

179 **MCCANN-ERICKSON INC. TOKYO** *Coca-Cola Company Japan*

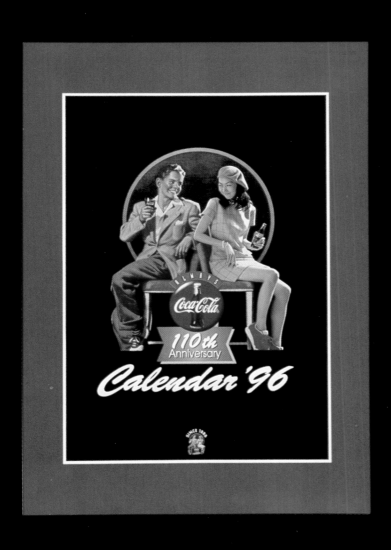

180 181

■ *180-185* **SANDSTROM DESIGN** *Pavlov Productions*

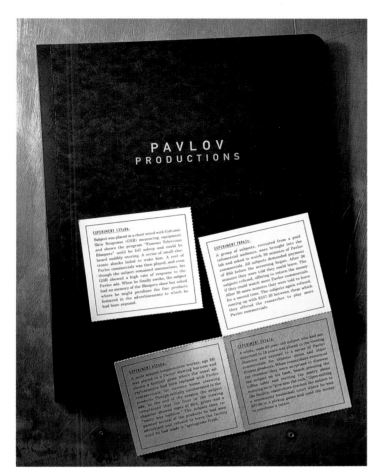

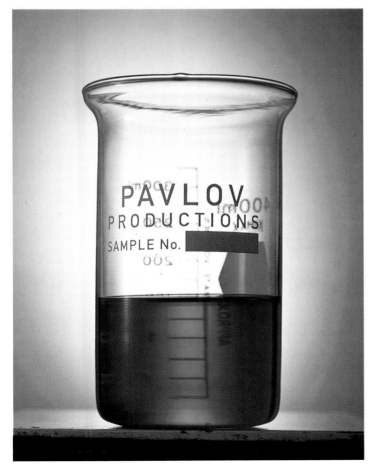
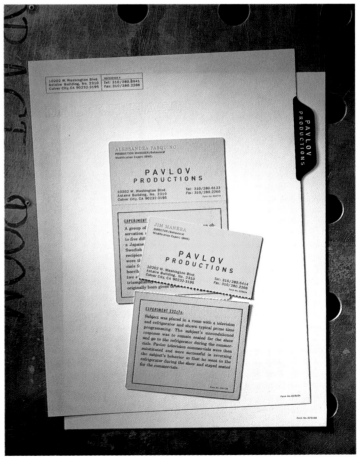

182 183

184 185

186 187

188 189

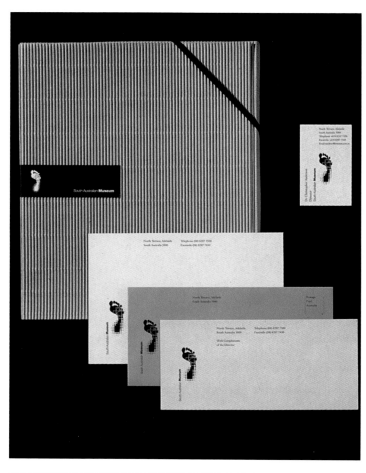
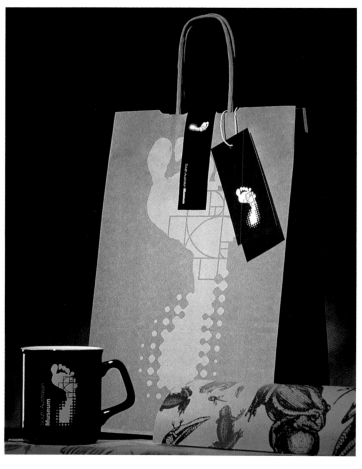

■ *186, 187* **IAN KIDD DESIGN PTY. LTD.** *South Australian Museum* ■ *188, 189* **HORNALL ANDERSON DESIGN WORKS** *Alki Bakery*

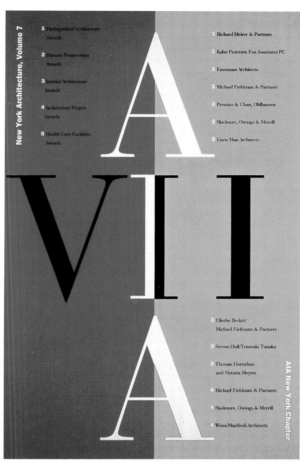

AIA New York Chapter

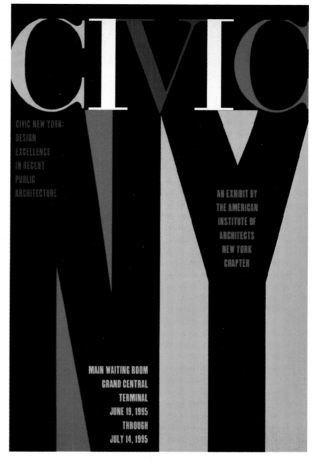

CIVIC NY

CIVIC NEW YORK: DESIGN EXCELLENCE IN RECENT PUBLIC ARCHITECTURE

AN EXHIBIT BY THE AMERICAN INSTITUTE OF ARCHITECTS NEW YORK CHAPTER

MAIN WAITING ROOM
GRAND CENTRAL
TERMINAL
JUNE 19, 1995
THROUGH
JULY 14, 1995

Annual Review 1995-1996

AIA New York Chapter

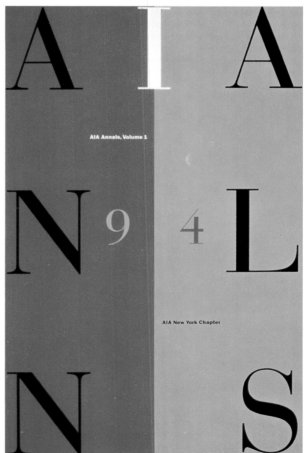

AIA Annals, Volume 1

ANNALS 94

AIA New York Chapter

190 191

192 193

■ *190-193* **PENTAGRAM DESIGN INC.** *American Institute of Architects*

194 195

196 197

198

Boise Cascade Office Products

Total Net Sales
Amounts in millions

$1,316

$909

$683

1993   1994   1995

199

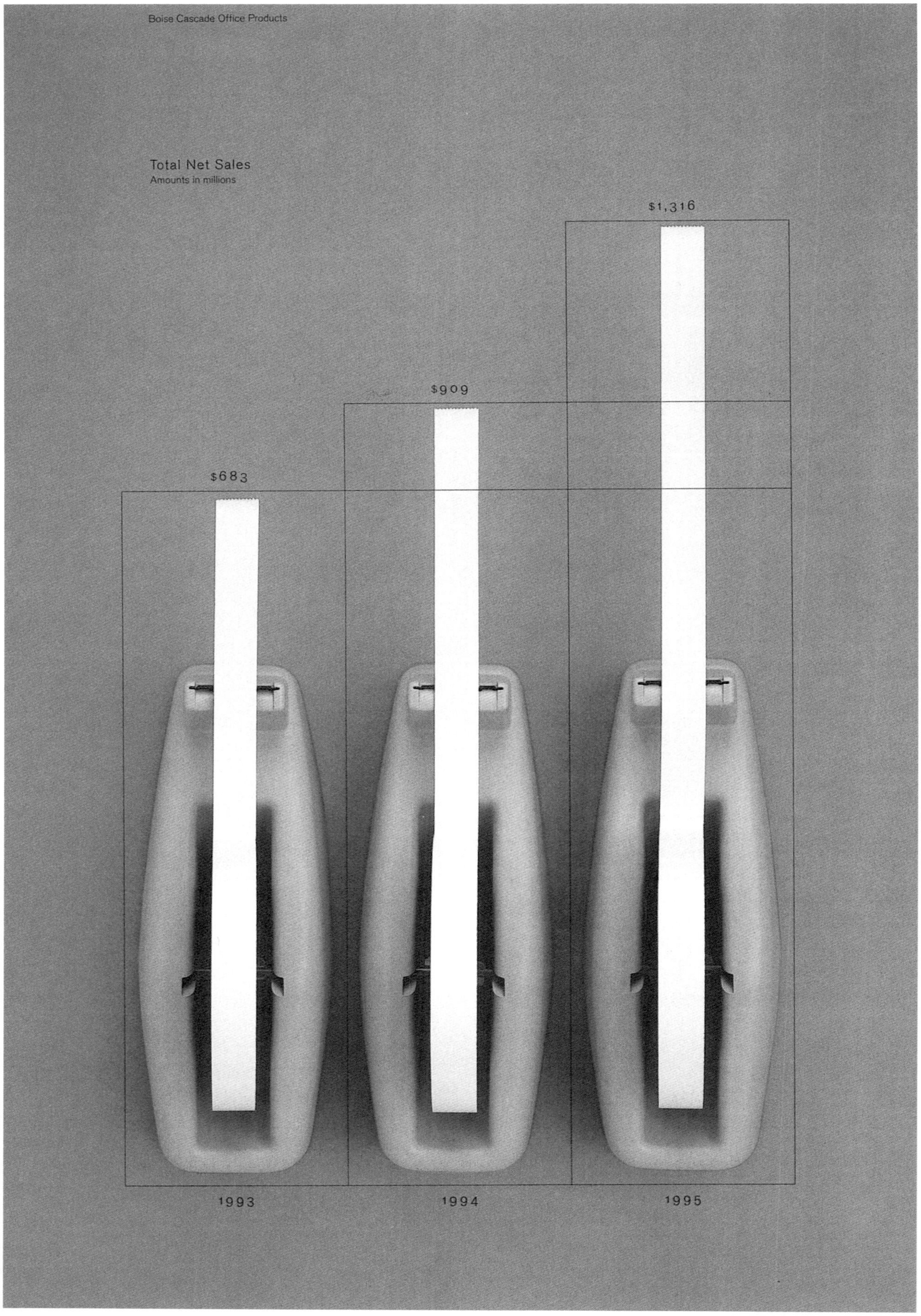

■ *199* **PETRICK DESIGN** *Boise Cascade Office Products*

202

HOLY ROLLER

J OSBORNE

A DOZEN male models in Mylar shorts is not what JOAN OSBORNE asked for from life, but she'll make do on this cloudy Liverpool morning. Once again she's about to perform her Grammy-nominated hit single "One of Us," this time for the kind of television talk show that features muscle-bound models to illustrate why more English women are watching soccer matches these days. The lads shiver as they trot from the studio's balcony-level waiting room to the taping area below. Osborne flirts with the hunks, shimmying a little as she walks by them in her Ann-Margret

FINDS SALVATION IN GOD AND GOOD SEX

BY ANN POWERS

44 · ROLLING STONE, MARCH 21, 1996

Photographs by MARK SELIGER

■ *203* **RICHARD BAKER** *US* ■ *204* **FRED WOODWARD, GERALDINE HESSLER** *Rolling Stone* ■ *205* **FRED WOODWARD, LEE BEARSON** *Rolling Stone* ■ *206* **FRED WOODWARD, GERALDINE HESSLER** *Rolling Stone* ■ *207, 208* **RICHARD BAKER** *US* ■ *209* **FRED WOODWARD, GERALDINE HESSLER** *Rolling Stone* ■ *210* **FRED WOODWARD** *Rolling Stone*

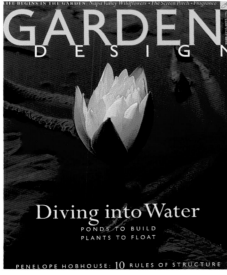

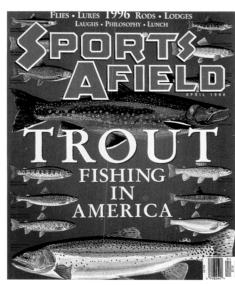

211 212 213

214 215 216

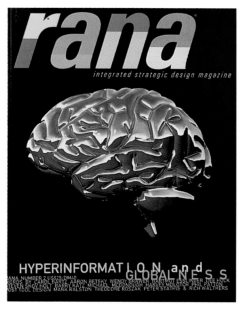

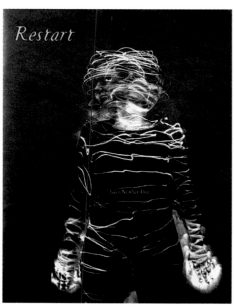

■ *211* **GARY GRETTER** *SPORTS AFIELD* ■ *212* **CHRISTIN GANGI, MICHAEL GROSSMAN** *GARDEN DESIGN* ■ *213* **MICHAEL LAWTON**
SPORTS AFIELD ■ *214* **FROGDESIGN** *RANA* ■ *215* **D.J. STOUT** *TEXAS MONTHLY* ■ *216* **THOMAS NOLLER, GARY VAN PATTER** *Restart Publishing*

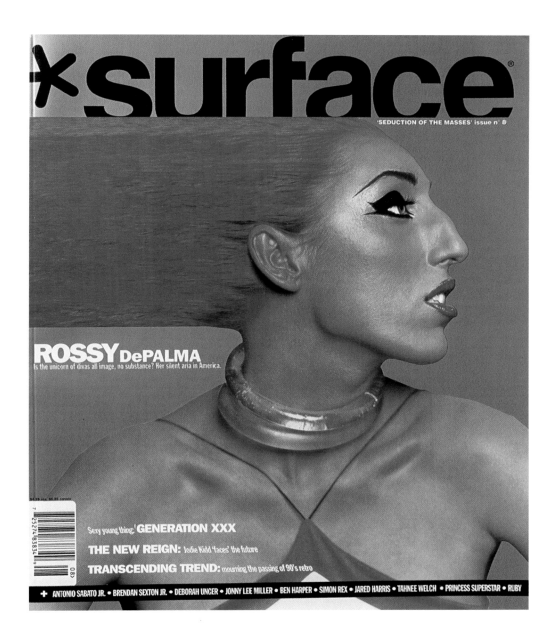

217

218 219

■ *221-227* **NAKAJIMA DESIGN** *rockin' on inc.*

221

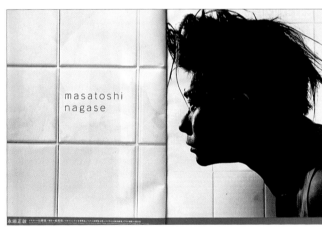

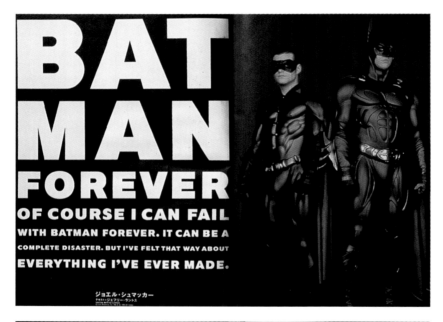

■ *228-233* **NAKAJIMA DESIGN** *rockin' on inc.*

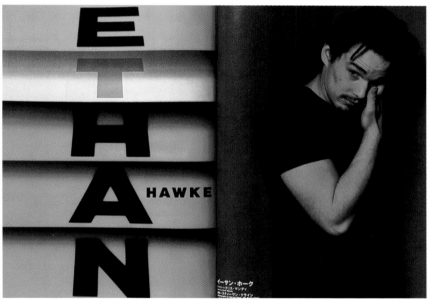

231

232

233

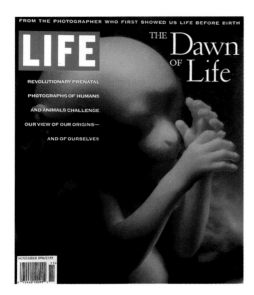

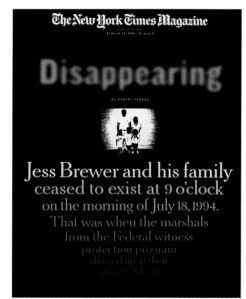

Büro: Die Bezeichnung für „Arbeits-, Amtszimmer" wurde im 17./18. Jh. aus *frz.* bureau entlehnt, das als Ableitung von *afrz.* bure bzw. burel wie diese ursprünglich einen „groben Wollstoff" bezeichnete, wie er u. a. zum Beziehen von [Schreib]tischen verwendet wurde, dann den „Schreibtisch" selbst und schließlich, weil der Schreibtisch als wesentliches Zubehör eines Arbeitszimmers gilt, die „Schreibstube". – Voraus liegt ein etymologisch undurchsichtiges Substantiv *vlat.* *bura (< *lat.* burra) „zottiges Gewand; Wolle". – Die Bildung **Bürokratie** wurde im 18./19. Jh. aus *frz.* bureaucratie entlehnt, eine Prägung des französischen Nationalökonomen Vincent de Gournay. Dazu stellen sich **Bürokrat** (aus *frz.* bureaucrate) und **bürokratisch** (aus *frz.* bureaucratique).

243 244

■ *243* **BAMDESIGN** *Brooklyn Academy of Music* ■ *244* **MANDEL, MUTH, WERBEAGENTUR, GMBH** *Voko Vertriebsstiftung Büroeinrichtungen KG*

8   9

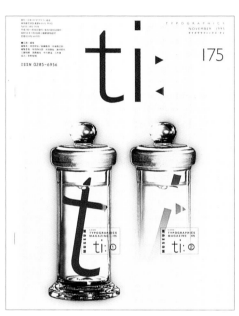

■ *245-253* **KOKOKUMARU CO., LTD.** *Japan Typography Association*

江戸文字の字形を比べる
桑山弥三郎

Kan Tai-keung   Hong Kong

251

252

253

Virtual Typo City

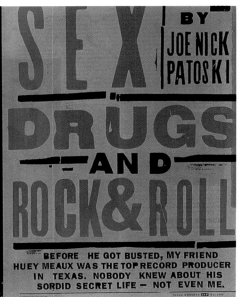

254

255

256

■ *254-256* **D.J. STOUT** *TEXAS MONTHLY*

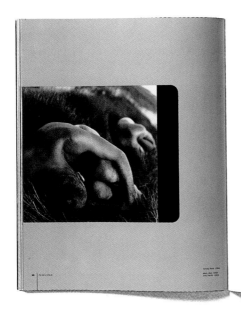
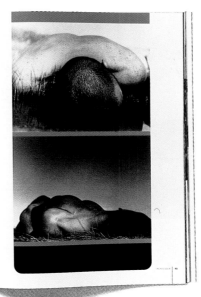

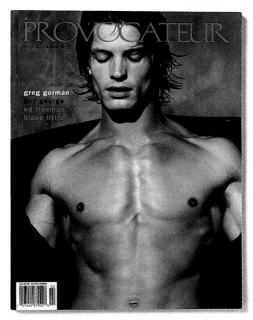

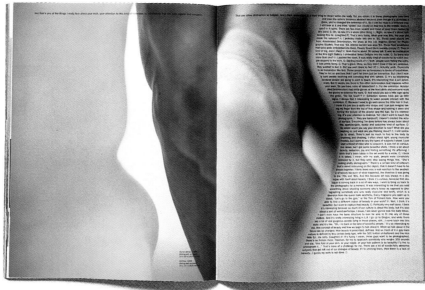

■ *257-259* **PHILIP PIROLO** *PROVOCATEUR*

260 261

262 263

264 265

■ *260-267* **POULIN & MORRIS** *Sony Music Entertainment Inc.*

268

269

■ *268* **ANTISTA FAIRCLOUGH DESIGN** *Texaco Refining & Marketing Inc.* ■ *269* **EMERY VINCENT DESIGN** *Denton Corker Marshall*

270 271

■ *270-271* **GRAPHICS & DESIGNING INC.** *G & D Management Inc.*

272

■ *272* **SQUIRES & COMPANY** *St. Pete's Dancing Marlin*

■ *273-278* **THE LEONHARDT GROUP/CORBIN DESIGN** *Recreational Equipment Inc.*

279 280

281 282

■ *279-282* **IMPACT GROUP INC.** *Maroon Creek Club*

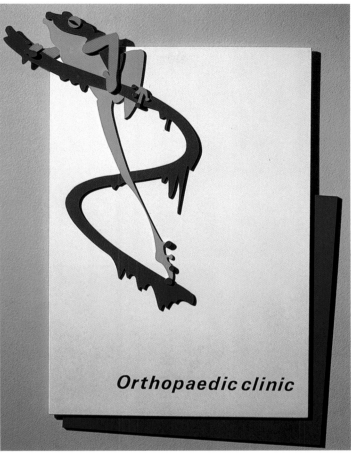

Orthopaedic clinic

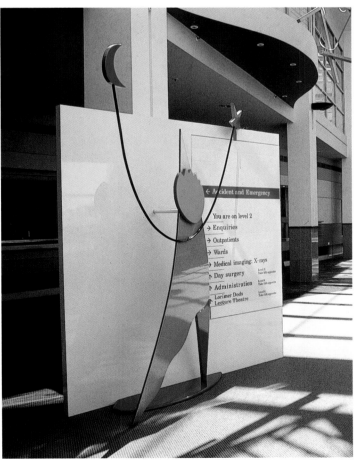

■ *283-286* **EMERY VINCENT DESIGN** *Royal Alexandra Children's Hospital*

■ *287, 288* **IMPACT GROUP INC.** *Heitman Financial/Snowmass Land Co.*

■ *289* **GRUPPE MAYLÄNDER WERBEAGENTUR** *Horst Wanschura*

32780

MELDEBESTÄTIGUNG

M.C.C.

WEISUNG

Diese Meldebestätigung informiert über eine Adressänderung. Sämtliche daraus resultierende administrative Anpassungen sind unverzüglich vorzunehmen. Diese Meldebestätigung gilt als Dokument und ist für die allfällige spätere Rücksendung an die zuständige Stelle aufzubewahren.

Form 2 68

Meldebestätigung.
Déclaration de domicile.
Avviso di notifica.

Name

WILD HEINZ

Ausstellungsort

WALD-KT.ZCH.

Karte

Nº 0.238 967-W

Amtsstelle **8005 Zürich 5, Industriequartier**

Zur sofortigen Weiterleitung an das Stadthaus, Büro 311

20.8

Frist bis

290

291

292

Introducing the BIGGEST NEW STAR on the HORIZON...
"AN AMAZING CREATURE..."
BORN from the FURTHEST DEPTHS of IMAGINATION!

CINEMA PORTRAITS presents
CRY OF THE **SHE-BABY**
BEHOLD!

NINE MONTHS IN THE MAKING!

KATRINA SUE BURKE
TOM & PEGGY BURKE
SUE NEUSCHOTZ

■ *290, 291* **WILD & FREY** *Heinz Wild* ■ *292* **WILLOUGHBY DESIGN** *Garrett Burke*

293

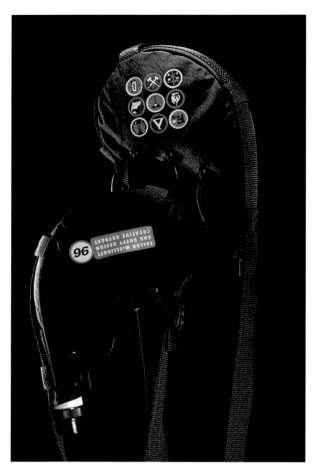

■ *294* **DUFFY DESIGN** *Fallon McElligott, Duffy Design* ■ *295* **SIETSEMA ENGEL PARTNERS** *(in-house)* ■ *296, 297* **DESIGNWORKS** *(in-house)*

298

299 300

301 302

303 304

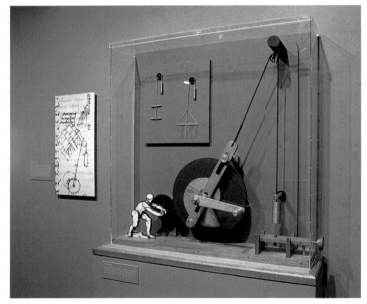

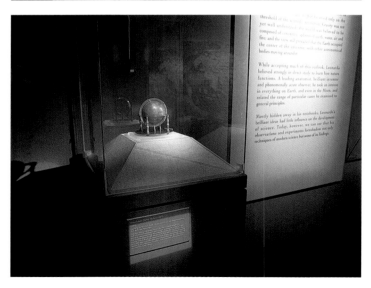

■ *299-304* **AMERICAN MUSEUM OF NATURAL HISTORY** *(in-house)*

305 306

307 308

■ *305-308* **2ND GLOBE** *(in-house)*

■ 309 **PENTAGRAM DESIGN INC.** *DuPont Company* ■ 310, 311 **PENTAGRAM DESIGN INC.** *Bausch & Lomb*

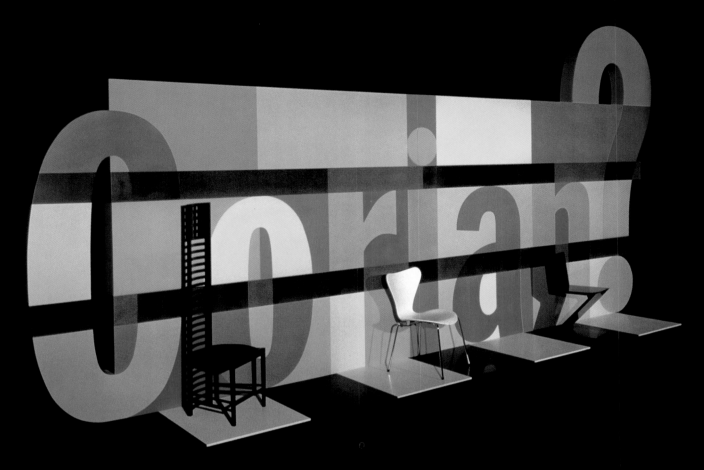

309

310 311

■ *309* **PENTAGRAM DESIGN INC.** *DuPont Company* ■ *310, 311* **PENTAGRAM DESIGN INC.** *Bausch & Lomb*

312

313

■ *312, 313* **FITCH INC.** *Chrysler Corporation*

314 315

316 317

■ *314-321* **NIKE IMAGE DESIGN** *Nike, Inc.*

318 319

320 321

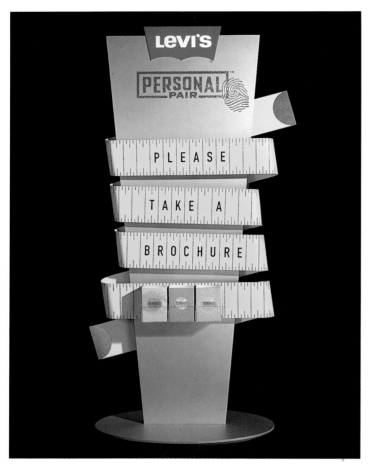

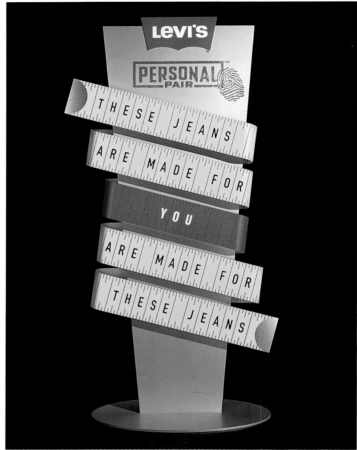

■ *322, 323* **TURNER DUCKWORTH** *Levi Strauss & Co.*

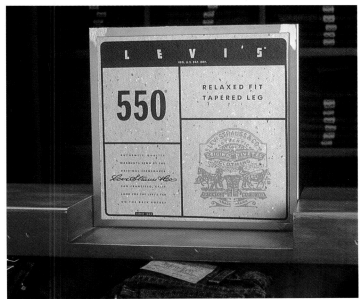

326 327

328 329

330 331

■ *324-331* **ZIMMERMANN CROWE DESIGN** *Levi Strauss & Co.*

332 333

334 335

■ *332-336* **SANDSTROM DESIGN** *Reebok*

336

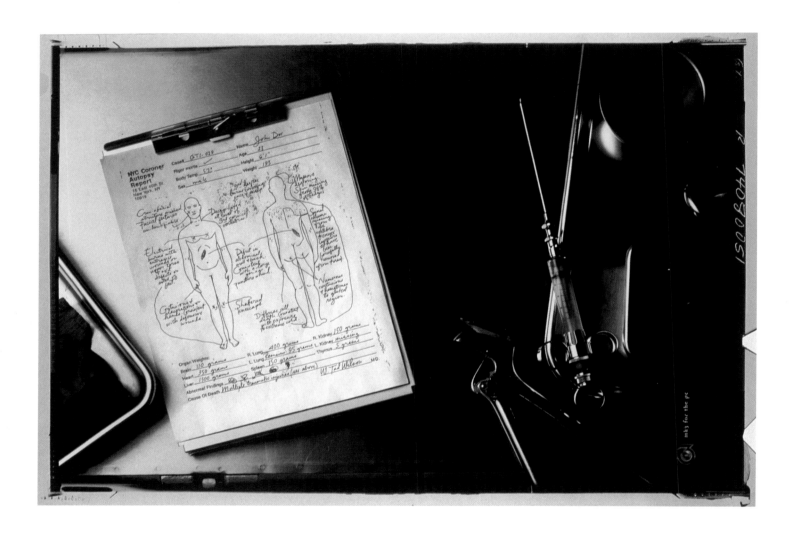

337

338

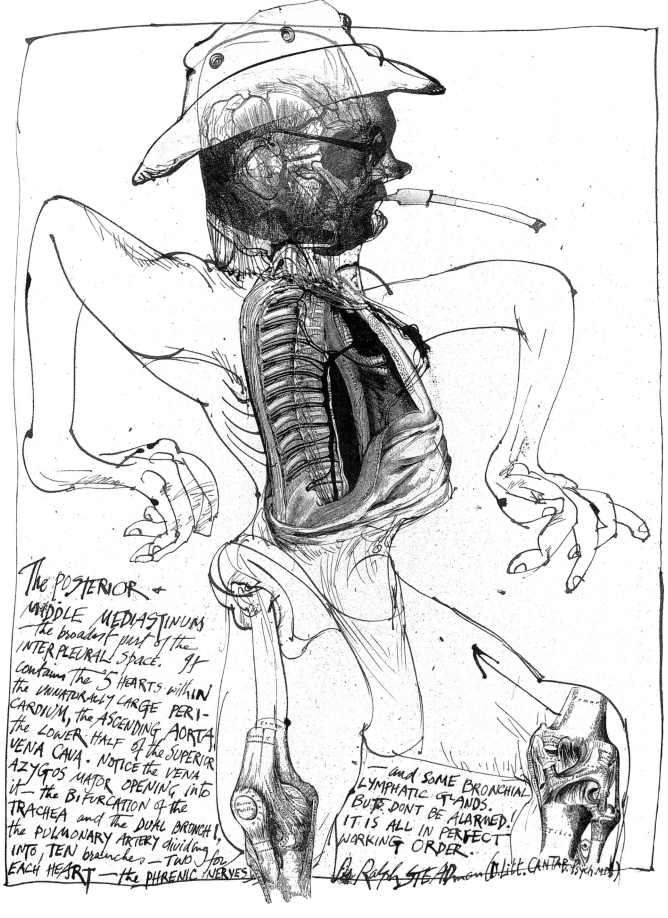

340

■ *340* **MILTON GLASER** *The New York Times Book Review*

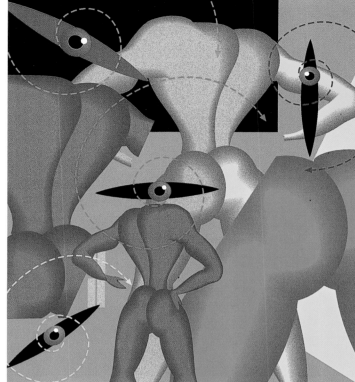

341 342

343 344

■ *341, 342* **SIEGMAR MÜNK** *Fischer Taschenbücher* ■ *343* **D. K. HOLLAND** *Rockport Allworth* ■ *344* **GREG TUCKER**

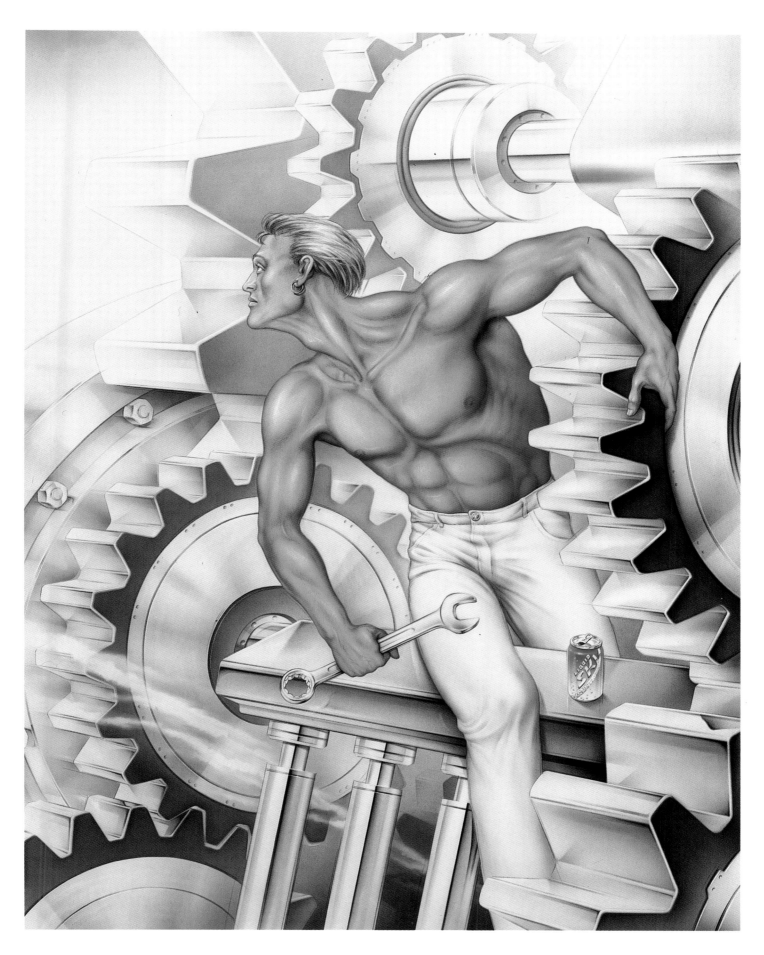

345

■ *345* **REINHARD HEROLD**

346

347

■ 346 **C.B. COMMUNICATIONS** *Garnett Inc.* ■ 347 **SANDRA HENDLER** *Self-promotion*

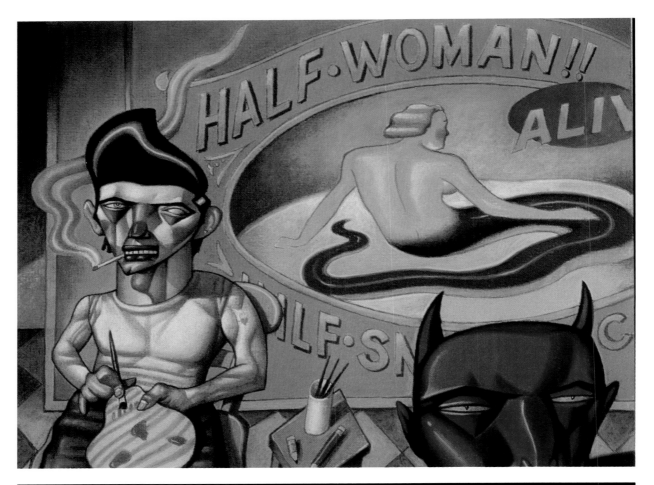

349

350

■ *349* **GREG TUCKER** ■ *350* **MIRES DESIGN** *Harcourt Brace & Co.*

351

352

353

■ *351* **TANGRAM STRATEGIC DESIGN** *Banca Popolare di Novara* ■ *352* **AMMIRATI PURIS LINTAS** *Seiko Epson* ■ *353* **MARA KURTZ STUDIO** *(in-house)*

354 355

356 357

■ *354* **JEFF KOEGEL** *WALKING Magazine* ■ *355* **JEFF KOEGEL** *PACKAGING WORLD Magazine* ■ *356* **CATHLEEN TOELKE** *GQ* ■ *357* **CATHLEEN TOELKE** *Simon & Schuster*

■ *358* **UNION DESIGN** *Henie-Onstad Art Center*

359

360

361

■ *359-362* **SANDSTROM DESIGN** *(in-house)*

The Adventures *of* Letter Head
Today, Letter Head discovers he has no arms or legs. Is he able to accept his fate? Or will he shred himself in a frenzy of self-pity and despair? Stay tuned, for another exciting episode of "*Letter Head!*" Sandstrom Design, 808 SW Third Avenue, Portland, Oregon 97204, Tel: 503.248.9466 Fax: 503.227.5035.

Sandstrom Design, Incorporated. Yeah, that's right. *Incorporated.* For your information, that means we're a corporation. A corporation with a lawyer. And an accountant. And a phone number: 503.248.9466. And a fax number: 503.227.5035. And an address. It's 808 SW Third Avenue in Portland, Oregon. The zip code is 97204. You can check it out if you want to. It's a real building. With a real elevator. And we have a receptionist who we pay money to every month to answer our phones. Because we get calls. Because we're a corporation.

I never realized just how easy it would be to kill someone who's waiting at the subway platform...They're mere inches from the tracks...one little push from behind and...But it's not like I would actually ever *do* that. Well, for *sure* I wouldn't do it to a client. Kathy Middleton, Sandstrom Design, 808 SW Third, № 610, Portland, Oregon 97204. Call: 503.248.9466, Fax: 503.227.5035.

I just think it's such a coincidence that I ended up at a place called Sandstrom Design. I mean, *come on* – what are the odds? Steve Sandstrom, 808 Southwest Third, № 610, Portland, Oregon 97204. Call: 503.248.9466, Fax: 503.227.5035.

You're probably wondering, "Just what is a Senior Designer?" Well, a Senior Designer can be someone who has worked in New York. A Senior Designer can be someone who is old. A Senior Designer can be a Junior Designer who threatens to leave if they don't get a promotion and you're thinking, "Okay, leave." Except their mom is your biggest, steadiest client so suddenly they're a Senior Designer. Or, as in the case of Sally Morrow, a Senior Designer can simply be an incredibly talented designer who has years of experience working with awesome clients, like Doc Marten's, Levi's and Microsoft, where Sally's mom, Velma Microsoft, works. Sandstrom Design, 808 SW Third, № 610, Portland, OR 97204. Call: 503.248.9466, Fax: 503.227.5035.

362

363

Skolos / Wedell

5 2 9

Main Street

Charlestown MA

0 2 1 2 9

ph : **617-242-5179**
fax: 617-242-**2135**

e.mail : swinc@skolwed.com

Skolos / Wedell

5 2 9

Main
Street

Charlestown

MA

0 2 1 2 9

ph : **617-242-5179**
fax: 617-242-**2135**

Nancy Skolos

5 2 9

Skolos / Wedell

Charlestown MA

Main
Street

0 2 1 2 9

swinc@skolwed.com

■ *363* **SKOLOS/WEDELL** *(in-house)*

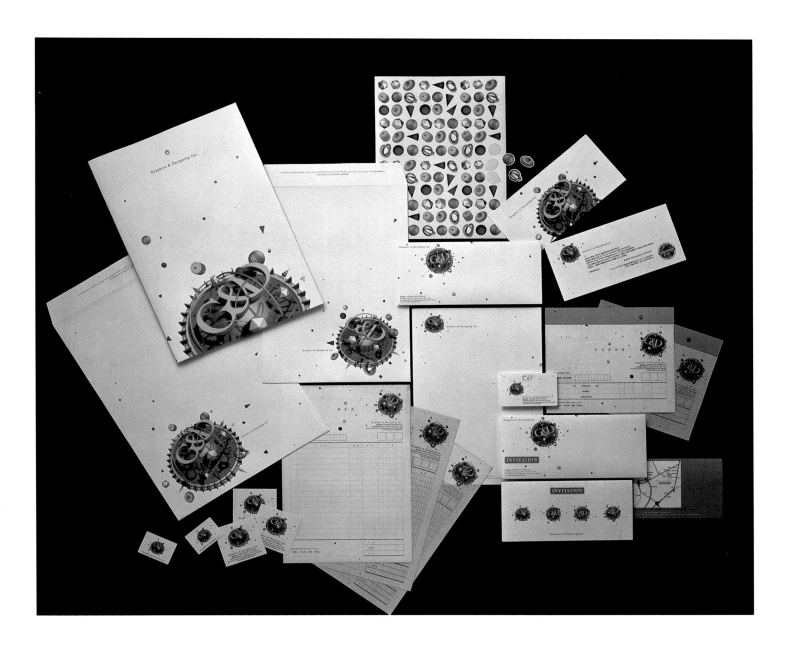

364

■ *364* **GRAPHICS & DESIGNING INC.** *G & D Management Inc.*

365 366 367

368 369 370

371 372 373

■ *365* **L3 CREATIVE** *The Dial Corp.* ■ *366* **MIKE SALISBURY COMMUNCATIONS INC.** *RAGE Magazine* ■ *367* **STORM DESIGN & ADVERTISING** *Paul West Photography*
■ *368* **TINGUELY CONCEPT** *Nidecker Snowboards* ■ *369* **FARNET HART DESIGN STUDIO** *Audubon Exploration* ■ *370* **TROY M. LITTEN DESIGN** *(in-house)*
■ *371* **HORNALL ANDERSON DESIGN WORKS** *Rhino Chasers* ■ *372* **PARTNERS DESIGN, INC.** *Canal Street Pub & Restaurant* ■ *373* **THE SLOAN GROUP** *Cafe Concepts*

■ *374* **SANDSTROM DESIGN** *Levi Strauss & Co.* ■ *375* **ZIMMERMANN CROWE DESIGN** *Levi Strauss & Co.* ■ *376* **SANDSTROM DESIGN** *Levi Strauss & Co.*

135

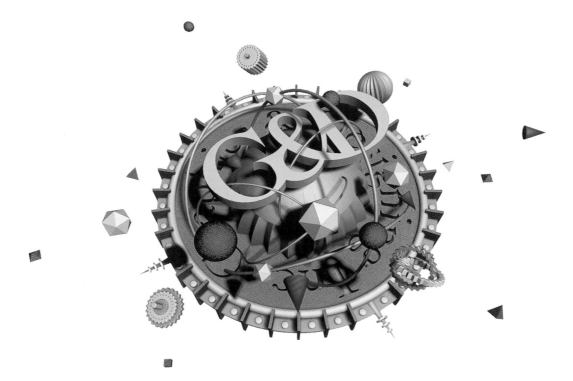

386

■ *386* **GRAPHICS & DESIGNING INC.** *G & D Management Inc.*

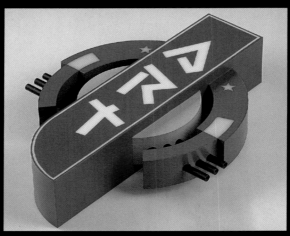

387

388

389

■ *387* **SMIT GHORMLEY LOFGREEN DESIGN** *Mesa Arts Center* ■ *388* **ART FORCE STUDIO** ■ *389* **DOO KIM DESIGN** *Korea International Trade Association*

390

391

392

393

394

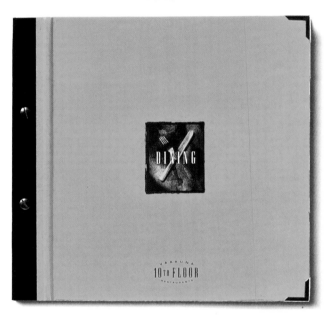

■ *395-397* **HASAN & PARTNERS** *Vaakuna 10th Floor Restaurants*

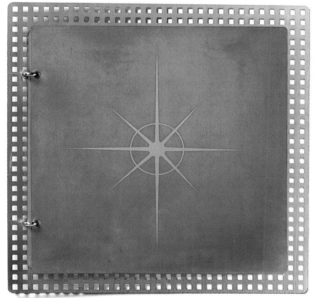

398

399

400

■ *398-400* **DES DESIGN** *Club B.A.S.E.*

401 402

403 404

■ *401* **DARE-ART** *Eye Q Music* ■ *402* **CAROL CHEN, GRAHAM ELIOT** *Sony Music* ■ *403* **CHIKA AZUMA** *Verve Records* ■ *404* **DARE-ART** *Eye Q Music*

142

405

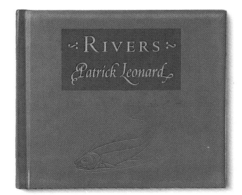

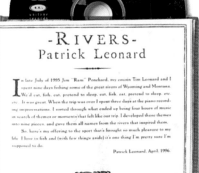

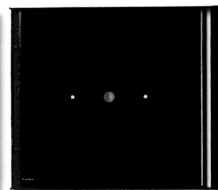

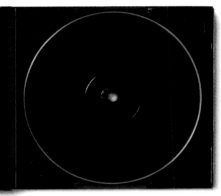

406 407

408 409

410 411

412 413

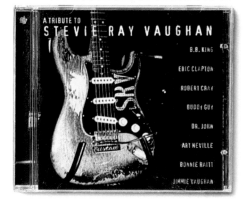

■ *406, 407* **DESIGN ART, INC.** *Unitone Records* ■ *408, 409* **SAGMEISTER INC.** *Warner Bros. Music* ■ *410-413* **SONY** *Sony Music*

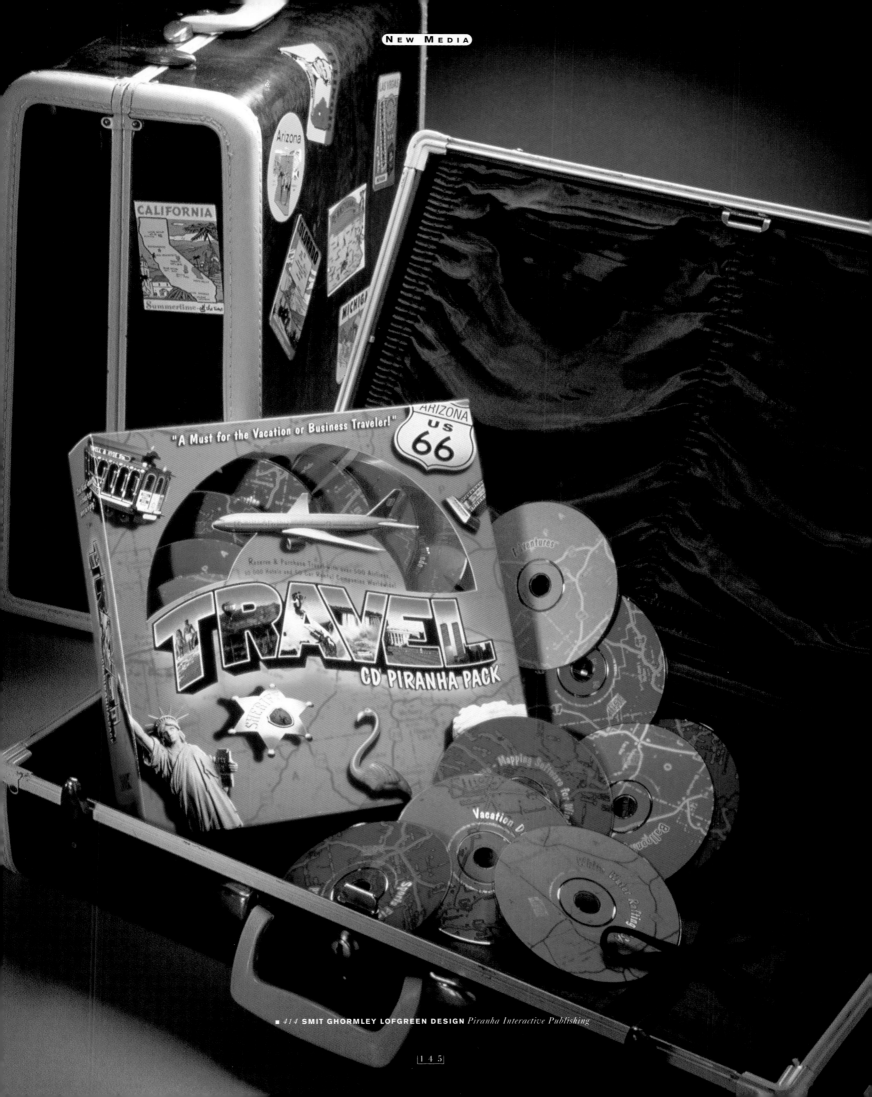

"A Must for the Vacation or Business Traveler!"

ARIZONA
US
66

Reserve & Purchase Tickets with over 500 Airlines,
10,000 Hotels and 50 Car Rental Companies Worldwide!

TRAVEL
CD PIRANHA PACK

SHERIFF

■ *414* **SMIT GHORMLEY LOFGREEN DESIGN** *Piranha Interactive Publishing*

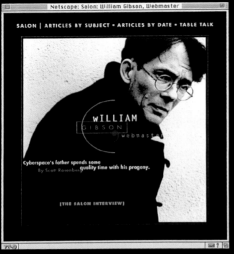

wILLIAM
GIBSON
webmaster

Cyberspace's father spends some
quality time with his progeny.
By Scott Rosenberg

[THE SALON INTERVIEW]

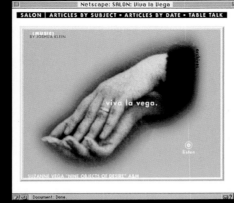

[MUSIC]
BY JOSHUA KLEIN

viva la vega.

listen

SUZANNE VEGA "NINE OBJECTS OF DESIRE" A&M

Document : Done.

MUSIC   ►by gavin mcnett◄

songs of
experience &

BILLY BRAGG / WILLIAM BLOKE / ELEKTRA ENTERTAINMENT

Document : Done.

MOVIES

from HIP HOP
TO HOLLYWOOD:
"SET IT OFF"
DIRECTOR
GARY GRAY

By DONNELL ALEXANDER

Music videos historically have been off the path of the serious filmmaker. But with the growing black market niche in both television and movies, that isn't true any more. Case in point: Director F. Gary Gray, whose stylish hip-hop videos gave him the opportunity to move to the bigger screen, making compelling, well-crafted feature films on urban themes.

A native of South Central Los Angeles, the 27-year-old Gray began his career seven years ago, gigging as a photographer on the young Fox network's rap video show "Pump it Up!" It was there that he met members of the seminal Los Angeles hip-hop group WC and the Maad Circle, who hired him to direct one of their videos. That work led to a prodigious video career, including his helming Coolio's "Fantastic Voyage" and Ice Cube's "Today was a Good Day," which was rated by

Document : Done.

IN THE NAME OF LOVE
OR A GREEN CARD

COURTNEY WEAVER

"would you marry me, Courtney?" John asked, looking deep into my eyes from across the table.

"I don't know what to say," I stammered. "I'm... I'm touched."

"I'm serious. I want to get married to you. I'd be brilliant."

We were at Orsino's, a trendy and expensive restaurant in West London,

MOVIES

RED riding hood
little
[revenge]

"Freeway" updates an old fairy tale with a tough, working class twist.

●

By CHARLES TAYLOR

when Vanessa (Reese Witherspoon), the teenage heroine of the wild and exhilarating black comedy, "Freeway," hunkers down to kiss her boyfriend Chopper (Bokeem Woodbine), she's voracious and blissfully content at the same time. Taking big sips from her honey's tasty lips, Vanessa has a blithe assurance. She acts as if nothing is going to change anytime soon, but life is about to turn into a pitching machine throwing her nothing but curveballs. Soon, to borrow a line from "All About Eve," she's got to deal with "everything but the hound dogs yappin' at

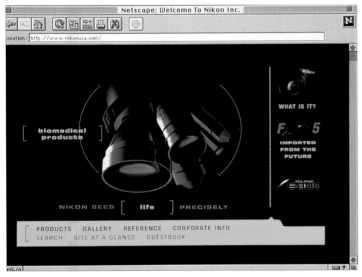

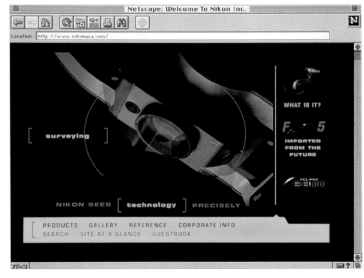

421 422

423 424

■ *421-424* **DUFFY DESIGN** *Nikon Inc.*

425 426

427

428 429

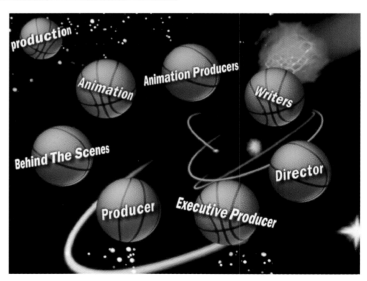

■ *425-429* **CBO MULTIMEDIA** *Warner Brothers*

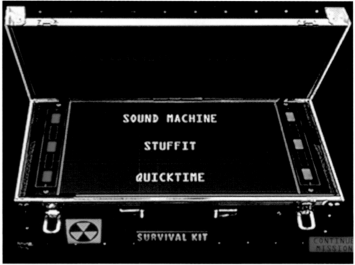
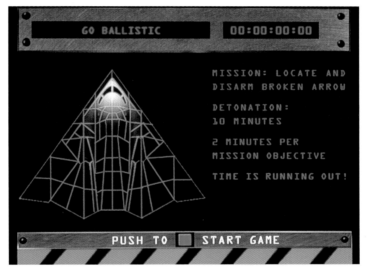

430 431

432

433 434

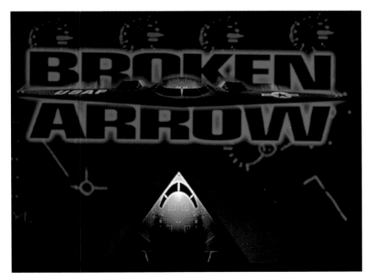

■ *430-434* **CBO MULTIMEDIA** *Twentieth Century Fox*

435 436
437 438
439 440

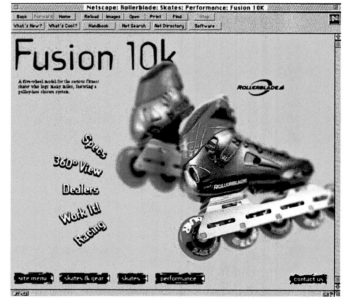

■ *435-440* **ADJACENCY: BRAND NEW MEDIA** *Rollerblade, Inc.*

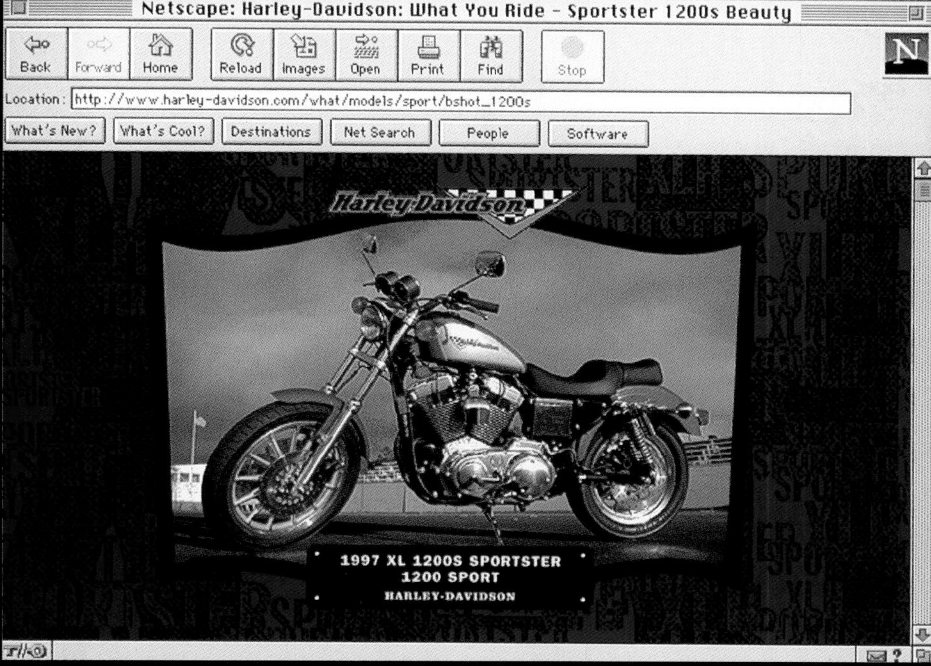

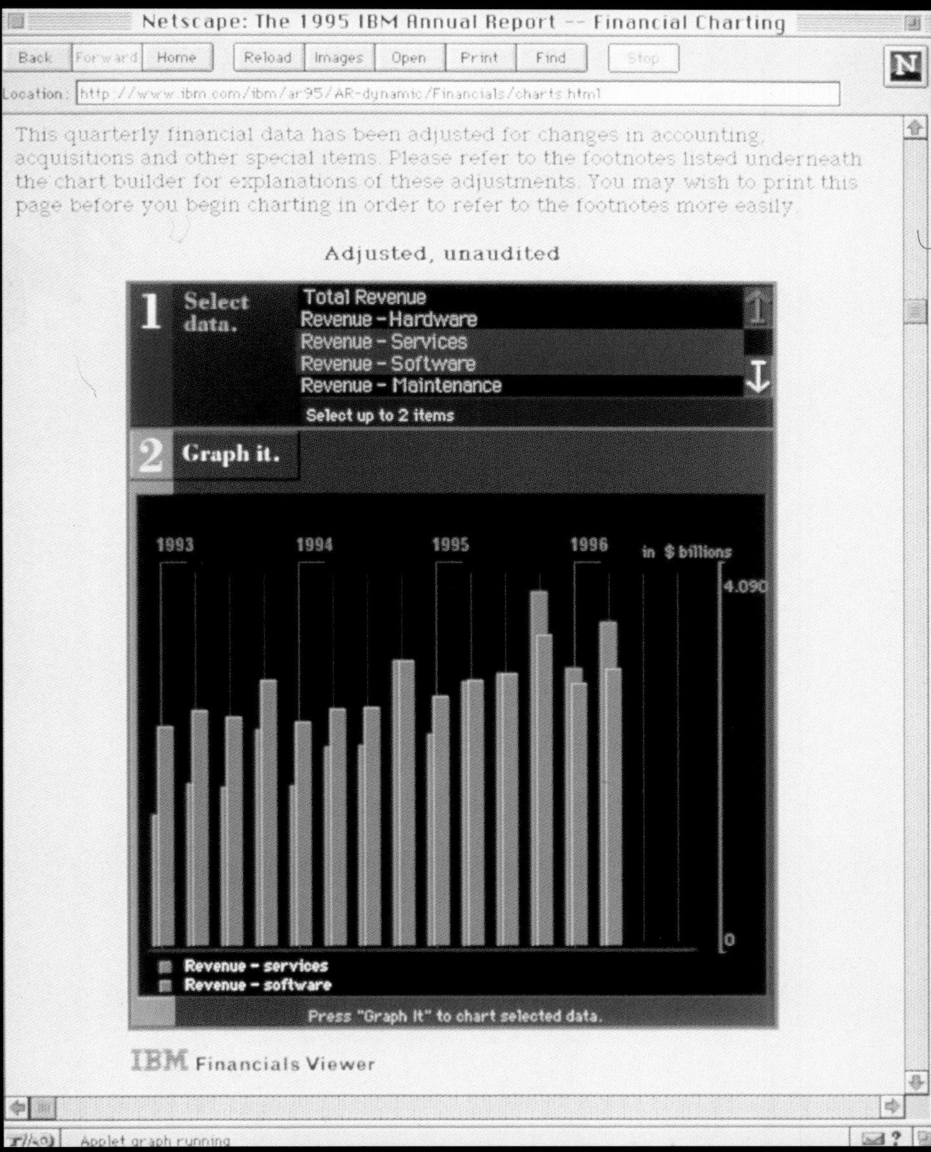

VSA PARTNERS, INC. *Harley-Davidson Inc.* ■ *442* ELEMENTAL INTERACTIVE DESIGN & DEVELOPMENT *IBM Cor*

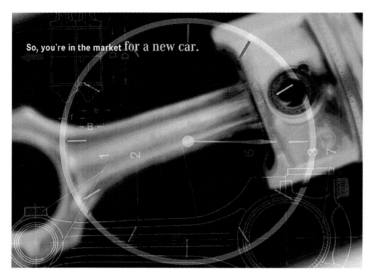

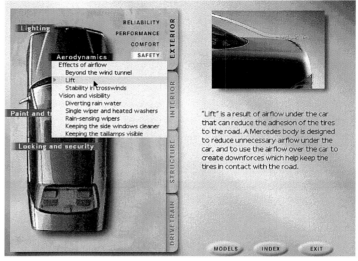

"Lift" is a result of airflow under the car that can reduce the adhesion of the tires to the road. A Mercedes body is designed to reduce unnecessary airflow under the car, and to use the airflow over the car to create downforces which help keep the tires in contact with the road.

MODELS   INDEX   EXIT

443 444
445 446
447 448

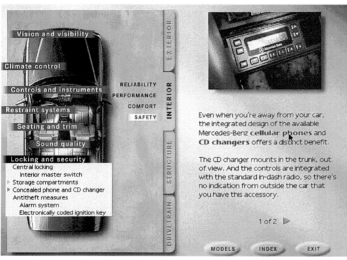

Even when you're away from your car, the integrated design of the available Mercedes-Benz cellular phones and CD changers offers a distinct benefit.

The CD changer mounts in the trunk, out of view. And the controls are integrated with the standard in-dash radio, so there's no indication from outside the car that you have this accessory.

1 of 2 ▷

MODELS   INDEX   EXIT

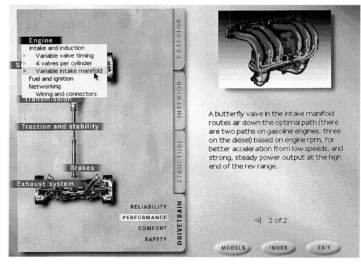

A butterfly valve in the intake manifold routes air down the optimal path (there are two paths on gasoline engines, three on the diesel) based on engine rpm, for better acceleration from low speeds, and strong, steady power output at the high end of the rev range.

◁ 2 of 2

MODELS   INDEX   EXIT

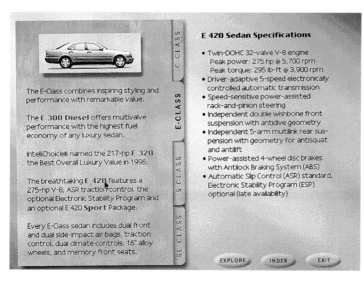

The E-Class combines inspiring styling and performance with remarkable value.

The E 300 Diesel offers multivalve performance with the highest fuel economy of any luxury sedan.

IntelliChoice® named the 217-hp E 320 the Best Overall Luxury Value in 1996.

The breathtaking E 420 features a 275-hp V-8, ASR traction control, the optional Electronic Stability Program and an optional E 420 **Sport** Package.

Every E-Class sedan includes dual front and dual side-impact air bags, traction control, dual climate controls, 16" alloy wheels, and memory front seats.

E 420 Sedan Specifications

- Twin-DOHC 32-valve V-8 engine
  Peak power: 275 hp @ 5,700 rpm
  Peak torque: 295 lb-ft @ 3,900 rpm
- Driver-adaptive 5-speed electronically controlled automatic transmission
- Speed-sensitive power-assisted rack-and-pinion steering
- Independent double wishbone front suspension with antidive geometry
- Independent 5-arm multilink rear suspension with geometry for antisquat and antilift
- Power-assisted 4-wheel disc brakes with Antilock Braking System (ABS)
- Automatic Slip Control (ASR) standard, Electronic Stability Program (ESP) optional (late availability)

EXPLORE   INDEX   EXIT

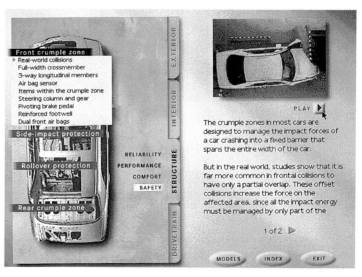

The crumple zones in most cars are designed to manage the impact forces of a car crashing into a fixed barrier that spans the entire width of the car.

But in the real world, studies show that it is far more common in frontal collisions to have only a partial overlap. These offset collisions increase the force on the affected area, since all the impact energy must be managed by only part of the

1 of 2 ▷

MODELS   INDEX   EXIT

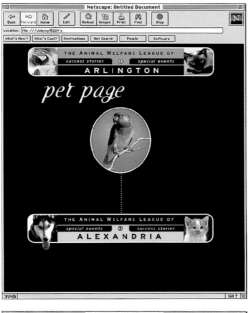

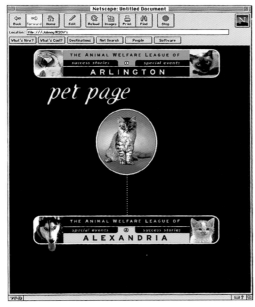

■ *449-454* **GRAFIK COMMUNICATIONS, LTD.** *Alexandria & Arlington Animal Shelters*

455

456

457

■ *455* **FOSSIL DESIGN STUDIO** *(in-house)* ■ *456* **CURTIS DESIGN** *Christopher Ranch* ■ *457* **FOSSIL DESIGN STUDIO** *(in-house)*

■ *459* **MIRES DESIGN** *Voit Sports*

459

■ *459* **MIRES DESIGN** *Voit Sports*

460 CLAUDIO NOVAES GRAPHIC DESIGN *Marabá Filmes*

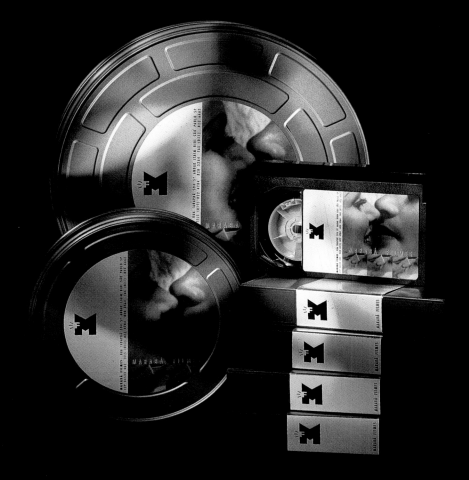

460

■ *460* **CLAUDIO NOVAES GRAPHIC DESIGN** *Marabá Filmes*

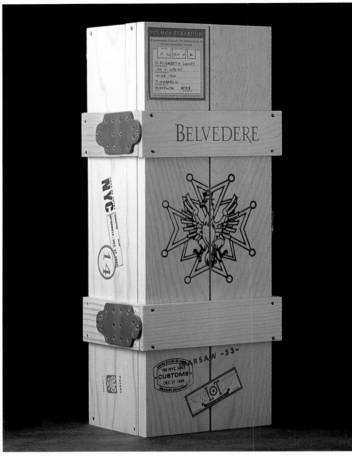

461 462

463 464

■ *461, 462* **PARACHUTE/CLARITY COVERDALE FURY** *Millennium Import Company* ■ *463* **MARK OLIVER, INC.** *Firestone Vineyard* ■ *464* **HAINES MCGREGORY** *IDV*

Dewar's
FINEST SCOTCH WHISKY

40%vol 75cl

466 467

■ *466* **DUFFY DESIGN** *Jim Beam Brands* ■ *467* **SBG PARTNERS** *Brown Forman*

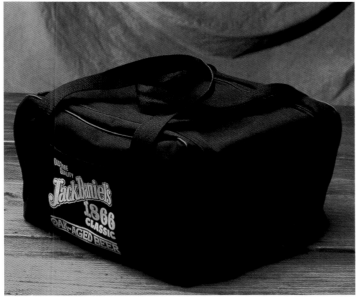

468 469

470 471

472 473

■ *468-473* **DYE, VAN MOL & LAWRENCE** *Jack Daniel's*

474 475

476 477

■ *474* **DUFFY DESIGN** *Molson Brewery* ■ *475* **EJE SOCIEDAD PUBLICITARIA** *Bacardi-Martini* ■ *476* **ANTISTA FAIRCLOUGH DESIGN** *Anheuser-Busch, Inc.*
■ *477* **MARK OLIVER, INC.** *Firestone Walker Brewing Co.*

478

479

■ *478, 479* **CAHAN & ASSOCIATES** *Boisset USA*

480 481

■ *480* **TUTSSELS** *Boots the Chemist* ■ *481* **PEARLFISHER** *(in-house)*

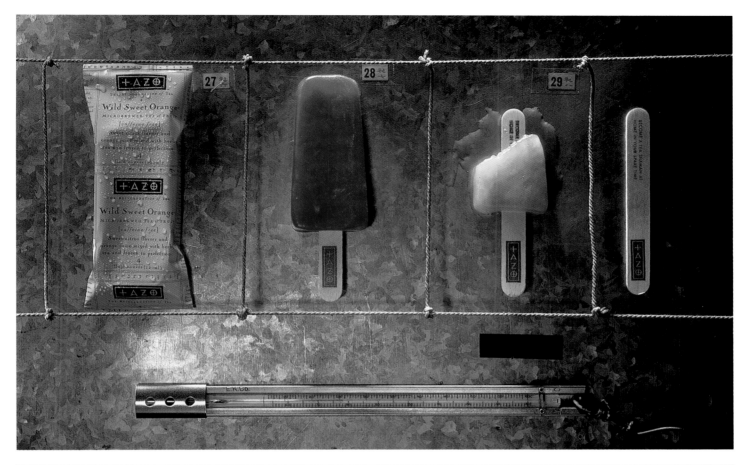

482

483

■ *482* **SANDSTROM DESIGN** *Tazo* ■ *483* **TURNER DUCKWORTH** *Levi Strauss & Co.*

484 485

486 487

■ *484* **DAVID LEMLEY DESIGN** *Brown & Haley* ■ *485* **NIKE IMAGE DESIGN** *Nike, Inc.* ■ *486, 487* **CHARLES S. ANDERSON DESIGN COMPANY** *K-Ration*

■ *488* **KAI MUI GROUP** *AKI S.p.A. Italia*

488

489

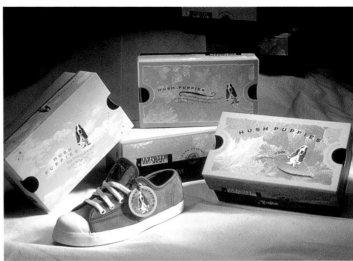

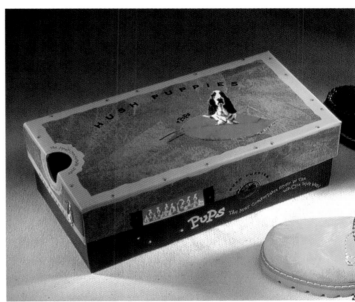

490 491

492 493

494 495

■ *490-495* **FITCH INC.** *Wolverine World Wide*

496

497

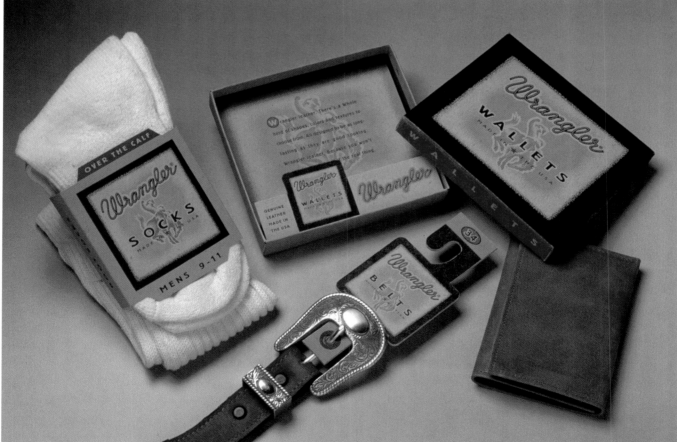

■ *496, 497* **DAVID POYTHRESS DESIGNS, LTD.** *Wrangler, Inc.*

498 499

■ *498* **BLACKBURN'S LTD.** *Gleneagle Spring Waters Co Ltd.* ■ *499* **ANTISTA FAIRCLOUGH DESIGN** *Sutton Place Gourmet*

500

501

■ *500* **SIEGEL & GALE** *S. D. Warren Company* ■ *501* **CROSBY ASSOCIATES INC.** *Champion International Corporation*

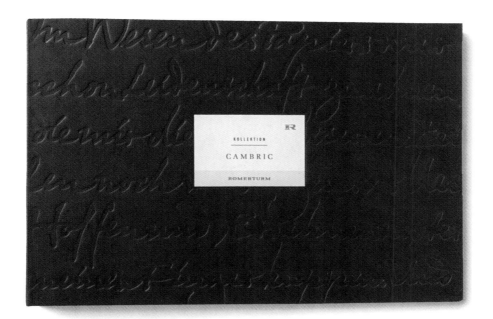

502

503

504

■ *502-504* **FACTOR DESIGN GMBH** *Römerturn Feinstpapier*

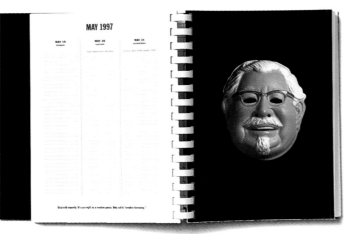

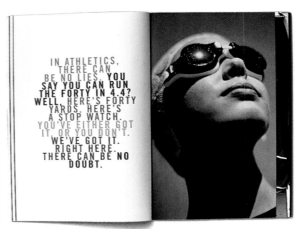

505 509

506 510

507 511

508 512

■ *505-508* **VSA PARTNERS, INC.** *Potlatch Corp.* ■ *509-512* **VAN DYKE COMPANY** *Simpson Coated Papers*

Wherever you want to go, Mohawk Navajo is the text and cover paper that can take you there. A smooth finish that's great to touch. 98 brightness whites that dazzle the eye. Navajo loves ink as much as you'll love printing on it. Because if you're used to settling for less than perfect reproduction to get the feel of a first-class uncoated sheet, your problems are over: Mohawk's patented Inxwell™ paper means lower dot gain, excellent ink holdout and improved opacity. Mohawk Navajo is recycled, with 20% post-consumer waste, and 100% acid free. And it's available the way you need it, from 24 lb. to 130 lb. double-thick, ready to go in cut sizes for digital applications, guaranteed for laser printing. No matter what you need to print, we've got the perfect vehicle: Mohawk Navajo.

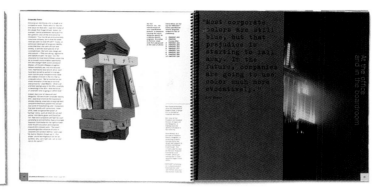

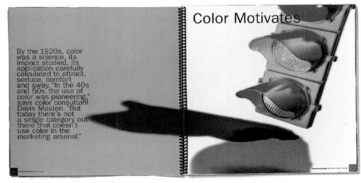

Color Motivates

By the 1920s, color was a science, its impact studied, its application carefully calculated to attract, seduce, comfort and sway. "In the 40s and 50s, the use of color was pioneering," says color consultant Davis Masten. "But today there's not a single category out there that doesn't use color in the marketing arsenal."

■ *513-516* **PENTAGRAM DESIGN INC.** *Mohawk Paper Mills* ■ *517-520* **DESIGNFRAME INC.** *Strathmore Papers*

521 522

IN THIS AGE OF DISPOSABLE, HIGH-SPEED, LO-RES CYBERHAZE,
THERE ARE TIMES WHEN USING PAPER IS A BETTER CHOICE.
AND WHEN IT COMES TO CHOOSING PAPER, THERE IS
THE OBVIOUS CHOICE:

Gleneagle
NO. 1 COATED PAPER

Consort Royal
SUPER PREMIUM COATED PAPER

SEE ON PAPER WHAT YOU SEE IN YOUR MIND.

■ *521, 522* **MANGOS INC.** *UK Paper North America*

523

524

525

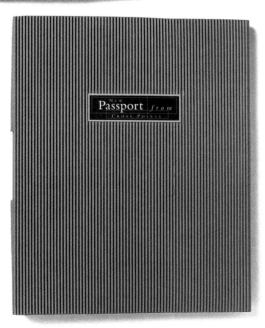

■ *523* **CHARLES S. ANDERSON DESIGN CO.** *French Paper Company* ■ *524, 525* **LITTLE & COMPANY** *Fraser Papers*

■ *526-529* **NIKE IMAGE DESIGN** *Nike, Inc.*

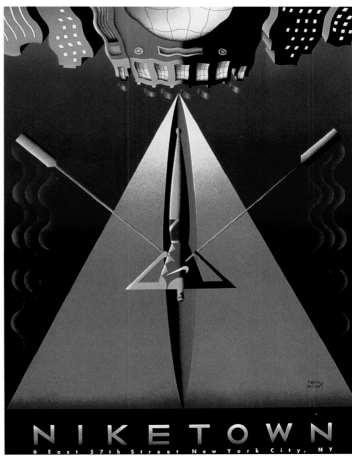

528 529

530

531

■ *530, 531* **BIG BANG IDEA ENGINEERING** *The Kalakala Foundation*

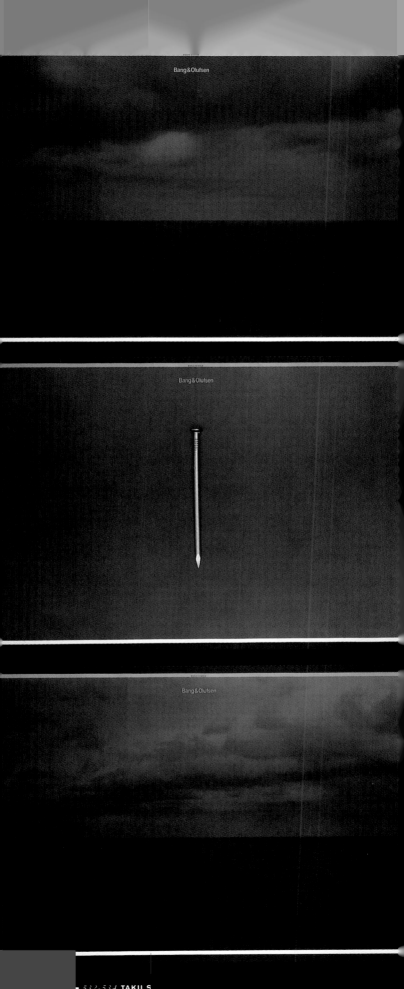

50 YEARS OF VESPA

MILTON GLASER INC, illustration

■ *536* ZIMMERMANN CROWE DESIGN *Levi Strauss & Co.*

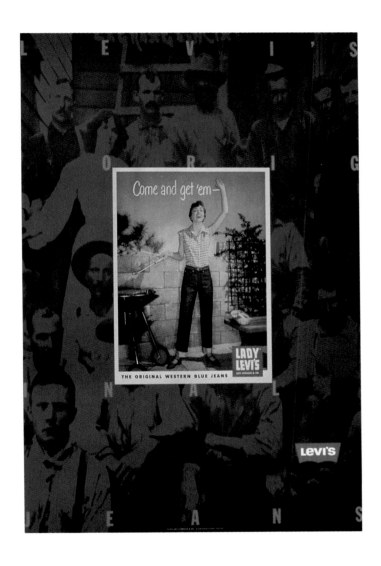

537 538

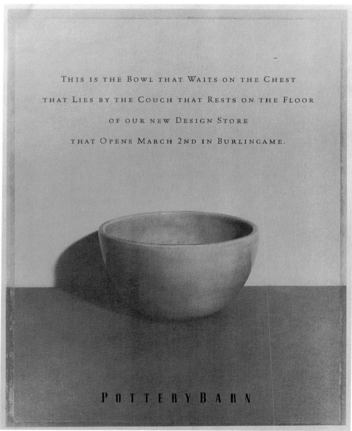

THIS IS THE FAN THAT STIRS THE DRAPE
THAT COOLS THE SHEET THAT BRUSHES THE FLOOR
OF OUR NEW DESIGN STORE
THAT OPENS ON JUNE 1ST IN SHORT HILLS.

POTTERY BARN

THIS IS THE BOWL THAT WAITS ON THE CHEST
THAT LIES BY THE COUCH THAT RESTS ON THE FLOOR
OF OUR NEW DESIGN STORE
THAT OPENS MARCH 2ND IN BURLINGAME.

POTTERY BARN

■ *537, 538* **EM DASH** *Pottery Barn*

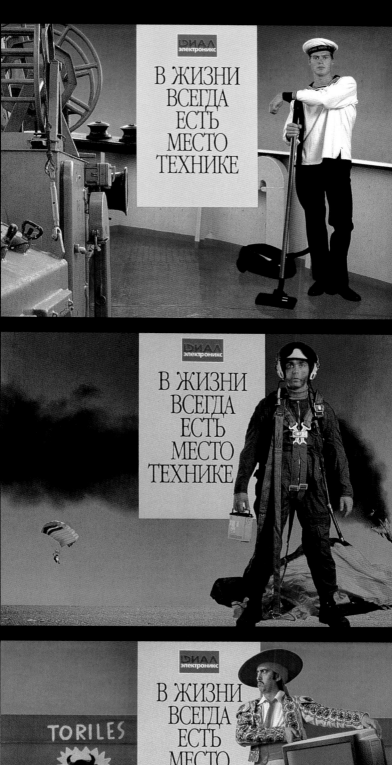

■ 539-541 **DESIGN BUREAU AGEY TOMESH** *Dial Electronics*

542 543

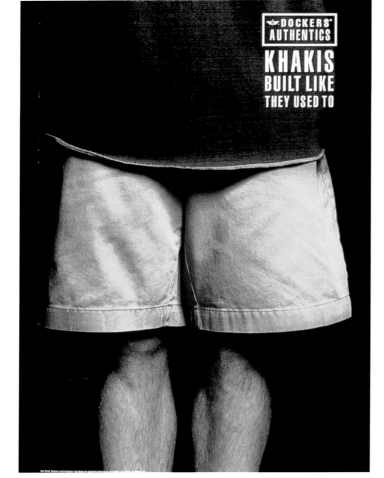

544

■ *544* **TAKU SATOH DESIGN OFFICE INC.** *(in-house)*

■ *545, 546* **FOOTE, CONE, & BELDING** *Levi Strauss & Co.*

547

548

549

■ *547-549* **SCHOLZ & FRIENDS** *FRANKFURTER ALLGEMEINE ZEITUNG*

550

551

■ *550* **SIMON & GOETZ** *adp.engineering GmbH* ■ *551* **FRIDOLIN BEISERT, MICHAEL SANS** *Art Center College of Design*

553-556 DALE FROMMELT DESIGN *(in-house)*

[192]

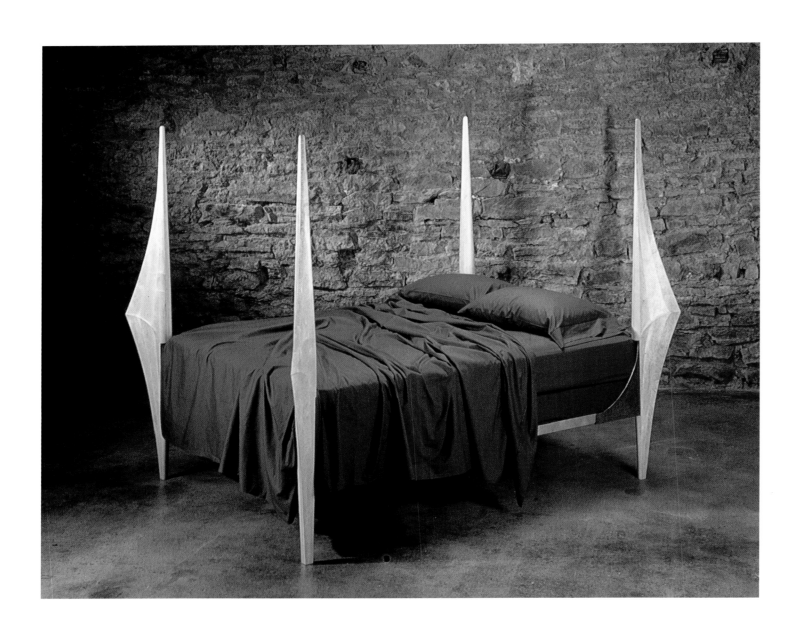

553

554

555

556

557 558

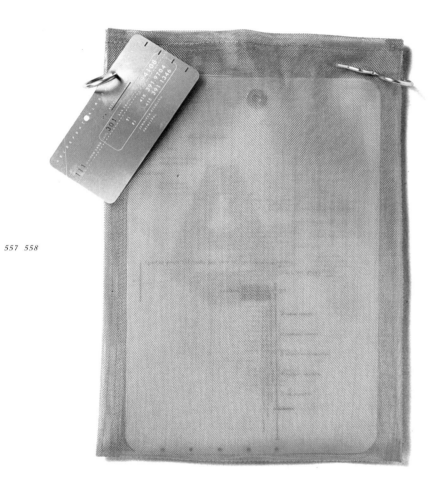
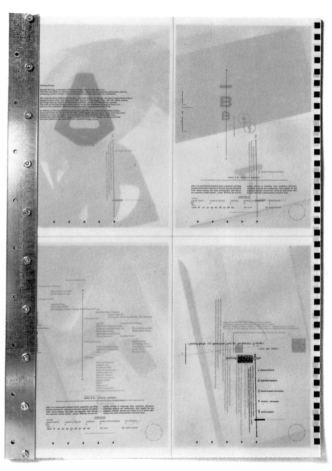

■ *557-561* **JENNIFER STERLING DESIGN** *(in-house)*

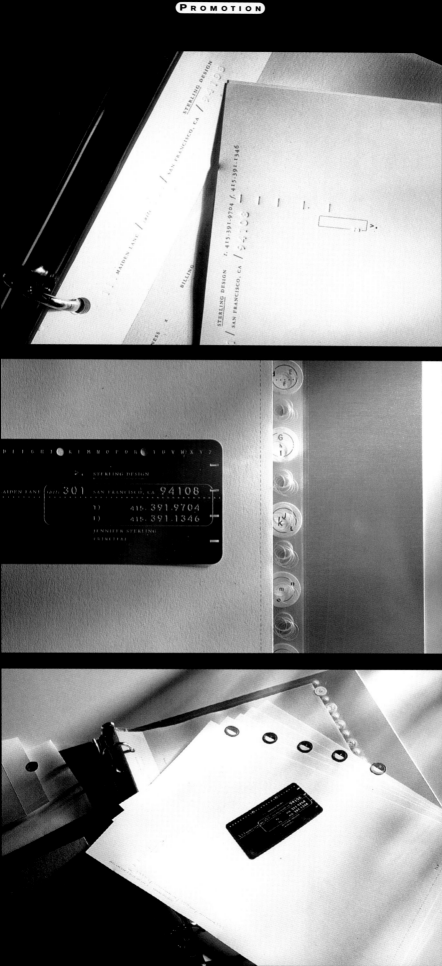

562

■ *562* **JENNIFER STERLING DESIGN** *Quickturn Design Systems Inc.*

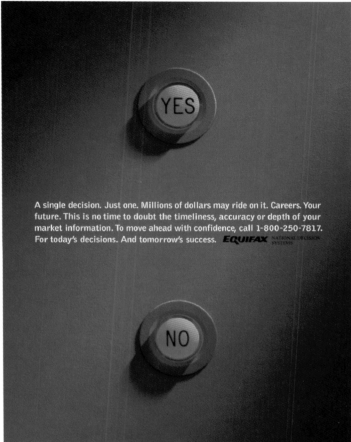

A single decision. Just one. Millions of dollars may ride on it. Careers. Your future. This is no time to doubt the timeliness, accuracy or depth of your market information. To move ahead with confidence, call 1-800-250-7817. For today's decisions. And tomorrow's success. **EQUIFAX** NATIONAL DECISION SYSTEMS

563   564

565   566

■ *563* **MIRES DESIGN** *Bordeaux Printers* ■ *564* **MIRES DESIGN** *Equifax Business Geometrics* ■ *565, 566* **CKS PARTNERS, INC.** *(in-house)*

567

568

569

■ *568* **NELEMAN STUDIO NYC** *(in-house)* ■ *569* **RITTA & ASSOCIATES** *BMW of North America Inc.*

571

■ *571* **ORIGIN DESIGN COMPANY LTD.** *(in-house)*

572 573

574 575

■ *572* **DESIGN GUYS** *Marshall Fields* ■ *573* **NIKE IMAGE DESIGN** *Nike, Inc.* ■ *574* **PACKAGE LAND CO., LTD.** *(in-house)* ■ *575* **PARHAM SANTANA INC.** *VH1*

576 NABATAME DESIGN OFFICE Nagaoka Kojimaya Co. Ltd.

576

577

578

579

580

■ *577* **Q30 DESIGN INC.** *Canada Post Corporation* ■ *578* **ESKIND WADDELL** *Canada Post Corporation* ■ *579* **SKOLOS/WEDELL** *United States Postal Service*
■ *580* **TAYBURN MCILLROY COATES** *Royal Mail National*

    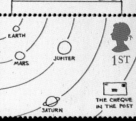

■ *581* **TUTSSELS** *Royal Mail National* ■ *582* **MICHAEL WOLFF** *Royal Mail National* ■ *583* **DESIGN HOUSE** *Royal Mail National*
■ *584* **MICHAEL NASH ASSOCIATES** *Royal Mail National* ■ *585* **SIMON CLAY** *Royal Mail National* ■ *586* **MOSELEY WEBB** *Royal Mail National*

587 588

589 590

■ *587* **MIRES DESIGN** *Hot Rod Hell* ■ *588* **MIRES DESIGN** *Harcourt Brace Co.* ■ *589* **TODD DAVID NICKEL** *(in-house)* ■ *590* **D. BETZ DESIGN** *Virtual Telemetrix*

591

592

■ *591, 592* **GRABARZ & PARTNER WERBEAGENTUR** *Self-promotion*

文字の物語が画面を行き交う。ことばを映像化する力が、漢字にはある。

文字の音楽が紙上を流れる。ひらがなの響きは、いつの時代も心に近い。

593
594

■ *593, 594* **SHINNOSKE INC.** *Morisawa & Co. Ltd.*

TRANSLATIONS AND CAPTIONS

ÜBERSETZUNGEN UND LEGENDEN

TRADUCTIONS ET LÉGENDES

(auf Seite 18 fortgesetzt) möchte. Wenn jemand wegen eines Jahresberichtes anruft, kommen Jahresberichte an den Anfang des Katalogs. Und wenn mir zum Beispiel in einem Jahr etwas nicht mehr gefällt, kann ich es einfach herausnehmen.» Der Aluminium-Katalog und die beigefügten Visitenkarten aus Metall passen in eine Tragtasche aus weichem Material. «Ich wollte ein Symbol für harte und weiche Gegenstände», sagt Sterling, die vor kurzem eine eigene Produktfirma gegründet hat, die Dinge wie Post-It-Notizzettel aus Aluminium anbietet. («Ich hasste die gelben Dinger, die überall auf meinen Unterlagen klebten», sagt sie.) Sterlings Name und Adresse sind in Blindprägung an der Seite ihrer Briefbogen angebracht. Das ist, wie sie sagt, «irgendwie typisch für meine Arbeit. Sie ist eher zurückhaltend.»

Jeff Larson, The Larson Group

Die Larson Group ist in Rockford, Illinois, in einem Industriegebiet westlich von Chicago zu Hause. Obgleich es Möglichkeiten genug gab, ist seine Designfirma gemäss Jeff Larson gewissen Aufträgen bewusst aus dem Weg gegangen, wie z.B. Broschüren für Firmen wie Pearson Fastener, die sich auf Schrauben spezialisiert haben (S. 59). «Sie sehen alle gleich aus», sagt Larson, «schwerfällig und uninteressant.» Aber dieses Mal sagte der Kunde, er wisse, was seine Konkurrenz mache, und er wolle etwas völlig anderes. «Es war eine Gelegenheit, das Produkt in seiner Rohform zu zeigen und es visuell attraktiv zu machen.» Larson konzentrierte sich auf die graphisch interessanten Formen der Schrauben selbst und verwendete nur wenig Text. «Wir zeigten das Endprodukt, und das erzählt die ganze Geschichte», sagt er. Da ausserdem alle Teile in den USA hergestellt werden, zeigt die Broschüre Arbeiter in der Fabrik, und damit war die Botschaft ohne viele Worte klar. Der geprägte, matt lackierte Kartonumschlag der 14seitigen Broschüre wurde mit Pearson-Verschlüssen zusammengehalten, was für eine ganz spezielle Wirkung sorgte.

Ted Leonhardt, The Leonhardt Group

Als die Leonhardt-Gruppe den Auftrag erhielt, für das Geschäft REI (S. 99), das Produkte für draussen verkauft, ein Beschilderungssystem zu entwerfen, war es naheliegend, sich Wanderwegschilder zum Vorbild zu nehmen, zumal die Verkaufsfläche des neu eröffneten REI-Flagship Stores in der City von Seattle über 25000m2 gross ist. «Angesichts der Grösse des Ladens mussten wir dafür sorgen, dass die Leute sich zurechtfinden», sagt Ted Leonhardt, Präsident der Designfirma aus Seattle. Statt wie jeder andere Supermarkt auszusehen, sollte das neue Geschäft von REI gemäss Leonhardt die Kultur der Firma reflektieren, inbesondere das Umweltbewusstsein. «Wir bemühten uns deshalb, Materialien zu verwenden, die entweder wiederverwertet oder natürlich waren, wie Holz, oxidiertes Metall und Stein. Das Hauptschild ist ein Felsblock, auf den REIs Logo sandgestrahlt wurde», sagt Leonhardt. Ein anderes Schild von Leonhardt, das viel beachtet wurde, war interessanterweise das Hinweisschild für die Damentoiletten. «Statt einer Frauenfigur mit einem Rock, die nur so dasteht, hatten wir eine aktive Frau beim Bergsteigen als Motiv ausgewählt – ausschreitend und mit schwingenden Armen. Es gibt natürlich staatliche Vorschriften für diese Art von Schildern, und wir mussten einiges tun, um es durchzusetzen», sagt Leonhardt.

Steve Sandstrom, Sandstrom Design

Pavlov Productions, eine Abteilung von Sony Entertainment, die vor allem TV-Werbespots produzieren, brauchten nicht nur ein visuelles Erscheinungsbild, als sie Steve Sandstrom von Sandstrom Design engagierten, sondern auch einen Namen. «Die Leute von Sony haben dank ihres Filmproduktionsstudios immense Möglichkeiten bei Spezialeffekten für ihre TV-Spots. Unser

Auftraggeber wollte auf keinen Fall einen Auftritt, der nur auf Technik beruht – typisch für die Spezialeffekt-Typen –, weil das ziemlich einschränkend ist», sagt Sandstrom, der Creative Director der Designfirma in Oregon ist. «Wir konnten uns auf Wissenschaftliches beziehen, aber wir machten es in jeder Hinsicht auf sehr witzige Art.» Der wissenschaftliche Aspekt des neuen Erscheinungsbildes für die Firma (S. 70, 71) ist nicht nur sehr direkt, sondern alle Sachen für Pavlov, von den (perforierten) Visitenkarten bis zu Video-Tape-Etiketten (die von Parktickets inspiriert wurden), zeichnen sich durch eine gewisse Naivität aus. «All das ist an Art Direktoren, Kreativ Direktoren, Texter, Rundfunk- und TV-Direktoren gerichtet, und wenn unser Design ein bisschen rauh aussieht, wissen diese Leute, dass es beabsichtigt ist. Es ist eigentlich Anti-Graphik. Wir haben Formen geschaffen, die so aussehen, als seien sie in einem Labor entstanden, eher in einer Behörde als in einer Welt, in der es um Stil geht.

Yoshimaru Takahashi, *Ti* Magazin

Bei der japanischen Zeitschrift *Ti* (S. 90, 91), die optisch aussergewöhnlich reizvoll ist, handelt es sich nicht einfach um ein weiteres geschäftliches Unternehmen – das zumindest behauptet Yoshimaru Takahashi, einer der fünf Art Direktoren, die das Redaktionsteam bilden. Es handelt sich um ein Projekt der Japan Typographers Association, das dank der ehrenamtlichen Mitarbeit von JTA-Mitgliedern und Unterstützung von draussen realisiert werden kann. Die Zeitschrift erscheint monatlich und soll «hervorragendes Design zeigen und damit auch erläutern, was gutes Design ist», sagt Takahashi. Von April 1995 bis März 1996 befasste sich das Magazin mit «dem Bildungskonzept. Die Idee dahinter war, dass jedes Element der Bildung sich aus der urbanen Erfahrung und Kommunikations-Design zusammensetzt», sagt Takahashi. «Jeden Monat wurde ein spezielles Thema aufgenommen, das ein weiterer Schritt auf dem Weg zum Verständnis war. Diese Ausgaben waren in unseren Augen Entdeckungsreisen in die Welt der Typographie und des Kommunikations-Designs.» Natürlich verursachen zu viele Köche manches Mal Hektik in der Küche, und selbst Takahashi gibt zu, dass «die Persönlichkeiten der Mitglieder ein Problem darstellten, wenn es darum ging, sich auf den Redaktionsschluss zu einigen. Wir haben das gelöst, indem jedes der fünf Mitglieder abwechselnd die Verantwortung für eine Ausgabe tragen musste.» Bei den fünf Redaktionsmitgliedern handelt es sich um Takahashi, Akio Okumura, Shinnosuke Sugisaki, Toshiyasu Nambu und Ken Miki.

Glenn Tutssel, Tutssels

Anlässlich des 150 jährigen Bestehens von Dewar's – Hersteller eines weltberühmten Scotch – beschloss Glenn Tutssel, Creative Director der Designfima Tutssels in London, eine von Schottlands ureigenen Ressourcen zu nutzen. Er lud Studenten der besten Design-Schulen des Landes ein, Dewar's' Flasche neu zu gestalten. Die Studentin Fiona Burnett gewann diesen Wettbewerb (S. 159). «Die Flasche zum Jahrestag von Dewar's wurde in einer streng limitierten Auflage von 1846 einzeln numerierten Stücken hergestellt», sagt Tutssel. Burnetts Entwurf «basiert auf der traditionellen schottischen Brosche und vermischt stilvolle, kosmopolitische Modernität mit traditionellen keltischen Motiven», sagt Tutssel. Das Broschenmotiv der Jubiläums-Karaffe «besteht aus hochwertigem Zinn und wurde auch als Kappe der Flasche verwendet. Das Zinn wurde in Email getaucht, und die Flasche wurde so gestaltet, dass die Spannung der Rundung den Clip festhält. Darunter ist ein Schraubverschluss», sagt Tutssel. Der Originalentwurf von Burnett war gemäss Tutssel noch ein bisschen dekorativer als das Endprodukt und sah ein Loch in der Mitte vor. Das sei jedoch nicht durchführbar gewesen, weil die Flasche keinen festen Stand gehabt hätte. Stattdessen wurde ein Loch mit Hilfe von Sandstrahlung simuliert.

Neil Zimmermann, Zimmermann Crowe Design

ZCD hat seit Jahren mit Levi's zusammengearbeitet», sagt Neal Zimmermann von der Designfirma Zimmermann Crowe Design in San Francisco. In letzter Zeit haben sie sich auf den dreidimensionalen Bereich konzentriert – Konzepte für Ladendesign, Präsentationsvorrichtungen und Displays. Levi's 'Traditional and Western'-Präsentationsprogramm (S. 115) wurde auf die Kleinstadtläden und Western-Läden zugeschnitten, die nicht so auf das rassigere, urbane Konzept, sondern eher auf des traditionelle Image von Levi's ansprechen», sagt Zimmermann. Die Idee hinter dem Levi's Heritage Shop war, Levi's als Erfinder der Blue Jeans zu präsentieren und die Geschichte der Firma in den Mittelpunkt zu stellen. Weil sich die Läden in Denver befinden, «arbeiteten wir mit dem Look der Industriearbeiter der 30er Jahre», statt mit dem Cowboy-Image, «das eher zu den Western-Konsumenten und nicht zum Jeans-Käufer passt», sagt Zimmermann. «Der Spass und die Einzigartigkeit lag in der persönlichen Bearbeitung der Schilder, einige wurden von einem Typen nach Hause genommen, der dann mit einer 38er auf sie schoss.» Zu Levi's Präsentationsgestell für das 'Wide Leg'-Modell «gehören Darstellungen und ein dreieckiges Element, das auf dem Logo basiert, wobei aufgehängte Jeans die Breite der Hosenbeine demonstrieren», sagt Zimmerman. Die Erdfarben des Americana-Displays, das für die Händler anlässlich der olympischen Sommerspiele in Atlanta entworfen wurde, «sollten einen Kontrast zu den rot-weiss-blauen Produktangeboten bilden».

Une Sélection des Meilleurs Designers de l'Année par Rynn Williams. Aujourd'hui indépendante, Rynn Williams est une ancienne rédactrice de Graphis.

Le processus créatif présente de nombreuses facettes. Beaucoup d'entre elles sont de nature subtile et intuitive – une certaine texture, une forme ou un caractère «fonctionnent» tout simplement, tandis que d'autres solutions paraissent démodées, fades ou banales. Des décisions plus importantes, en termes de distribution ou de positionnement, peuvent sembler plus difficiles à prendre, parce qu'elles ont trait à l'évolution stratégique. Mais en fin de compte, chaque aspect revêt son importance, en particulier si l'on considère qu'un design doit sortir du lot. ▲ Dans le cadre de la préparation de Graphis Design 98, Graphis a également dû prendre des décisions difficiles. Il a fallu trancher parmi les centaines de travaux sélectionnés pour représenter ce qui se fait de mieux en matière de design international. Finalement, notre choix s'est arrêté sur 13 projets répertoriés dans les différentes catégories: design environnemental, présentoirs, promotions, panneaux d'affichage, design rédactionnel et brochures. Tous se distinguent par leur pertinence, leur fonctionnalité et leur aspect résolument novateur. Au fil de nos entretiens avec les créatifs à l'origine de ces superbes travaux, nous avons essayé de cerner le processus créatif qui sous-tend leur approche respective, le chemin parcouru, de l'idée de base au produit final, magnifique.

Hideki Nakajima, magazine Cut

Son travail pour le magazine pop japonais Cut (page 84-87) montre clairement que Hideki Nakajima, graphiste de Tokyo, s'oppose à l'infographie omniprésente. «Les budgets dont disposent les magazines pour notre travail sont généralement modestes et c'est pourquoi je ne délègue rien à l'extérieur. Je fais les prises de vue dans mon studio, qui est minuscule. Cela dure souvent jusqu'à minuit ou jusqu'à l'aube. Ainsi, je parviens à réduire les coûts au minimum tout en essayant de faire quelque chose d'original. J'espère que mon travail exprime d'une certaine manière ma résistance face à l'omnipotence de la PAO.» La production de la couverture présentant la star islandaise Björk est un bon exemple de la façon de travailler de Nakajima: «Nous avons fait ces prises de vue dans un hôtel de Tokyo. Nous avons simplement recouvert le mur d'un drap et en un quart d'heure, tout était terminé. J'avais apporté des fraises, parce qu'on m'avait dit qu'elle aimait ça.» Pour la couverture présentant Patricia Arquette, Nakajima s'est contenté de poser une boule-miroir de 40 cm de diamètre sur un toit et d'y placer la lettre A. «Le bleu est le reflet du ciel», explique-t-il, avant d'ajouter, «nous devions trouver un espace entièrement dégagé, la boule reflétant tout ce qui l'entoure.»

Dale Frommelt, Dale Frommelt Design

La parenté entre les cathédrales et les galeries n'a pas échappé à Dale Frommelt, ces lieux étant tous deux destinés à la contemplation. C'est pourquoi, lorsque l'on demanda à ce designer originaire de Kansas City, aujourd'hui installé dans le Missouri, de créer des meubles (page169) pour un penthouse d'artiste situé au-dessus de la Grand Arts Gallery de Kansas City, il décida de réaliser dans les hautes pièces blanches une chambre à coucher de style gothique. «L'essentiel est que le regard soit dirigé vers le ciel. Les quatre piliers en marbre du lit rappellent les flèches d'une cathédrale», explique Frommelt. De plus, afin de renforcer cette impression aérienne, «chaque pilier a sa propre forme et est rattaché au matelas.» Par contre, les tables et les chaises qu'il a conçues pour la galerie elle-même sont le résultat d'une réflexion pragmatique. «C'est la première fois que j'essaie de créer des produits principalement fabriqués à l'aide de matériaux recyclés et que l'on peut démonter ou plier afin de les ranger à plat.» Les pièces des meubles peuvent ensuite être combinées différemment afin de créer de nouveaux objets. «Ce sont des 'meubles-lego'.» La chaise est en outre équipée de roulettes qui fonctionnent comme une articulation lorsque l'on rabat la chaise vers l'arrière et qui disparaissent lorsqu'elle est en position normale.

Olaf Stein, Factor Design

«Notre objectif est de convaincre le client que les solutions créatives, risquées, peuvent être très efficaces, car elles attirent l'attention des groupes-cibles», dit Olaf Stein de Factor Design, Hambourg. «Si, dans ce monde fou, on ne parvient pas à atteindre les groupes-cibles, on gaspille l'argent du client.» Römerturm Feinstpapier, l'un des plus grands fabricants de papier allemands, est satisfait de la manière dont a été investi son argent. Intitulé «Die Kollektionen», le système de présentation que Factor Design a réalisé pour ses produits (page 173) est à la fois très élégant et très efficace. Il est constitué de 17 livres d'échantillons contenant tous les papiers proposée et d'un ouvrage présentant sous forme de fichier les différentes couleurs et qualités disponibles. «Nous avons utilisé un exemple imprimé qui illustre les différentes techniques d'impression comme la quadrichromie, la thermogravure ou le gaufrage», explique Stein. «Cela permet de comparer le rendu de l'image sur les diverses qualités de papier.» «Die Kollektionen» est destiné d'une part à être envoyé à des clients potentiels et, d'autre part, à être présenté par le service extérieur de Römerturm à des agences de publicité et à des studios de graphisme, ce qui explique la présence d'une poignée intégrée. «Nous faisons nous-mêmes partie du public-cible», ajoute Stein «et c'est pourquoi nous avons développé quelque chose qui correspond exactement à nos besoins.»

Jaimie Alexander, Fitch Inc.

«A l'époque où nous discutions du relookage de leur image pour les années 90 (page 169), nous nous demandions s'il fallait garder le joli petit chien. Or, nous en sommes arrivés à la conclusion que le chien était l'élément le plus positif pour les consommateurs», dit Jaimie Alexander, DA de Fifth Inc., société installée à Worthington, Ohio, chargée de retravailler le packaging du fabricant de chaussures Hush Puppies. «En ce qui concerne l'identité visuelle de l'entreprise, nous voulions décliner l'image du chien de manière plus moderne.» C'est ainsi que les emballages des articles pour enfants ont été entièrement remaniés «parce que nous avons remarqué que les enfants, dès l'âge de quatre ans, ont une influence sur ce que leurs parents leur achètent», explique Alexander. L'ouverture qui permet de voir ce qu'il y a dans la boîte a été placée au dos de l'emballage, car des études ont montré qu'ainsi, il est plus résistant, mais elle a été «intégrée au design de sorte à devenir un signe distinctif de la marque.» Il est clair que le nouveau look s'adresse en priorité aux enfants. «Mais il est exigeant, ce qui fait qu'il accroche aussi les parents», poursuit Alexander. «L'emballage de ce genre de produits est souvent présent dans les magasins, il doit donc à la fois être fonctionnel et représentatif.»

Toshihiro Onimaru, Graphics and Designing Inc.

Lorsque l'on évoque la cuisine japonaise, on ne pense pas forcément aux quiches et aux tartes, ce qui n'a certainement pas facilité le travail de Toshihiro Onimaru, DA de Graphics and Designing Inc., Tokyo, lorsqu'il s'est agi de concevoir le papier à en-tête (page 97, 137) de G&D Management Inc. Dans un même temps, il disposait ainsi d'une plus grande liberté. G&D Management Inc. est une filiale de la société de design qu'a ouvert le premier café-restaurant «Quiche & Tart» au Japon. «Au Japon, les quiches et les tartes ne sont pas populaires. C'est pourquoi, afin d'éveiller la curiosité des Japonais, j'ai choisi d'utiliser une illustration plutôt qu'une photo, pensant que cette solution était plus efficace», explique Onimaru. «D'aucuns trouvent peut-être ce logo trop classique, voire démodé. Mais le concept du restaurant est bien de proposer une version moderne de la tarte maison, et il me semblait donc indispensable d'exprimer ce concept au niveau visuel.» Onimaru n'aime pas la nostalgie et il a donc «décidé de choisir un caractère et des couleurs qui correspondent à la sensibilité des Japonais modernes.» A ce jour, G&D Management Inc. possède un restaurant à Tokyo. Mais il est prévu d'en ouvrir un deuxième en automne. «Ils nous offrent une excellente occasion d'essayer dans la pratique tout ce que nous concevons et produisons», conclut Onimaru.

Mark Crawford, Intralink Film Graphic Design

A Hollywood, Sunset Boulevard est jalonné d'immenses panneaux d'affichage. Pour attirer l'attention des passants blasés sur l'affiche du film à grand-spectacle «Twister» (page 155), Mark Crawford et Anthony Goldschmidt, directeurs créatifs d'Intralink Film Graphic Design, savaient donc qu'il fallait trouver quelque chose de vraiment original. «Nous avons pensé qu'il pourrait être intéressant de travailler sur l'idée de la destruction et de la force qu'il faut pour causer de tels dégâts», explique Crawford. Au lieu d'opter pour quelque chose de classique – par exemple une photo tirée du film qui montrerait la tornade ('twister') – Intralink décida donc de construire une sorte de relief duquel émergent des bouts de bois, des pneus et des pièces métalliques, «comme si une tornade s'était abattue sur Sunset Boulevard et avait projeté ces objets sur le panneau d'affichage.» L'«affiche» ainsi réalisée a été placée avant même la sortie du film et elle sautait littéralement aux yeux, se distinguant de toutes les autres. «C'était très émotionnel», poursuit Crawford. L'affiche est immense, «mais comme nous montrions les dégâts causés par la tornade et non la tornade elle-même, elle paraissait encore plus grande.»

Jennifer Sterling, Jennifer Sterling Design

«L'organisation prévient l'ennui», affirme Jennifer Sterling, installée à San Francisco. Il y a deux ans, lorsqu'elle s'attaqua à la conception d'un outil de promotion pour sa propre société (page 194, 195), elle choisit de prendre pour exemple les dossiers qu'elle constitue pour ses clients. «Je voulais créer quelque chose qui soit typique de ce que je fais pour mes clients, quelque chose d'avantageux qui puisse être remanié, adapté en fonction de l'évolution de la situation», explique-t-elle. «Le catalogue est constitué de cinq chapitres que je peux mettre dans l'ordre que je veux, en fonction du client. Si quelqu'un me contacte pour un rapport annuel, je place les rapports annuels au début du catalogue. Et si, par exemple, dans un an, quelque chose ne me plaît plus, je le retire.» Le catalogue en aluminium et les cartes de visite en métal qui l'accompagnent peuvent être rangés dans une mallette souple. «Je voulais que ça symbolise les matériaux durs et les matériaux souples», dit Sterling qui a récemment créé une société de fabrication proposant notamment des «post-it» en aluminium. («Je détestais tous ces petits bouts de papier jaunes qui dépassaient de mes dossiers.») Pour imprimer son nom et son adresse sur son papier à en-tête, elle a choisi un gaufrage neutre qui longe le bord de la feuille. «Cela reflète assez bien mes travaux, plutôt discrets», résume-t-elle.

Jeff Larson, The Larson Group

Le Larson Group est installé à Rockford, Illinois, à l'ouest de Chicago, au cœur d'une zone industrielle, ce qui aurait pu lui permettre de réaliser de nombreuses brochures pour des entreprises comme Pearson Fastener, un fabricant de vis (page 59). «Mais nous avons consciemment évité ce genre de commandes», explique Jeff Larson, «car ces catalogues se ressemblent tous, ils sont lourds et inintéressants.» Cette fois-ci pourtant, le responsable de Pearson Fastener a appelé Larson en affirmant qu'il savait ce que faisait la concurrence et qu'il voulait quelque chose de résolument différent. «C'était une occasion de montrer le produit à l'état brut et de le mettre en valeur visuellement.» Larson s'est ainsi concentré sur la forme des vis, sur leur graphisme particulier, et a limité le texte. «Nous avons simplement montré le produit fini, car il raconte toute son histoire», ajoute-t-il. Toutes les pièces étant en outre fabriquées aux Etats-Unis, la brochure présente également des ouvriers au travail, ce qui permet de faire passer le message sans grandes explications. Enfin, pour la couverture gaufrée en carton mat de cette brochure de 14 pages, Larson a utilisé des fermetures Pearson pour obtenir un effet visuel original.

Ted Leonhardt, The Leonhardt Group

Lorsque les magasins REI demandèrent au Leonhardt Group, Seattle, de concevoir un système de signalétique, Ted Leonhardt pensa immédiatement qu'il fallait s'inspirer des panneaux qui balisent les promenades dans les forêts américaines (page 99). En effet, REI vend des articles destinés à la vie en plein air et, de plus, le magasin que la société vient d'ouvrir au centre de Seattle a une surface de 25 000 m2. «Etant donné la taille du magasin, il fallait être sûr que les gens n'allaient pas se perdre», explique Leonhardt. D'autre part, pour se distinguer des autres supermarchés, le magasin REI devait refléter la culture de l'entreprise et tout particulièrement son souci de l'environnement. «C'est pourquoi nous avons choisi des matériaux recyclés ou naturels comme le bois, le métal oxydé ou la pierre. Le panneau principal est un bloc de pierre sur lequel le logo de REI a été dessiné au jet de sable», poursuit Leonhardt. Dans un même esprit, il a également cherché des solutions originales pour des panneaux moins importants, par exemple celui des toilettes pour dames. «Au lieu d'y faire figurer la silhouette d'une femme immobile en jupe, nous avons choisi une femme active qui fait de l'escalade. Mais apparemment, il existe des réglementations assez strictes pour ce genre de panneaux et nous avons dû nous battre pour le faire passer.»

Steve Sandstrom, Sandstrom Design

Lorsqu'ils s'adressèrent à Steve Sandstrom, Pavlov Productions, un département de Sony Entertainment qui produit principalement des spots télévisés, était à la recherche d'une identité visuelle. Mais ce n'était pas tout. A l'époque, cette société n'avait pas encore de nom. «Pour leurs spots TV, les gens de chez Sony ont, grâce à leurs studios de cinéma, des possibilités quasi illimitées en ce qui concerne les effets spéciaux. Pourtant, les responsables de ce département voulaient à tout prix éviter d'avoir une identité visuelle qui n'évoquerait que la technique – du genre 'Ah voilà les types des effets spéciaux' – pour ne pas être confinés dans ce domaine», explique Steve Sandstrom, directeur créatif de la société Sandstrom Design installée à Portland, Oregon. «Nous nous sommes certes inspirés de la science, mais toujours avec une touche d'humour.» L'aspect scientifique de la nouvelle identité de Pavlov (page 70, 71) est ainsi à la fois très direct et empreint d'une certaine naïveté, qu'il s'agisse des cartes de visite perforées ou des étiquettes pour cassettes vidéo, inspirées des tickets de parking. «Tout cela est destiné à des directeurs artistiques, à des directeurs créatifs, à des rédacteurs, à des responsables de chaînes télévisées ou de stations de radio, et ils savent que nous avons consciemment choisi un design un peu brut. En fait, c'est de l'antigraphisme. Nous avons créé des formes qui semblent sortir d'un laboratoire, qui paraissent avoir été conçues plutôt par des fonctionnaires que par des artistes.»

Yoshimaru Takahashi, magazine Ti

Pour Takahashi, l'un des cinq directeurs artistiques qui forment son équipe rédactionnelle, le magazine japonais Ti (page 90, 91), visuellement très séduisant, n'est pas un produit commercial comme les autres. Il s'agit en effet d'un projet de la Japan Typographers Association qui a vu le jour grâce à l'engagement et au travail bénévole des membres de l'association et de ceux qui la soutiennent. Le mensuel Ti a pour but de «présenter ce qui se fait de mieux dans le domaine du graphisme et du design afin de montrer ce qu'est un bon design», dit Takahashi. Entre avril 1995 et mars 1996, le magazine s'est intéressé au «concept de la culture. L'idée qui sous-tendait cette recherche était que chaque élément de la culture est constitué de l'expérience urbaine et du design de communication», explique Takahashi.

«Tous les mois, nous avons choisi un thème précis permettant de mieux comprendre le fond du problème. Pour nous, ces numéros étaient comme les étapes d'un voyage qui nous emmène à la découverte du monde de la typographie et du design de communication.» Il est clair que, parfois, quand il y a trop de cuisiniers, le travail en cuisine devient difficile, et Takahashi reconnaît que «les membres de l'équipe rédactionnelle ont parfois du mal à s'entendre à la veille du bouclage. Nous avons résolu ce problème en nous chargeant à tour de rôle de la réalisation d'un numéro.» Outre Takahashi, la rédaction est constituée d'Akio Okumura, de Shinnosuke Sugisaki, de Toshiyasu Nanbu et de Ken Miki.

Glenn Tutssel, Tutssels

A l'occasion du 150e anniversaire de Dewar's, fabricant d'un scotch mondialement célèbre, Glenn Tutssel, directeur de la création de la société de design londonienne Tutssels, a décidé de faire appel aux forces vives du pays d'origine de cet alcool. C'est ainsi qu'il a demandé aux élèves des meilleures écoles de design écossaises de redessiner la bouteille Dewar's. Le concours a été remporté par Fiona Burnett (page 159). «Cette bouteille a été produite en série limitée. Nous avons fabriqué 1846 exemplaires numérotés», explique Tutssel. «La bouteille conçue par Burnett s'inspire de la broche écossaise traditionnelle, elle allie une modernité cosmopolite et d'anciens motifs celtes. La broche de la 'carafe anniversaire' est en étain et elle sert de bouchon. L'étain a été trempé dans de l'émail, et la bouteille a été dessinée de manière à ce que la tension de l'arrondi maintienne le clip. En-dessous, il y a une fermeture à vis.» En fait, l'original de Burnett était encore plus décoratif que le produit fini, et il y avait un trou au milieu de la bouteille. Mais cette idée n'a pas pu être réalisée, car la bouteille aurait manqué de stabilité. On a donc préféré imiter un trou en opacifiant la partie centrale de la bouteille au jet de sable.

Neil Zimmermann, Zimmermann Crowe Design

«ZCD travaille depuis des années avec Levi's», dit Neal Zimmermann de Zimmermann Crowe Design, San Francisco. Ces derniers temps, ZCD s'est concentré sur des réalisations tridimensionnelles (design de magasins, systèmes de présentation). C'est ainsi que «le programme de présentation Levi's 'Traditional and Western' (page 115) a été conçu pour les magasins installés dans des petites villes et les boutiques western plus proches de l'image traditionnelle de Levi's que de son image actuelle, plus urbaine», poursuit Zimmermann. L'idée principale des Levi's Heritage Shops était de présenter Levi's comme l'inventeur du blue jean et d'évoquer l'histoire de l'entreprise. Ces magasins étant installés à Denver, «nous avons travaillé sur le look des ouvriers des années 30 et non sur celui des cow-boys qui correspond plus aux clients 'western' qu'aux acheteurs de jeans. Ce qui nous a amusés – et c'est ce qui rend ce concept original – c'était de retravailler à notre manière les différents éléments. Un des types a par exemple pris un panneau chez lui et a tiré dessus avec un 38. Pour le système de présentation du modèle Wide Leg, nous avons utilisé des illustrations et un élément triangulaire qui rappelle le logo, des jeans suspendus soulignant la largeur des jambes», dit Zimmermann. Quant aux couleurs chaudes du présentoir Americana, conçu à l'occasion des J.O. d'Atlanta, «elles avaient pour but de contraster avec le bleu, le blanc et le rouge des produits.»

PAGE 2 DESIGN FIRM/ILLUSTRATOR: *Sandra Hendler* CLIENT: *Usiskin Contemporary Art* ■ *This image suggests the solitude of making music in a wild place with only hidden listeners: the animals.* ● *Die Einsamkeit der Musiker in der Natur — mit versteckten Tieren als einzigen Zuhörern.* ▲ *Image évoquant la solitude du musicien dans la nature avec pour seuls auditeurs les animaux cachés.*

PAGE 4 ART DIRECTOR/DESIGNER: *John Ball* DESIGN FIRM: *Vanderschuit Studio* ■ *Water is the metaphor used to illustrate the business opportunity of providing fast Internet service.* ● *Wasser dient hier als Metapher für die wirtschaftlichen Chancen, die ein schneller Internet-Service bietet.* ▲ *L'eau, métaphore illustrant le potentiel économique d'un service Internet rapide.*

PAGE 20; #1, 2 ART DIRECTORS: *Woody Pirtle, John Klotnia* DESIGNER: *Ivette Montes de Oca* DESIGN ASSISTANT: *Seung Il Choi* DESIGN FIRM: *Pentagram Design, Inc.* ILLUSTRATORS: *Lori Anzalone, Dugald Stermer, Kevin Torline, Barbara Kelly* CLIENT: *National Audubon Society* PRINTER: *Sandy Alexander Inc.* ■ *This annual report for National Audubon Society focuses on birds' wildlife, and habitat.* ● *Thema dieses Jahresberichtes für die National Audubon Society sind die Vö gel und ihr Lebensraum.* ▲ *Les oiseaux et leur habitat, tel était le thème du rapport annuel de la National Audubon Society.*

PAGE 21; #3-5 ART DIRECTOR/DESIGNER: *Jennifer Sterling* DESIGN FIRM: *Jennifer Sterling Design* PHOTOGRAPHER/ILLUSTRATOR: *Jennifer Sterling* COPYWRITER: *Robert Pollie* CLIENT: *Quickturn Design Systems Inc.* PRINTER: *Active Graphics* ■ *Quickturn is an emulation and design verification provider for software and hardware. The annual report is filled with facts regarding the benefits (in both time and money) for testing products.* ● *Quickturn ist ein Serviceunternehmen für Software und Hardware. Der Jahresbericht liefert zahlreiche Fakten über die Vorteile von Produkttests, und zwar in terminlicher wie in finanzieller Hinsicht.* ▲ *Quickturn est une société de services spécialisée dans les logiciels et le matériel informatique. Le rapport annuel présente avec moult faits à l'appui les avantages que procurent les tests de produits en termes de temps et d'argent.*

PAGE 22; #6-9 ART DIRECTOR: *Jurek Wajdowicz* DESIGNERS: *Lisa Larochelle, Jurek Wajdowicz* DESIGN FIRM: *Emerson, Wajdowicz Studios* PHOTOGRAPHERS: *J. Blair, J. Brockmann, H. Caux* COPYWRITER: *David Konigsberg* CLIENT: *United Nations Office for Project Services* PRINTER: *H. MacDonald Printing* ■ *This annual report's rhythm and photojournalistic design approach features powerful photos, and the typography of a report "from the front."* ● *Der photojournalistische Stil, der in den eindrucksvollen Aufnahmen wie auch im Design und der Typographie zum Ausdruck kommt, macht diesen Jahresbericht zu einem «Bericht von der Front».* ▲ *Réalisé dans le style du photojournalisme qui se traduit à travers les images fortes, le graphisme et la typographie, ce rapport annuel se présente comme un «rapport du front».*

PAGE 22; #10-13 ART DIRECTOR/DESIGNER: *Kerry Leimer* DESIGN FIRM: *Leimer Cross Design* PHOTOGRAPHER: *Tyler Boley* COPYWRITER: *Nick Carter, Kerry Leimer* CLIENT: *Zurich Reinsurance Centre Inc.* PRINTER: *Lithographix Inc.* ■ *This annual report was created to orient employees to the requirements of surviving in a changing insurance industry.* ● *Der Jahresbericht dient der Orientierung des Personals über die Massnahmen, die notwendig sind, um den neuen Anforderungen der Versicherungsbranche gerecht zu werden.* ▲ *Rapport annuel visant à orienter le personnel sur les mesures à prendre pour s'adapter et faire face aux nouvelles exigences du marché des assurances.*

PAGE 23; #14-17 ART DIRECTOR/DESIGNER: *Michael Gunselman* DESIGN FIRM: *Michael Gunselman Inc.* PHOTOGRAPHER: *Ira Wexler* COPYWRITER/CLIENT: *Corporation for Public Broadcasting* PRINTER: *GraphTec* ■ *This annual report reinforces the client's commitment to creating new learning opportunities through technology.* ● *Thema des Jahresberichtes ist das Engagement des Kunden im Bereich der Ausbildungsmö glichkeiten durch Technologie.* ▲ *Rapport annuel mettant en avant l'engagement du client dans le domaine de la création de nouvelles possibilités de formation grâce à la technologie.*

PAGE 23; #18-21 ART DIRECTOR/DESIGNER: *Neal Ashby* DESIGN FIRM/CLIENT: *Recording Industry Association of America* PHOTOGRAPHER: *Amy Guip* COPYWRITERS: *Neal Ashby, Fred Guthrie* PRINTER: *Steckel* ■ *This annual*

report for the Recording Industry Association of America uses the motif of a cassette player to examine the past year and the future of the association. It tackles difficult subjects like music censorship and copyright protection on the information superhighway with powerful imagery, and stark black-and-white typography. ● *Dieser Jahresbericht für den Verband der Tonträgerindustrie Amerikas benutzt das Motiv eines Kassettengerätes, um das vergangene Jahr und die Zukunft des Verbandes zu analysieren. Hier werden schwierige Themen wie Zensur in der Musik und Urheberrechtsschutz im Informations-Superhighway angesprochen, und zwar mit Hilfe von eindrucksvollen Bildern und schlichter Typographie in Schwarzweiss.* ▲ *Ce rapport annuel de l'Association américaine de l'industrie du disque prend un lecteur cassettes comme sujet pour analyser le passé et l'avenir de l'association. Il soulève des thèmes délicats, tels que la censure dans la musique et la protection des droits d'auteur sur Internet. Des images fortes et une typo noir et blanc sobre créent l'impact souhaité.*

PAGE 24; #22 ART DIRECTOR: *Dana Arnett* DESIGNERS: *Melissa Waters, Adam Smith* DESIGN FIRM: *VSA Partners, Inc.* EDITOR: *Mike Fernandez* CLIENT: *Eastman Kodak Company* PRINTER: *Case Hoyt Corp.* ■ *A "gallery" of images from each of the divisions was positioned at the beginning of the annual report followed by a collection of essays and product vignettes. The overall effect was a clear, compelling image of Kodak in 1996.* ● *Eine «Galerie» von Bildern aus jedem der verschiedenen Unternehmensbereiche wurde an den Anfang des Jahresberichtes gestellt, gefolgt von einer Reihe von Textbeiträgen und Produktvignetten. Der Gesamteindruck war ein klares, überzeugendes Bild von Kodak im Jahre 1996.* ▲ *Les différents services de l'entreprise sont présentés comme des «galeries» d'images au début du rapport annuel. Une série de textes et de vignettes produit complète le rapport. Le résultat donne une image positive de Kodak en 1996.*

PAGE 24; #23 ART DIRECTOR: *Jurek Wajdowicz* DESIGNERS: *Jurek Wajdowicz, Lisa Rochelle* DESIGN FIRM: *Emerson, Wajdowicz Studios* PHOTOGRAPHERS: *J. Becker, T. Sennett, D. Rest* CLIENT: *The Rockefeller Foundation* PRINTER: *H. MacDonald Printing* ■ *The effective art direction, use of vibrant photographs (featuring the Foundation's recent beneficiaries) and elegant but understated typography express the Foundation's positive and active approach to diverse international and national concerns in the areas of science-based development, equal opportunity, school reforms, arts and humanities.* ● *Das aktive Engagement dieser Stiftung in verschiedenen Bereichen — wissenschaftliche Projekte, Chancengleichheit, Schulreformen, Kunst und Humanwissenschaften — ist Gegenstand dieses Jahresberichtes. In lebendigen Bildern werden die Begünstigten aus jüngerer Zeit vorgestellt. Die schlichte, elegante Typographie und das Design unterstützen die Wirkung der Aufnahmen.* ▲ *L'engagement actif de la Fondation Rockefeller dans des domaines variés — développement de la science, égalité des chances, réformes de l'éducation, arts, sciences humaines... — est l'objet de ce rapport annuel superbement réalisé. Des images vivantes présentent les récents bénéficiaires de la Fondation, et la typographie se caractérise par son élégance sobre.*

PAGE 24; #24 ART DIRECTOR/DESIGNER: *Robert Achten* DESIGN FIRM: *Origin Design Company Ltd.* PHOTOGRAPHER: *John Daley* COPYWRITER: *Sue Wood & Associates* CLIENT: *Trans/Power New Zealand Ltd.* ■ *This annual report serves as the company's flagship document, launching its new logo and corporate colors.* ● *In diesem Jahresbericht, dem wichtigsten Kommunikationsmittel des Unternehmens, werden das neue Logo und die Firmenfarben vorgestellt.* ▲ *Principal outil de communication de l'entreprise, ce rapport annuel présente le nouveau logo et le code-couleur de la société.*

PAGE 24; #25 ART DIRECTOR: *Howard Brown* DESIGNERS: *Howard Brown, Mike Calkins* DESIGN FIRM/CLIENT: *Urban Outfitters* PHOTOGRAPHERS: *Steve Belkowitz, Charles Peterson* COPYWRITERS: *Ken Cleeland, Richard Haynes* PRINTER: *The Taylor Group*

PAGE 25; #26 ART DIRECTOR: *John Brady* DESIGNER: *Christine Mcintyre* DESIGN FIRM: *John Brady Design Consultants* PHOTOGRAPHERS: *John Wee, Julie Poskie* COPYWRITER: *David Gardener* CLIENT: *Greater Pittsburgh Council, Boy Scouts* PRINTER: *Reed & Witting* ■ *The directive was to produce a report that conveyed the timeless values of the Boy Scouts with environmen-*

tally friendly tools: digital photos and recycled papers. ● *Aufgabe war es, die zeitlosen Werte der Pfadfinder mit umweltfreundlichen Mitteln - digitalen Photos auf Umweltpapier — zum Ausdruck zu bringen.* ▲ *Photos numériques sur papier recyclé. L'objectif était d'évoquer les valeurs immuables des éclaireurs en recourant à des moyens écologiques.*

PAGE 26; #27-30 ART DIRECTOR/DESIGNER/COPYWRITER: *Kerry Leimer* DESIGN FIRM: *Leimer Cross Design* PHOTOGRAPHER: *Eric Myer* CLIENT: *Expeditors International of Washington, Inc.* PRINTER: *H. MacDonald Printing* ■ *This report expresses commitment to customer service through the people at Expeditors.* ● *Thema dieses Jahresberichtes ist der gute Kundenservice des Unternehmens.* ▲ *Rapport annuel axé sur la qualité du service à la clientèle, une priorité de l'entreprise.*

PAGE 27; #31 ART DIRECTOR: *Tim Hale* DESIGNERS: *Stephen Zhang, Casey McGarr* DESIGN FIRM: *Fossil Design Studio* PHOTOGRAPHER/ILLUSTRATOR: *Rick Bryant* COPYWRITER: *Merk Harbor* CLIENT: *Fossil* PRINTER: *Bucannan Printing* ■ *The mission was to present a company that is stable, conscious of its position and committed to the creativity and insight that had brought them this far.* ● *Hier ging es um die Darstellung der Firma als stabiles Unternehmen, das sich seiner Position bewusst ist, die es der Kreativität und dem Fachwissen der Mitarbeiter verdankt.* ▲ *L'objectif était de présenter la société comme une entreprise solide et consciente de sa position qu'elle doit à la créativité et au savoir-faire de ses collaborateurs.*

PAGE 28; #32 ART DIRECTOR: *Chuck Creasy* DESIGNERS: *Chuck Creasy, Kevin Hinson* DESIGN FIRM: *Dye, Van Mol and Lawrence* PHOTOGRAPHER: *Michael W. Rutherford* CLIENT: *Middle Tennessee Council, Boy Scouts of America* ■ *Drawing on scouting's traditional focus on the outdoors and the provocative design possibilities involving a child's inherent fascination with insects, this annual report takes "bugs" as its central design concept and creates something playful and endearing, like scouting itself.* ● *Angesichts der Verbundenheit mit der Natur und der Faszination, die Käfer auf Kinder ausüben, boten diese das ideale Thema für den Jahresbericht der Pfadfinder. Der spielerische, liebenswerte Gesamteindruck des Designs entspricht ganz der Idee der Pfadfinderbewegung.* ▲ *Les insectes, qui fascinent les enfants et évoquent l'idée de nature associée au scoutisme, étaient le sujet central de ce rapport annuel des Boy Scouts of America. Le design, plaisant et ludique, traduit bien l'esprit du scoutisme.*

PAGE 29; #33-36 ART DIRECTOR: *Damiá Mathews* DESIGNERS: *Damiá Mathews, Samuel Gonzales, Cheché Murillo* DESIGN FIRM: *Ediciones B, in-house design studio* PUBLISHER: *Ediciones B S.A.* ■ *The idea was to create a simple but identifiable look for a series of books, some of which had already been published by the same company, updating and unifying the design that in most cases was simply an adaptation of the original American artwork, and aiming it at Spanish marketing, management, and business students.* ● *Hier ging es darum, einen einfachen, aber unverkennbaren Auftritt für eine Serie von Büchern zu schaffen. Einige der Bücher waren bereits vorher vom Verlag publiziert worden, wobei viel von der Gestaltung der amerikanischen Originalausgaben übernommen worden war. Es ging im Prinzip um die Auffrischung und Vereinheitlichung der Reihe, die für Marketing-, Management und Betriebswirtschaftstudenten in Spanien bestimmt ist.* ▲ *Création d'une identité visuelle simple et aisément identifiable pour une collection d'ouvrages spécialisés (marketing, gestion, hautes études commerciales), dont certains avaient déjà été publiés. Il s'agissait de rafra"chir et d'uniformiser la présentation directement inspirée des éditions américaines originales, et de l'adapter au public cible des étudiants espagnols.*

PAGE 30; #37 ART DIRECTOR: *Paul Buckley* DESIGNER: *Martin Ogolter* DESIGN FIRM/ PUBLISHER: *Viking/Penguin* AUTHOR: *Robyn Davidson* ■ *The design for the book evokes the feeling of a notebook that the author bought in India (where the memoir takes place) and began writing and gluing pictures into, thereby making it her own personal object. The title type follows the same concept, suggesting the author could have drawn the letterforms herself, inspired by the local type treatments and visual forms.* ● *Dieses Buch handelt von Erinnerungen an Indien, wo die Autorin ein Notizbuch kaufte, in dem sie ihre Eindrücke nicht nur in Worten, sondern auch in Bildern festhielt, die sie hineinklebte und es so*

zu einem ganz persö nlichen Gegenstand machte. Das Design des Buches nimmt den Notizbuchcharakter auf, wobei der Titel so wirkt, als habe ihn die Autorin, inspiriert von indischer Kultur, selbst entworfen. ▲ *Livre de souvenirs sur l'Inde où l'auteur acheta un cahier pour consigner ses impressions sous forme de notes et d'images qu'elle colla, faisant de son journal un objet très personnel. Les caractères choisis pour le titre du livre traduisent l'esprit du journal et pourraient laisser croire que l'auteur, inspirée par la culture indienne, les a créés elle-même.*

PAGE 30; #38 DESIGNER: *Marja-Leena Muukka* DESIGN FIRM: *WSOY/Studio* AUTHOR: *Pekka Himanen* PHOTOGRAPHER: *Studio Pekka Himanen* PUBLISHER: *WSOY Printers and Publishers*

PAGE 31; #39-42 ART DIRECTOR: *Michael Bierut* DESIGNERS: *Emily Hayes, Esther Bridavsky* DESIGN FIRM: *Pentagram Design Inc.* PUBLISHER: *Monacelli Press* ■ *Monograph of buildings designed by architect Robert A. M. Stern.* ● *Eine Monographie über den Architekten Robert A. M. Stern.* ▲ *Monographie de l'architecte Robert A. M. Stern.*

PAGES 32, 33; #43-48 ART DIRECTOR: *D.J. Stout* DESIGNERS: *D.J. Stout, Nancy McMillen* PHOTOGRAPHER: *Keith Carter* AUTHOR: *Greil Marcus* PUBLISHER: *Rice University Press*

PAGE 34; #49 ART DIRECTOR: *Joe Duffy* DESIGNER: *KOBE* DESIGN FIRM: *Duffy Design* ILLUSTRATORS: *KOBE, Jeff Johnson, Ed Bennet, Michelle Hill* COPYWRITER: *Mike Lescarbo* CLIENT: *Childen's Defense Fund* PRINTER: *Heritage Press*

PAGE 34; #50 ART DIRECTOR/DESIGNER/ILLUSTRATOR: *Joe Duffy* DESIGN FIRM: *Duffy Design* POETRY: *William Butler Yeats* WRITER: *Pat Fallon* PUBLISHER/PRINTER: *Heritage Press*

PAGE 35; #51 ART DIRECTOR/DESIGNER: *Paul Buckley* DESIGN FIRM/ PUBLISHER: *Penguin USA* PRINTER: *Coral Graphics* ■ *Since a cigar box is a key piece of evidence in this novel, it seemed natural to make it the complete cover and transform the book into "the box."* ● *In dieser Geschichte spielt eine Zigarrenkiste eine wesentliche Rolle, es lag daher nahe, das ganze Buch quasi zu einer Zigarrenkiste zu machen.* ▲ *Une boîte de cigares jouant un rôle-clé dans l'intrigue de ce roman, l'idée de présenter le livre comme une boîte de cigares s'imposa tout naturellement.*

PAGE 36; #52-55 ART DIRECTOR/DESIGNER: *Douglas Martin* DESIGN FIRM: *Design & Direction Inc.* PUBLISHER: *Smart Art Press* PRINTER: *Jomagar*

PAGE 36; #56-59 DESIGN FIRM/PUBLISHER: *Chronicle Books* DESIGN MANAGER: *Jill Jacobsen* DESIGNER: *Brian Lee Hughes* AUTHOR: *Risa Mickenberg*

PAGE 37; #60-63 ART DIRECTOR: *Steven Hankinson* DESIGN FIRM: *Arnell Group* PHOTOGRAPHER: *Peter Arnell* WRITER: *Sara Arnell* PUBLISHER: *Rapoport Printing*

PAGE 37; #64-67 GENERAL COORDINATORS: *Elizabeth Monascal, Rafael Castro* TECHNICAL EDITOR: *Gisela Goyo* DESIGNER: *Eduardo Chumaceiro* DESIGN FIRM: *Fundación Polar* WRITER: *Lelia Delgado* ■ *"The weaving of tradition: contemporary indigenous basket weaving of Venezuela." This catalog was designed to accompany an exhibition at the cultural center of Casa Alejo Zuloaga in Venezuela.* ● *Katalog für eine Ausstellung im Kulturzentrum der Casa Alejo Zuloaga über das noch heute gepflegte traditionelle Kunsthandwerk der Korbflechterei in Venezuela.* ▲ *La vannerie, un artisanat traditionnel au Venezuela. Catalogue d'une exposition présentée au centre culturel de la Casa Alejo Zuloaga.*

PAGE 38; #68-70 ART DIRECTOR: *Malcolm Waddell* DESIGNERS: *Maggi Cash, Gary Mansbridge, Malcolm Waddell* DESIGN FIRM: *Eskind Waddell* COPYWRITER: *Leslie Elizabeth Ebbs* PUBLISHER: *Canada Post Corporation* ■ *The book was designed to present each postage stamp issued in Canada during 1996 in the context of an illustrated story explaining, in a bilingual format, its background and historical significance. Also included is a chapter of technical* *details about each stamp for the more knowledgeable collector.* ● *Dieses Buch zeigt alle 1996 in Kanada herausgegebenen Briefmarken im Rahmen einer illustrierten Geschichte, die über den Hintergrund und die historische Bedeutung (in zwei Sprachen) Auskunft gibt. Ein Sonderkapitel informiert den ernsthaften Sammler über technische Details einer jeden Marke.* ▲ *Ce livre présente tous les timbres poste édités au Canada en 1996 à travers une histoire illustrée expliquant le contexte et la signification historique. Le texte est en deux langues, et un chapitre consacré aux détails techniques complète l'ouvrage.*

PAGE 39; #71, 72 ART DIRECTOR: *Michael Bierut* DESIGNERS: *Michael Bierut, Esther Bridavsky* DESIGN FIRM: *Pentagram Design Inc.* PUBLISHER: *Monacelli Press* ■ *The book is a monograph and collection of critical essays about the Aronoff Center for Design and Art at the University of Cincinnati, designed by Peter Eisenmann. The building is constructed of dynamically joined boxes colliding and connecting in space; the book approximates this experience of the building with ample photography and a visible grid, or series of boxes for the reader/viewer to move through.* ● *Dieses Buch, das eine Sammlung kritischer Aufsätze enthält, befasst sich mit dem von Peter Eisenmann entworfenen Aronoff Center for Design and Art der University of Cincinnati. Das Gebäude besteht aus einer dynamischen Konstruktion verschiedener Kuben, die miteinander kollidieren bzw. verbunden sind. Der Band entspricht dieser speziellen Erfahrung des Gebäudes mit Hilfe von aufschlussreichen Photos und einem sichtbaren Raster bzw. einer Reihe von Boxen, durch die sich der Betrachter/Leser hindurchbewegen kann.* ▲ *Monographie regroupant des essais critiques sur l'Aronoff Center for Design and Art de l'Université de Cincinnati conçu par Peter Eisenmann. Le bâtiment consiste en une construction dynamique de différents cubes qui entrent en collision ou s'assemblent dans l'espace. Le livre, à l'image de cette expérience architectonique, est illustré de nombreuses photos et présente une trame apparente, soit une série de boîtes à travers lesquelles le lecteur peut se déplacer.*

PAGES 40, 41; #73-78 ART DIRECTORS: *David Turner, Bruce Duckworth* DESIGNER: *Jeff Fassnacht* DESIGN FIRM: *Turner Duckworth* CLIENT: *Levi Strauss & Co.* PRINTER: *Colorbar*

PAGE 42; #79 ART DIRECTOR: *Halasi Zoltan* DESIGN FIRM: *Art Force Studio* PHOTOGRAPHER/ILLUSTRATOR: *Bakcsy A'rpa'd* CLIENT: *Füzfö i Papir Ltd.*

PAGE 43; #80, 81 DESIGN FIRM: *Le Petit Didier* PHOTOGRAPHER/ILLUSTRATOR: *Michel Wirth* PUBLISHER: *Arsenal/Yan Zoritchak*

PAGE 44; #82-84 ART DIRECTORS: *Doug Herbert, Al Gluth, John Weaver* DESIGNER: *Doug Herbert* DESIGN FIRM/CLIENT: *Gluth Weaver Design* PHOTOGRAPHER: *Paul Aresu* COPYWRITER: *Molly Glentzer* PRINTER: *Champagne/Wetmore* ■ *The promotion was designed to explain four key philosophies of the firm and show work in an easily updatable manner.* ● *Thema dieser Werbebroschüre sind die vier wichtigsten Grundsätze der Firma. Die Broschüre ist so konzipiert, dass sie sich leicht mit neuen Arbeiten ergänzen lässt.* ▲ *Brochure illustrant les quatre principes-clés de l'entreprise, conçue de sorte à pouvoir être facilement réactualisée.*

PAGE 45; #85 ART DIRECTOR: *Garry Emery* DESIGN FIRM/CLIENT: *Emery Vincent Design* COPYWRITER: *Garry Emery, Peter Steidl* ■ *A little book on a selection of corporate identities.* ● *Ein kleines Buch mit einer Auswahl von Firmenlogos.* ▲ *Petit livre illustrant une série choisie d'identités visuelles.*

PAGE 46; #86-89 ART DIRECTOR/DESIGNER: *Dan Richards* DESIGN FIRM: *Nike Image Design* PHOTOGRAPHER: *Kevin Irby* ILLUSTRATOR: *Bob Bredemeier* COPYWRITER: *Neil Webster* PRINTER: *Graphic Arts Center* ■ *The directive was to design a catalog to launch a new roller hockey product that is both sophisticated and approachable.* ● *Gewünscht war ein anspruchsvoller und dabei leicht zugänglicher Katalog für die Einführung eines neuen Hockey-Rollschuhs.* ▲ *Le client souhaitait un catalogue à la fois sophistiqué et convivial pour le lancement de nouveaux rollers.*

PAGE 46; #90-93 ART DIRECTOR: *Bill Cahan* DESIGNER: *Bob Dinetz* DESIGN FIRM: *Cahan & Associates* COPYWRITER: *Danny Altman* CLIENT: *GVO* PRINTER: *Graphic Arts Center*

PAGE 47; #94-97 CREATIVE DIRECTORS: *Paul Curtin, Rob Price, Woody Nelson* DESIGNERS: *Jan Webber, Peter Locke* DESIGN FIRM: *Goodby, Silverstein & Partners* COPYWRITER: *Bill Day* CLIENT: *The Sharper Image*

PAGE 47; #98-101 ART DIRECTOR/DESIGNER: *Reiner Hebe* DESIGN FIRM/CLIENT: *HEBE: Werbung & Design* PHOTOGRAPHER/ILLUSTRATOR: *Mike Loos* COPYWRITER: *Reiner Hebe* PRINTER: *Druckhaus Munster*

PAGE 48; #102 ART DIRECTOR: *René Payne* DESIGN FIRM: *Cipriani Kremer Design* PHOTOGRAPHERS: *John Shotwell (cover & back), stock* COPYWRITER: *Brian Flood* CLIENT: *Lotus Corporation* ■ *The purpose of this piece was to literally and figuratively demonstrate to computer manufacturers that the product would increase their sales.* ● *Hier ging es darum, Computer-Hersteller zu überzeugen, dass das Produkt ihre Verkäufe fördern wird.* ▲ *L'objectif était de démontrer aux fabricants d'ordinateurs — au sens propre comme au figuré — que le produit vanté allait stimuler leurs ventes.*

PAGE 48; #103 ART DIRECTOR/DESIGNER: *Ron Dumas* DESIGN FIRM: *Nike Image Design* COPYWRITER: *Bob Lambie* PRINTER: *Irwin Hodson* ■ *This piece communicates a directional change for Nike's corporate identity to sales representatives and employees. The image of the Hummer vehicle on the cover communicates the irreverence of the company, while showing a dynamic visual for the "Swoosh" only approach.* ● *Mit der Broschüre sollte das Nike-Personal einschliesslich des Aussendienstes über neue Direktiven hinsichtlich des Markenauftritts informiert werden. Das Bild des Fahrzeugs (ein 'Hummer') auf dem Umschlag symbolisiert die Unbekümmertheit des Unternehmens und demonstriert gleichzeitig die dynamische Wirkung der neuen Art, den Nike-Haken allein, ohne jeglichen Zusatz, zu zeigen.* ▲ *Brochure informant les employés et les concessionnaires Nike des nouvelles directives de la maison en matière d'identité visuelle. L'image du véhicule sur la couverture illustre l'insouciance de la société et l'effet dynamique créé par le crochet Nike lorsqu'il apparaît seul, sans texte.*

PAGE 49; #104 ART DIRECTOR/DESIGNER: *Peter Scholl* DESIGN FIRM: *Graphiste ASG/SGV* PHOTOGRAPHER: *Diverse* CLIENT: *Théâtre de Vevey*

PAGE 49; #105 DESIGNER: *Michael Vanderbyl* DESIGN FIRM: *Vanderbyl Design* ILLUSTRATOR: *Eric Donelan* COPYWRITER: *David Betz* CLIENT: *Keilhauer* ■ *This small promotion piece is aimed at architects and designers, and makes fun of the "design speak" often used in front of clients to sell ideas.* ● *Diese kleine Werbebroschüre richtet sich an Architekten und Designer. Sie mockiert sich über die typische «Design-Sprache», die oft benutzt wird, um Kunden Ideen zu verkaufen.* ▲ *Petite brochure destinée aux architectes et aux designers et tournant en dérision le jargon de la branche, souvent utilisé pour vendre une idée aux clients.*

PAGE 49; #106 ART DIRECTOR: *James Pyott* DESIGNERS: *James Pyott, Marc Ward, Martin Bacon* DESIGN FIRM: *Pyott Design Consultants* COPYWRITER/CLIENT: *Tony Stone Images* ■ *This catalogue was designed so that it would be treasured and valued by recipients. It was their property and for their eyes only. It communicates the innovative and creative nature of the company using anti-design metaphors such as photobooth photography and degenerated text and design.* ● *Die Empfänger dieses Katalog sollten vor allem Spass an ihm haben, und den Wunsch verspüren, ihn aufzuheben. Die innovativen und kreativen Qualitäten der Firma kommen hier durch Anti-Design-Metaphern zum Ausdruck: die Photos stammen aus Automaten, Text und Design sind sehr rudimentär.* ▲ *L'objectif était de créer un catalogue séduisant que le client ait envie de conserver. L'esprit novateur et créatif de la société est illustré par des métaphores antidesign: les images proviennent de photomatons, le texte et le design sont réduits à leur plus simple expression.*

PAGE 49; #107 ART DIRECTOR/DESIGNER: *Michael Brock* DESIGN FIRM: *Michael Brock Design* CLIENT: *Los Angeles Times* PRINTER: *Alan Lithograph* ■ *The directive was to produce a brochure which positions the Sunday magazine as a leader in its category and to aid ad sales.* ● *Aufgabe war es, das Sonntagsmagazin der Los Angeles Times als führend in dieser Kategorie darzustellen und somit die Anzeigenverkäufe zu fördern.* ▲ *L'objectif était de présenter le magazine du dimanche du Los Angeles Times comme le numéro un de ce type de publications et de stimuler les ventes d'annonces.*

PAGE 50; #108-110 ART DIRECTOR: *John Bjerg Nielsen* DESIGN FIRM: *Jørn Moesgård A/S* CLIENT: *Bent Krogh A/S* ■ *This modest retrospective of a furniture designer is printed in two colors on recycled paper and uses existing photographs, a metal cover homemade at the designer's factory. The result is a curious little book, which stands out because of its modesty.* ● *Dieser eigenwillige kleine Katalog, der sich durch seine Bescheidenheit auszeichnet, zeigt die Arbeiten eines Mö bel-Designers. Es wurden vorhandene Photos verwendet, und der Metallumschlag wurde im Atelier des Designers hergestellt. Der Katalog ist zweifarbig auf Umweltpapier gedruckt.* ▲ *Ce petit livre au concept résolument minimaliste présente les réalisations d'un designer de meubles. Des photos qui existaient déjà ont servi aux illustrations, et la couverture métallique a été réalisée dans l'atelier du designer. Impression bichrome sur papier recyclé.*

PAGE 51; #111-113 ART DIRECTOR: *Valerie Taylor Smith* DESIGNER: *Michael Hernandez* DESIGN FIRM: *Nike Image Design* PHOTOGRAPHER/ILLUSTRATOR: *Terry Allen* COPYWRITER: *Bob Lambie*

PAGES 52, 53; #114, 116 ART DIRECTORS: *Jennifer Jerde, Jennifer Breeze* DESIGNERS: *Jennifer Jerde, Jennifer Breeze, Julie Cristello, Michael Braley* DESIGN FIRM: *Elixir Design, Inc.* PHOTOGRAPHERS: *Deborah Jones, Tony Stromberg* COPYWRITERS: *Shane Brentham, Emily Shephard* CLIENT: *Elixir Design, Inc.* ■ *The primary objective of this promotion is to act as an encapsulated portfolio, but it also exhibits the firm's commitment to indelible design through collaboration.* ● *Diese Broschüre sollte in erster Linie als Arbeitsmappe dienen, gleichzeitig aber demonstriert sie auch das Anliegen der Firma, durch Zusammenarbeit zu eindrucksvollen Designlö sungen zu gelangen.* ▲ *Réalisée sous la forme d'un porte-documents, cette brochure illustre la philosophie d'une société de design qui s'attache à rechercher des solutions originales grâce à la collaboration.*

PAGES 52, 53; #115, 117 ART DIRECTOR: *Nancy Hoefig* DESIGNER: *Nancy Hoefig, Cinthia Wen* DESIGN FIRM: *Landor Associates* PHOTOGRAPHER: *Michael Friel* COPYWRITER: *Donata Maggipinto* CLIENT: *Williams/Sonoma* PRINTER: *Alden Printers* ■ *The ad creates awareness of a registry service for kitchen-related wedding gifts using product to illustrate the classic wedding adage, "Something old, something new, something borrowed, something blue."* ● *Mit dieser Anzeige wird auf den Hochzeitsgeschenk-Service eines Geschäftes für Küchenartikel aufmerksam gemacht. Produkte illustrieren einen klassischen amerikanischen Hochzeitsspruch: "Something old, something new, something borrowed, something blue." («Etwas Altes, etwas Neues, etwas Geborgtes, etwas Blaues.»* ▲ *Publicité pour un magasin de cadeaux de mariage spécialisé dans les articles de cuisine. Les produits illustrent un vieux dicton américain sur le mariage: «Something old, something new, something borrowed, something blue.» («Du vieux, du neuf, du prêté, du bleu.»)*

PAGE 54; #118-121 ART DIRECTOR/DESIGNER: *Fanon Giriano* DESIGN FIRM: *Fan On Design Communication* PHOTOGRAPHER/ILLUSTRATOR: *Cario Miriani Fulcis* COPYWRITER: *Giriano Fanon* CLIENT: *Benetton Sport System* PRINTER: *Artegrafila*

PAGE 54; #122-125 ART DIRECTOR/DESIGNER: *Jeff Barnes* DESIGN FIRM: *Barnes Design Office* PHOTOGRAPHER: *Welzenbach Photography* ILLUSTRATORS: *Steve Ravenscraft, Karen Pattee David*

PAGE 55; #126-129 ART DIRECTOR: *Paula Scher* DESIGNER: *Lisa Mazur* DESIGN FIRM: *Pentagram Design Inc.* PHOTOGRAPHERS: *Michael Daniel, Richard Avedon* CLIENT: *Public Theater, NYC* ■ *The varied but cohesive graphic language reflects street typography: it's extremely active, unconventional, and almost graffiti-like. Applications to print and promotional materials utilize Victorian wood typefaces which are emblematic of the theater.* ● *Die abwechslungsreiche und doch homogene graphische Sprache reflektiert die Typographie der Strasse: sie ist extrem lebendig, unkonventionell und sieht fast wie ein Graffiti aus. Für Drucksachen und anderes Werbematerial wurden viktorianische Holzschnitt-Schriften verwendet, die in Bezug auf das Theater sinnbildlichen Charakter haben.* ▲ *Riche mais cohérent, le langage graphique reflète la typographie de la rue qui, pleine de vie et anticonformiste, ressemble à un graffiti. Imprimés et matériel publicitaire ont été composés avec des caractères en bois victoriens qui évoquent l'esprit du théâtre.*

PAGE 55; #130-133 ART DIRECTORS/DESIGNERS:: *Eric Urmetzer, Walter Schönauer* CREATIVE DIRECTORS: *Kurt George Dieckert, Robert Wohlgemuth, Jan Ritter* DESIGN FIRM: *Springer & Jacoby* LITHOGRAPHY: *BRK Reproduktion/Ruck Reproduktionstechnik* PHOTOGRAPHERS: *Peter Lindbergh, Michele Comte, Eberhard Sauer, Marcus Bolsinger* CLIENT: *Mercedes-Benz AG* PRINTER: *Druckerei* ■ *This design presents the world of the SLK with special emphasis on the uniqueness of the concept of the vehicle, and intends to excite the potential SLK-buyer as well as the press.* ● *Die Welt der Mercedes-SLK-Fahrer und das einzigartige Konzept des Fahrzeugs stehen hier im Mittelpunkt, wobei sowohl potentielle Käufer als auch die Presse angesprochen werden sollen.* ▲ *Pour séduire la presse et de nouveaux clients, l'agence a choisi de présenter le monde de la Mercedes SLK en mettant l'accent sur le concept unique du véhicule.*

PAGE 56; #134 ART DIRECTOR: *Fulvio Metri* DESIGNERS: *Ettore Tosi, Tipolito Maggioni* DESIGN FIRM: *Tosi Associati* COPYWRITER: *Fulvio Metri* CLIENT/PRINTER: *Tipolito Maggioni* ■ *The design shows how to achieve a graphic product and not the necessary technology for its achievement.* ● *Hier geht es nicht um die Technik, sondern um das graphische Endprodukt.* ▲ *L'accent est mis sur l'aspect graphique du produit fini et non sur ses caractéristiques techniques.*

PAGE 57; #135 ART DIRECTORS/DESIGNERS: *Dan Richard, Webb Blevins* DESIGN FIRM: *Nike Image Design* PHOTOGRAPHER: *Kevin Irby* ILLUSTRATORS: *Webb Blevins, Mike Pfenning* COPYWRITER: *Neil Webster* PRINTER: *Graphic Arts Center* ■ *This owner's manual also serves as an image piece for Nike hockey skates.* ● *Dieses Benutzer-Handbuch dient auch als Image-Broschüre für Eishockey-Schlittschuhe von Nike.* ▲ *Manuel destiné au consommateur servant aussi à promouvoir l'image des patins à glace Nike.*

PAGE 57; #136 ART DIRECTORS: *Ian Newlands, Christine Arden* DESIGNER: *Ian Newlands* DESIGN FIRM: *BNA Design Ltd.* PHOTOGRAPHY: *stock* COPYWRITER: *Mary Mountier* CLIENT: *New Zealand Post Ltd.* ■ *This stamp book celebrating famous New Zealand racehorses had to appeal to both philatelic collectors as well as enthusiastic racegoers.* ● *Dieser Briefmarkenkatalog, dessen Thema berühmte Rennpferde Neuseelands sind, sollte sowohl Briefmarkensammler als auch das Publikum von Pferderennen ansprechen.* ▲ *Catalogue de timbres consacré à de célèbres chevaux de course de Nouvelle-Zélande. L'objectif était de séduire à la fois les philatélistes et les turfistes.*

PAGE 57; #137 ART DIRECTOR/DESIGNER: *Haesun Kim Lerch* DESIGN FIRM: *Pennebaker.LMC* PHOTOGRAPHER: *Haesun Kim Lerch* CLIENT: *The BUZZ 107.5* PRINTER: *Champagne Fine Printing* ■ *Playing off the idea of what the radio station would look like visually, the agency took music artists' portraits and digitized them to use as divider sheets throughout the book.* ● *Digitalisierte Porträts von Musikern dienen als Zwischenblätter im gesamten Katalog für einen Radio-Sender.* ▲ *Portraits numérisés de musiciens utilisés comme pages de séparation dans cette publication consacrée à la radio the BUZZ.*

PAGE 57; #138 ART DIRECTORS: *Michele Melandri, Eric Helser* DESIGNER: *Michele Melandri* DESIGN FIRM: *Nike Image Design* PHOTOGRAPHER: *Morgan Henry* ILLUSTRATORS: *Annette De Waal, Jan Beran, Lena James, Michele Melandri* COPYWRITERS: *Emily Brew, Betsy Pitschka, Eric Helser, Thalia Fajans* PRINTER: *Irwin Hodson* ■ *The directive was to break down the merchandising process into its three different systems. The first half of the manual shows all three systems without product — photos are treated as duotones so that focus is on the fixture system. The second half also shows all three systems, but with product and in full color so that the product merchandised on fixtures is highlighted.* ● *Im ersten Teil dieses Handbuchs werden alle drei Merchandising-Systeme ohne Produkte vorgestellt. Die Photos sind im Duoton gedruckt, so dass das Auge auf die Verkaufsständer gelenkt wird. Der zweite Teil zeigt ebenfalls die drei Systeme, aber hier stehen die Produkte dank der mehrfarbigen Wiedergabe im Mittelpunkt.* ▲ *La première partie de ce manuel présente les trois systèmes de merchandising sans produit. L'agence a opté pour des photos bicolores afin d'attirer le regard sur les présentoirs. La deuxième partie illustre également les trois systèmes, mais cette fois, les produits tiennent la vedette grâce à l'impression couleur.*

PAGE 58; #139 ART DIRECTOR/DESIGNER: *Nicole Bryan* DESIGN FIRM: *Werk 3, Graphic Design* CLIENT: *Nils Holger Moormann GmbH* ■ *This catalog for a designer/furniture manufacturer needed to be pocket-sized, yet also contain a great deal of text in two languages. The solution uses colored boxes for the text with no white space at all.* ● *Dieser Katalog für einen Hersteller von Designer-Möbeln sollte Taschenformat haben, dabei aber eine Menge Text in zwei Sprachen enthalten. Die Lösung bestand in farbigen Feldern für den Text, wobei ganz auf weisse Flächen verzichtet wurde.* ▲ *Réalisé pour un fabricant de meubles design, ce catalogue devait se présenter dans un format de poche et contenir beaucoup de texte en deux langues. La solution consista à créer des encadrés de différentes couleurs et à renoncer à tout espace blanc.*

PAGE 58; #140 ART DIRECTOR/DESIGNER: *Milton Glaser* DESIGN FIRM: *Milton Glaser Inc.* PHOTOGRAPHER: *Matthew Klein* CLIENT: *Windows on the World*

PAGE 58; #141 ART DIRECTORS: *David Stokes, Gayle Pastrick* CREATIVE DIRECTORS: *Dean Van Eimeren, Gayle Pastrick* DESIGNER: *Karen Knecht-Squires* DESIGN FIRM: *Saatchi & Saatchi/Pacific* PHOTOGRAPHER: *Paul Taylor (cover and inside cover); Rick Rusing, Harry Varnos (balance of book)* ILLUSTRATOR: *Kevin Hulsey* COPYWRITER: *Jon Jay* CLIENT: *Toyota Motor Sales, U.S.A., Inc.*

PAGE 58; #142 ART DIRECTORS: *David Stokes, Gayle Pastrick* CREATIVE DIRECTORS: *Dean Van Eimeren, Gayle Pastrick* DESIGN FIRM: *Saatchi & Saatchi/Pacific* PHOTOGRAPHER: *Paul Taylor (cover/inside cover); Rick Rusing, David LeBon (balance of book)* ILLUSTRATOR: *Kevin Hulsey* COPYWRITER: *Jon Jay* CLIENT: *Toyota Motor Sales, U.S.A., Inc.* ■ *The covers of these brochures were meant to be as graphic and colorful as possible, while using a single secondary object to symbolize the life-style each vehicle facilitates. The first inside spreads then play off the graphic covers with the full product revealed in an environment that includes the secondary objects.* ● *Die Umschläge dieser Broschüren sollten so graphisch und farbig wie möglich wirken, wobei ein einziges zusätzliches Objekt den Lebensstil symbolisiert, der mit den einzelnen Fahrzeugen in Verbindung gebracht wird. Auf den ersten Seiten wird dann jeweils der Umschlag wiederholt, dieses Mal aber mit dem Auto in einem Umfeld, zu dem auch das zusätzliche, bereits gezeigte Objekt gehört.* ▲ *Les couvertures de ces brochures devaient être aussi graphiques et colorées que possible. A chaque fois, un seul objet symbolise le style de vie associé à chaque véhicule. Les premières pages reprennent le sujet de la couverture, mais cette fois-ci, le véhicule est présenté dans un environnement qui intègre l'objet de référence du véhicule.*

PAGE 59; #143-145 ART DIRECTOR/DESIGNER: *Jeff Larson* DESIGN FIRM: *The Larson Group* PHOTOGRAPHER: *Steve Pitkin* CLIENT: *Pearson Fastener* ■ *In order to stand out from the other look-alike brochures in the fastener industry, this brochure uses a hard-bound cover held together by fasteners to create an industrial mood which is softened by elegant product photos.* ● *Der feste, von Verschlüssen zusammengehaltene Umschlag soll diesem Katalog für Verschlüsse einen industriellen Touch geben, der wiederum durch elegante Produktaufnahmen gemildert wird.* ▲ *Pour démarquer cette brochure des produits concurrents et lui conférer une touche industrielle, l'agence a opté pour une couverture rigide maintenue par des fermetures, dont l'effet est adouci par l'élégance des photographies de produits.*

PAGE 60; #146 ART DIRECTOR/DESIGNER: *Jennifer Sterling* DESIGN FIRM/CLIENT: *Jennifer Sterling Design.*

PAGE 60; #147 ART DIRECTOR/DESIGNER: *Trey Speegle* DESIGN FIRM: *Trey Speegle Designs* ARTIST/CLIENT: *Hedy Klineman* PRINTER: *Studio Gribaudo* ■ *The idea was not only to reproduce the paintings but to create an object that reflects the sensibility of the work.* ● *Hier ging es nicht nur um die Präsentation der Malerei, der Katalog sollte auch die Stimmung der Bilder reflektieren.* ▲ *L'objectif n'était pas seulement de reproduire des peintures, mais de rendre l'atmosphère évoquée par les Œuvres présentées.*

PAGE 61; #148-153 ART DIRECTOR: *Byron Jacobs* DESIGNERS: *Byron Jacobs, Mei Lee Chan* DESIGN FIRM: *PPA Design Ltd.* PHOTOGRAPHERS: *Christopher Wormell, Stock* COPYWRITER: *Dominic Purvis* CLIENT: *Swire Properties*

PRINTER: *HK Prime Printing Co.* ■ *Butterfields is a Hong Kong commercial tenants club based on a colonial theme concept revolving around the late 19th century to early twentieth-century time period.* ● *Butterfields ist ein Club für Geschäftsleute in Hongkong. Das Konzept basiert auf dem Kolonialstil der Jahrhundertwende.* ▲ *Butterfields est un club d'hommes d'affaires à Hongkong. Le concept se base sur le style colonial fin de siècle.*

PAGE 62; #154 ART DIRECTOR: *Le Petit Didier Michel* DESIGN FIRM: *Le Petit Didier* CLIENT: *Arsenal*

PAGE 63; #155, 156 ART DIRECTOR: *Rüdiger Goetz* DESIGNERS: *Rüdiger Goetz, Christian Dekant* DESIGN FIRM: *Simon & Goetz* PHOTOGRAPHER: *Rui Camillo* CLIENT: *Fichtel & Sachs GmbH* ■ *The design language of Elan communicates a futuristic idea of movement and blends well into the general Sachs bicycle design language. The formal quality of the brochure showcases the technical features of the product.* ● *Die futuristische Auffassung von Bewegung, die hier zum Ausdruck kommt, entspricht dem Designkonzept der Sachs-Fahrräder. Im Mittelpunkt dieser Broschüre sehen die technischen Eigenschaften des Produktes.* ▲ *La représentation futuriste du mouvement développée ici correspond au design des cycles Sachs. La brochure devait mettre l'accent sur les caractéristiques techniques du produit.*

PAGE 64; #157 ART DIRECTORS: *Robert Achten, Tim Bright* DESIGNER: *Ravindra Manhaas* DESIGN FIRM: *Origin Design Co. Ltd.* ILLUSTRATOR: *Adam Errington* CLIENT: *Charta Packaging*

PAGE 65; #158-165 DESIGNER/PHOTOGRAPHER: *Seymour Chwast* DESIGN FIRM: *The Pushpin Group* CLIENT: *The Pushpin Group, Mohawk Paper* PRINTER: *Berman Printing* ■ *The directive was to present the theme of cars in as many different styles as possible.* ● *Das Thema Auto sollte hier auf möglichst viele Arten dargestellt werden.* ▲ *Le thème de la voiture décliné sous toutes ses formes.*

PAGE 66; #166-168 ART DIRECTOR/DESIGNER: *Min Byung-Geol* DESIGN FIRM/CLIENT: *Ahn Graphic* PRINTER: *Samwha Color Ltd.* ■ *In this calendar for the digital age, dates in the binary system used in computer science were used rather than the usual decimal system format.* ● *In diesem Kalender für das digitale Zeitalter wurde das Kalendarium entsprechend dem binären System des Computers konzipiert statt nach dem üblichen Dezimalsystem.* ▲ *Dans ce calendrier consacré à l'ère numérique, les dates sont consignées selon le système binaire propre aux ordinateurs et non pas selon le système décimal.*

PAGE 67; #169 ART DIRECTORS: *David Turner, Bruce Duckworth* DESIGNERS: *Jeff Fassnacht, Eden Fahlen* DESIGN FIRM: *Turner Duckworth* CLIENT: *Levi Strauss & Co.* PRINTER: *Bauer Engraving* ■ *These personalized directories were created for the Levi's marketing department.* ● *Persönliche Adressbücher für die Marketing-Abteilung von Levi's.* ▲ *Carnets d'adresse personnalisés conçus pour le service marketing de Levi's.*

PAGE 68; #170-178 ART DIRECTORS/COPYWRITERS: *Achim Falkenthal, Hubertus Adam* DESIGNER: *Hubertus Adam* DESIGN FIRM: *Falkenthal, Adam, TV Druck* PHOTOGRAPHER/ILLUSTRATOR: *Achim Falkenthal*

PAGE 69; #179 ART DIRECTOR/DESIGNER: *Ikuo Toyama* DESIGN FIRM: *McCann-Erickson Inc. Tokyo* ILLUSTRATOR: *Shoji Sekiguchi* CLIENT: *Coca-Cola Japan Company* PRINTER: *Light Printing Inc.* ■ *The design used classic Coca-Cola art as the main visual, with one character from the past but another from today's youth added using computer graphic techniques.* ● *Klassische Coca-Cola-Motive stehen hier im Mittelpunkt, wobei jeweils eine Figur aus der Vergangenheit digital mit einem heutigen Jugendlichem kombiniert wurde.* ▲ *Motifs Coca-Cola classiques bien que des éléments du passé aient été associés à un jeune d'aujourd'hui à l'aide de l'ordinateur.*

PAGES 70, 71; #180-185 ART DIRECTOR/DESIGNER/ILLUSTRATOR: *Steve Sandstrom* DESIGN FIRM: *Sandstrom Design* COPYWRITER: *Steve Sandoz* CLIENT: *Pavlov Productions* PRINTER: *Premier Press* ■ *Sony Commercial Productions needed to distinguish their group and create an identity appealing to top creative advertising agencies and producers. The company was renamed* and all the communication materials were developed around "behavioral modification" and "conditioned response" themes that are associated with the name. ● Die Sony-Werbefilmproduktion brauchte ein Erscheinungsbild, das kreative Werbeagenturen und Regisseure ansprechen würde. Die Firma erhielt einen neuen Namen, und das gesamte Kommunikationsmaterial basiert auf den Begriffen Beweglichkeit und Anpassungsfähigkeit, Eigenschaften, die diese Firma charakterisieren. ▲ La société de production de spots publicitaires Sony avait besoin d'une identité à même de séduire les meilleures agences de publicité et les réalisateurs. A cet effet, elle a été rebaptisée, et tout le matériel de communication se base désormais sur les thèmes "modification du comportement" et "réponse conditionnée", soit la flexibilité et la faculté d'adaptation, deux qualités associées au nom de cette société.

PAGE 72; #186, 187 ART DIRECTOR/COPYWRITER: *Ian Kidd* DESIGNERS: *Matthew Remphrey, Ian Kidd* DESIGN FIRM: *Ian Kidd Design Pty. Ltd.* ILLUSTRATOR: *Matthew Remphrey* CLIENT: *South Australian Museum of Natural History* ■ Since civilization has always been fascinated with the footprint, from Neolithic man to Robinson Crusoe to Neil Armstrong, the mark for this museum of natural history is a foot. The heel is out of focus, representing discovery but not answers. At the instep is the "golden spiral" which is at the center to many answers to the universe. And at the toes, the image is defined, representing the clarity of problems solved. ● Da Fussabdrücke die Menschheit zu allen Zeiten fasziniert haben, wurde ein Fuss als Zeichen für das Naturhistorische Museum gewählt. Die Hacke ist verschwommen, was soviel wie Entdeckungen statt Antworten heissen soll. Beim Spann befindet sich die "goldene Spirale", die im Zentrum vieler Antworten auf das Universum steht. Das Bild der Zehen ist gestochen scharf, womit die Klarheit gelöster Probleme zum Ausdruck gebracht werden soll. ▲ Depuis toujours, les empreintes exercent une grande fascination sur l'homme. Pour cette raison, une empreinte de pied a été choisie pour symboliser le Musée d'histoire naturelle. Le talon est caché, ce qui signifie que l'on part à la découverte de quelque chose. Au niveau du coup-de-pied se trouve la "spirale dorée", qui est au centre de nombreuses réponses sur l'univers. Les orteils sont reproduits avec une grande netteté, ce qui indique que tout est clair, les problèmes ont été résolus.

PAGE 72; #188, 189 ART DIRECTOR: *Jack Anderson* DESIGNERS: *Jack Anderson, David Bates* DESIGN FIRM: *Hornall Anderson Design Works* ILLUSTRATOR: *David Bates* CLIENT: *Alki Bakery* ■ The "A" logo depicts the bakery's old world style of baking through the illustration of a wooden bread peel being placed in an oven. The mascot logo reflects the bakery's beach side locale by combining the baker's image with a wave. ● Das "A"-Logo mit der Darstellung eines hölzernen Brotschiebers, der in den Ofen geschoben wird, illustriert die alte Backtradition der Bäckerei. Das Maskottchen, das aus einer Bäckerfigur und einer Welle besteht, weist auf die Lage der Bäckerei am Meer hin. ▲ Le logo "A", une pelle de boulanger en bois poussée à l'intérieur d'un four, reflète la tradition et le savoir-faire du maître-boulanger. La mascotte à l'effigie du boulanger est complétée par une vague qui indique la situation en bord de mer de la boulangerie.

PAGE 73; #190-193 ART DIRECTOR: *Michael Gericke* DESIGNERS: *Michael Gericke, Edward Chioutucto* DESIGN FIRM: *Pentagram Design Inc.* CLIENT: *American Institute of Architects*

PAGES 74, 75; #194-198 ART DIRECTOR/DESIGNER: *Gaby de Abreu* DESIGN FIRM: *KSDP Pentagraph* CLIENT: *Sun International*

PAGE 76; #199 ART DIRECTOR: *Robert Petrick* DESIGNERS: *Robert Petrick, Laura Ress* DESIGN FIRM: *Petrick Design* PHOTOGRAPHER: *Chuck Shotwell* CLIENT: *Boise Cascade Office Products* PRINTER: *The Hennegan Company* ■ This graph for the annual report of an office products company uses common products in an unusual way. ● Diese Graphik für den Jahresbericht einer Büroartikelfirma zeigt gewöhnliche Gegenstände auf ungewöhnliche Art. ▲ Créé pour le rapport annuel d'un fabricant de meubles de bureau, ce graphique présente des objets usuels sous un jour nouveau.

PAGE 77; #200 ART DIRECTOR/DESIGNER: *Fred Woodward* DESIGN FIRM/PUBLISHER: *Rolling Stone Magazine* PHOTOGRAPHER: *Mark Seliger* PHOTO EDITOR: *Jodi Peckman*

PAGE 77; #201 ART DIRECTOR/DESIGNER: *Fred Woodward* CLIENT/PUBLISHER: *Rolling Stone Magazine* PHOTOGRAPHER: *Albert Watson* PHOTO EDITOR: *Jodi Peckman*

PAGE 78; #202 ART DIRECTOR: *Fred Woodward* DESIGNERS: *Fred Woodward, Geraldine Hessler* CLIENT/PUBLISHER: *Rolling Stone Magazine* PHOTOGRAPHER: *Mark Seliger* PHOTO EDITOR: *Jodi Peckman*

PAGE 79; #203 ART DIRECTOR/DESIGNER: *Richard Baker* CLIENT/PUBLISHER: *US Magazine* PHOTOGRAPHER: *Lance Staedler*

PAGE 79; #204 ART DIRECTOR: *Fred Woodward* DESIGNERS: *Fred Woodward, Geraldine Hessler* CLIENT/PUBLISHER: *Rolling Stone Magazine* PHOTOGRAPHER: *Mark Seliger* PHOTO EDITOR: *Jodi Peckman*

PAGE 79; #205 ART DIRECTOR: *Fred Woodward* DESIGNERS: *Fred Woodward, Lee Bearson* CLIENT/PUBLISHER: *Rolling Stone Magazine* PHOTOGRAPHER: *Mary Ellen Mark* PHOTO EDITOR: *Jodi Peckman*

PAGE 79; #206 ART DIRECTOR: *Fred Woodward* CLIENT/PUBLISHER: *Rolling Stone Magazine* PHOTOGRAPHER: *Albert Watson* PHOTO EDITOR: *Jodi Peckman*

PAGE 79; #207 ART DIRECTOR/DESIGNER: *Richard Baker* CLIENT/PUBLISHER: *US Magazine* PHOTOGRAPHER: *Peggy Sirota*

PAGE 79; #208 ART DIRECTOR/DESIGNER: *Richard Baker* CLIENT/PUBLISHER: *US Magazine* PHOTOGRAPHER: *Mark Seliger*

PAGE 79; #209 ART DIRECTOR: *Fred Woodward* DESIGNERS: *Fred Woodward, Geraldine Hessler* CLIENT/PUBLISHER: *Rolling Stone Magazine* PHOTOGRAPHER: *Mark Seliger* PHOTO EDITOR: *Jodi Peckman*

PAGE 79; #210 ART DIRECTOR/DESIGNER:: *Fred Woodward* CLIENT/PUBLISHER: *Rolling Stone Magazine* PHOTOGRAPHER: *Matthew Rolston* PHOTO EDITOR: *Jodi Peckman*

PAGE 80; #211 ART DIRECTOR: *Michael Lawton* DESIGNER: *Gary Gretter* CLIENT/PUBLISHER: *Sports Afield Magazine* ■ The cover image needed to be classic, handsome, and still have good newsstand appeal. ● Das Titelbild sollte klassisch und ansprechend sein und doch auffällig genug, um sich am Kiosk durchzusetzen. ▲ La couverture devait être à la fois classique et séduisante, et accrocher le regard dans les kiosques.

PAGE 80; #212 ART DIRECTORS: *Christin Gangi* CREATIVE DIRECTOR: *Michael Grossman* PHOTO EDITOR: *Susan Goldberger* CLIENT/PUBLISHER: *Garden Design Magazine* PHOTOGRAPHER: *Andre Baranowski*

PAGE 80; #213 DESIGN DIRECTOR/DESIGNER: *Gary Gretter* CLIENT/PUBLISHER: *Sports Afield Magazine* ILLUSTRATOR: *James Prosek*

PAGE 80; #214 DESIGN FIRM/PUBLISHER: *frogdesign* PHOTOGRAPHERS: *frogdesign Team, Dietmar Henneka, Randall Ingalls, Daniel Proctor* ARTISTS: *Thomas Preston Dævall, Alfons Noltgreve, MC. ILL* ■ This magazine takes its inspiration from a unique fusion of analog, traditional, and digital media, and seeks to define a new level of appropriate communication based on youth-culture inspired visual literacy. ● Die Ästhetik dieser Zeitschrift basiert auf einer Verbindung traditioneller und digitaler Medien. Sie bemüht sich um die Schaffung einer neuen angemessenen Kommunikationsebene, die auf dem visuellen Vokabular der Jugendkultur basiert. ▲ Magazine combinant médias traditionnels et numériques. Il s'agissait de créer un nouveau style de communication, qui reprenne le langage visuel des jeunes.

PAGE 80; #215 ART DIRECTOR: *D. J. Stout* DESIGNERS: *D. J. Stout, Nancy McMillen* CLIENT/PUBLISHER: *Texas Monthly* PHOTOGRAPHER: *Danny Turner* ■ This cover for an annual "Twenty Texans" issue was influenced by old pulp western action magazine covers from the fifties which graphically meshed well with the image of Chuck Norris dressed like an old gunfighter. ● Dieser Umschlag für die jährliche Sonderausgabe der Zeitschrift Texas Monthly mit dem Titel "Zwanzig Texaner" ist vom Stil der Umschläge von Westernmagazinen der fünfziger Jahre inspiriert, der ausgezeichnet zum dem Bild passt, das Chuck Norris als alten Revolverhelden zeigt. ▲ Couverture de l'édition spéciale, "Vingt Texans", du magazine Texas Monthly. Elle s'inspire du graphisme des magazines western des années 50, qui correspond en tous points à l'image de Chuck Norris, présenté ici comme un as de la gachette.

PAGE 80; #216 ART DIRECTOR: *Thomas Noller* DESIGNERS: *Thomas Noller, Garry U. Van Patter* DESIGN FIRM: *Restart Publishing* PUBLISHER: *Garry U. Van Patter* ■ *This low-budget, high-quality magazine on issues in design education was published initially for Pratt Institute students.* ● *Dieses anspruchsvolle Magazin, das sich mit Fragen der Designausbildung befasst und mit einem kleinen Budget produziert wird, wurde ursprünglich von Studenten des Pratt Institute herausgegeben.* ▲ *Publié à l'origine par des étudiants du Pratt Institute, ce magazine à petit budget contient des articles pointus sur la formation dans le domaine du design.*

PAGE 81; #217 ART DIRECTORS: *Richard Klein, Riley John-Donnell* DESIGNER: *Riley John-Donnell* DESIGN FIRM: *Exquisite Corps* PHOTOGRAPHER: *Paco Navarro* RETOUCHING: *Tom Pitts, Nina Alter* PUBLISHER: *Surface Magazine* ■ *Surface's cover images spotlight the diva icons of the media age. The covers are dramatically retouched to exaggerate shape and form, as well as to reinforce the portrait as iconography. The metallic green ink and orange body paint were selected in order to emphasize Rossy dePalma's unique profile.* ● *Auf den Umschlägen dieses Magazins figurieren die Divas des Medienzeitalters. Die Darstellungen werden massiv retuschiert, um die Formen zu überzeichnen und den Ikonen-Charakter der Porträts zu unterstreichen. Das Metallic-Grün und die orangefarbene Kö rperbemalung sollen Rossy dePalmas einzigartige Silhouette hervorheben.* ▲ *Les couvertures de ce magazine illustrent les divas de l'ère des médias. Elles ont fait l'objet d'importantes retouches pour "gonfler" les formes et souligner le caractère iconique des portraits. Le vert métallisé et l'orange utilisés pour peindre le corps de Rossy de Palma soulignent son profil, unique.*

PAGES 82, 83; #218-220 ART DIRECTOR: *Simon Attila* DESIGN FIRM: *Art Force Studio* PHOTOGRAPHER: *A'rpa'd Bakcsi* PUBLISHER: *Felix Film and Mai Nap*

PAGES 84-87; #221-233 ART DIRECTOR: *Hideki Nakajima* EDITOR: *Ken Sato* DESIGN FIRM: *Nakajima Design* PUBLISHER: *rockin' on, Inc.* PHOTOGRAPHERS: *Itaru Hirama (#221, 230, 233, artwork photos #222, 223, 226), Michel Itghe (#222), Dewey Nicks (#223), Takahashi Homma (#224, 227), Akira Matsuo (#225), Jean Baptiste Mondino (#226), Albert Watson (#228), Mark Seliger (#231), Steven Klein (#232)*

PAGE 88; #234 DIRECTOR OF DESIGN/DESIGNER: *Tom Bentkowski* DESIGN FIRM/PUBLISHER: *Life Magazine* PHOTOGRAPHER: *Lennart Nilsson* PRINTER: *Judd's* ■ *This arrangement of Lennart Nilsson's photographic experiments was meant to clearly show his explorations into comparative biology.* ● *Darstellung der photographischen Experimente von Lennart Nilsson.* ▲ *Présentation des expériences photographiques de Lennart Nilsson.*

PAGE 88; #235 DIRECTOR OF DESIGN: *Tom Bentkowski* DESIGNER: *Mimi Park* DESIGN FIRM/PUBLISHER: *Life Magazine* IMAGE CREATION: *Rob Silvers* PRINTER: *Judd's* ■ *This unique image for the 60th anniversary of Life magazine acknowledges the history of the magazine, while incorporating an element of modern technology.* ● *Dieses Bild zum 60jährigen Bestehen des Life Magazine bezieht sich auf die Geschichte der Zeitschrift.* ▲ *Réalisée pour le 60ᵉ anniversaire de Life Magazine, cette image en retrace l'histoire.*

PAGE 88; #236 DIRECTOR OF DESIGN: *Tom Bentkowski* ART DIRECTOR/DESIGNER: *Mimi Park* DESIGN FIRM/PUBLISHER: *Life Magazine* PRINTER: *Judd's* ■ *The simple format of this design leads the reader through a pictoral history of the automobile, and provides for occasional off-road excursions into longer essays.* ● *Die Bilder erzählen die Geschichte des Automobils, ergänzt durch ausführliche zum Thema.* ▲ *Les images racontent l'histoire de l'automobile et sont complétées par des articles de fond.*

PAGE 88; #237-239 ART DIRECTOR/DESIGNER: *John Muller* DESIGN FIRM:

Muller & Company ILLUSTRATOR: *Mike Weaver* CLIENT: *Sportscar Vintage Racing Association* ■ *These covers use an art deco style of illustration to show the beauty of the race cars and to depict cars in motion as pieces of artwork.* ● *Auf diesen Umschlägen mit Art Deco-Illustrationen werden Rennwagen als Kunstwerke präsentiert.* ▲ *Couvertures de style art déco présentant des voitures de course comme des Ïuvres d'art.*

PAGE 88; #240 ART DIRECTOR: *Janet Froelich* DESIGNER: *Catherine Gilmore-Barnes* DESIGN FIRM: *The New York Times Magazine* CLIENT: *The New York Times Company*

PAGE 88; #241 ART DIRECTOR: *Janet Froelich* DESIGNER: *Joel Cuyler* DESIGN FIRM: *The New York Times Magazine* PHOTOGRAPHERS/ARTISTS: *Rimma Gerlovina, Valeriy Gerlovin* CLIENT: *The New York Times Company*

PAGE 88; #242 ART DIRECTOR: *Janet Froelich* DESIGNERS: *Joel Cuyler, Lisa Naftolin* DESIGN FIRM: *The New York Times Magazine* ARTIST: *Gerhard Richter* CLIENT: *The New York Times Company*

PAGE 89; #243 ART DIRECTORS: *Rafael Weil* EDITOR: *James Truman* DESIGNERS: *Jason Ring* DESIGN CONSULTANT: *Michael Bierut* DESIGN FIRM: *BAMdesign* PHOTOGRAPHER: *Brigitte Lacombe* CLIENT: *Brooklyn Academy of Music* PRINTER: *Finlay Brothers* ■ *The design represents the leap from an academic coffee table book format to a kinetic magazine format. This fusion of visual identity and editorial direction creates a strong new voice that both welcomes the public and articulates the energy of this performing arts institution.* ● *Der akademische, traditionelle Stil dieser Publikation einer Musikakademie wich einem lebendigen Magazinformat. Die neue redaktionelle und gestalterische Ausrichtung reflektiert die Lebhaftigkeit der Musikakademie und lädt das Publikum zum Studium des Inhalts ein.* ▲ *Publication traditionnelle d'une académie de musique revue et corrigée: le format du magazine, l'orientation éditoriale et conceptuelle reflètent le dynamisme de cette académie et invitent le public à en découvrir le contenu.*

PAGE 89; #244 ART DIRECTOR: *Jürgen Mandel* DESIGNERS: *Jürgen Mandel, Frank Koschembar, Bea Bug* DESIGN FIRM: *Mandel, Muth, Werbeagentur, GmbH* PHOTOGRAPHER: *David Hall, Karsten De Riese* ILLUSTRATOR: *Sibylle Schwarz* COPYWRITER: *Wilfried Korfmacher, Jürgen Mandel* CLIENT: *VOKO Vertriebsstiftung Büroeinrichtungen KG* PRINTER: *Germany* ■ *This original promotional magazine addresses existing and potential new customers.* ● *Diese aussergewö hnliche Publikation richtet sich an vorhandene und potentielle neue Kunden.* ▲ *Publication originale visant à séduire de nouveaux lecteurs.*

PAGES 90, 91; #245-253 ART DIRECTORS/DESIGNERS: *Ken Miki, Toshiyasu Nanbu, Akio Okumura, Shinnosuke Sugisaki, Yoshimaru Takahashi* DESIGN FIRM: *Kokokumaru Co., Ltd.* CLIENT: *Japan Typography Association*

PAGE 92; #254 ART DIRECTOR/DESIGNER: *D. J. Stout* DESIGN FIRM/PUBLISHER: *Texas Monthly* ILLUSTRATOR: *Matt Mahurin* WRITER: *Robert Draper* ■ *The childlike, scrawled type was meant to convey the primitive violence of an incident in which a group of bored kids attacked a horse and beat it to death with sticks.* ● *Die kindliche Krackelschrift sollte die primitive Gewalttätigkeit einer Gruppe gelangweilter Kinder zum Ausdruck bringen, die ein Pferd mit Stö cken zu Tode geprügelt hat.* ▲ *L'écriture enfantine et maladroite reflète la violence primitive qui a conduit des enfants cruels, en proie à l'ennui, à tuer un cheval à coups de bâton.*

PAGE 92; #255 ART DIRECTOR/DESIGNER: *D. J. Stout* DESIGN FIRM/PUBLISHER: *Texas Monthly* ILLUSTRATOR: *John Collier* WRITER: *Joe Nick Patoski* ■ *The type for this opening spread for a story on a famous music producer from East Texas was influenced by an old, cheap silkscreened music poster off the walls of an old building.* ● *Ein altes, im Siebdruckverfahren hergestelltes Musikplakat an der Wand eines alten Gebäudes inspirierte zu der Schrift der einleitenden Doppelseite für eine Geschichte über einen berühmten Musikproduzenten aus Texas.* ▲ *Le caractère utilisé pour la double page d'introduction à l'histoire d'un célèbre producteur de musique texan s'inspire d'une ancienne affiche de musique, une sérigraphie, placardée sur le mur d'un vieil immeuble.*

PAGE 92; #256 ART DIRECTOR: *D.J. Stout* DESIGNERS: *D.J. Stout, Nancy McMillen* DESIGN FIRM/PUBLISHER: *Texas Monthly* PHOTOGRAPHER: *Rick Patrick* WRITER: *Anne Dingus* ■ *The art of the belt buckle is the focal point of this design which utilizes clear, simple photography and straightforward layout.* ● *Kunstvolle Gürtelschnallen, wie man sie vor allem in Texas findet, stehen hier im Mittelpunkt.* ▲ *Boucles de ceinture mises en valeur par le style simple et direct des photographies et le layout épuré.*

PAGE 93; #257-259 ART DIRECTOR/DESIGNER: *Philip Pirolo* DESIGN FIRM: *Alluvial Publishing* WRITER: *Ted Bouloukos* CLIENT: *Provocateur* PRINTER: *Pacific Rim International* ■ *The repeated image was used in this spread to illustrate JFK Jr. as an icon of pop culture and a symbol of dynamic change.* ● *John F. Kennedy Jr. wird hier als eine Ikone der Pop-Kultur und Symbol dynamischer Veränderungen präsentiert.* ▲ *John F. Kennedy Jr. est présenté ici comme une icône de la culture pop, un symbole du changement et du dynamisme.*

PAGES 94, 95; #260-267 ART DIRECTOR: *Richard Poulin* DESIGNERS: *Richard Poulin, J. Graham Hanson* DESIGN FIRM: *Poulin & Morris* CLIENT: *Sony Music Entertainment Inc.* ■ *This architectural sign program uses a color-coded, modular panel system derived from the standard jewel box CD case.* ● *Die Standardverpackung für CDs diente als Ausgangsbasis für dieses architektonische Beschilderungssystem, das mit Farbkodierungen und Versatzstücken arbeitet.* ▲ *Inspiré du packaging standard d'un CD, cette signalétique architectonique repose sur un système de panneaux modulaires et un code-couleur.*

PAGE 96; #268 ART DIRECTORS/DESIGNERS: *Thomas Fairclough, Tom Antista* DESIGN FIRM: *Antista Fairclough Design* CLIENT: *Texaco Refining & Marketing Inc.* ■ *This new Texaco station design features softer curves and lighter, brighter colors.* ● *Sanftere Linien und leuchtendere Farben kennzeichnen die neue Gestaltung der Texaco-Tankstellen.* ▲ *Des lignes plus douces et des couleurs plus vives caractérisent les nouvelles stations d'essence Texaco.*

PAGE 96; #269 ART DIRECTOR: *Garry Emery* DESIGN FIRM: *Emery Vincent Design* CLIENT: *Denton Corker Marshall* ■ *This 450 meter exhibition space features graphics produced on large oblique blades which serve as entry markers to an exhibition space.* ● *Bei der Gestaltung einer riesigen Ausstellungshalle dienten grosse, schräge Schilder als Hinweis auf die verschiedenen Eingänge.* ▲ *Ces grands panneaux obliques ont été utilisés pour signaler les différentes entrées d'une énorme halle d'exposition.*

PAGE 97; #270-271 ART DIRECTOR/ILLUSTRATOR: *Toshihiro Onimaru* DESIGNER: *Do* DESIGN FIRM: *Graphics & Designing Inc.* PHOTOGRAPHER:/COPYWRITER: *Nil* CLIENT: *G & D Management Inc.* ■ *This visual identity for a cafe in Tokyo works well in multiple and single color palettes and targets customers who enjoy a "casual but fashionable" lifestyle.* ● *Dieses Erscheinungsbild für ein Café in Tokio wirkt in einfarbiger Ausführung ebenso wie in mehrfarbiger. Es soll vor allem ein Publikum ansprechen, das einen "legeren und doch trendigen" Lifestyle schätzt.* ▲ *Unicolore ou multicolore, cette identité visuelle pour un café à Tokyo s'adresse à un public-cible qui apprécie un style de vie "décontracté et dans le coup".*

PAGE 98; #272 ART DIRECTOR/DESIGNER: *Paul Black* DESIGN FIRM: *Squires and Company* CLIENT: *St. Pete's Dancing Marlin Restaurant* ■ *The identity and signage for this restaurant maintains the spirit of both the old brick warehouse district in which it is located and the young, hip, professional clientele it caters to.* ● *Auftritt und Beschilderung für dieses Restaurant entsprechen einerseits dem Stil der alten Backsteinlagerhäuser der Umgebung, andererseits auch dem Geschmack der Kundschaft, die aus jungen, berufstätigen Leuten besteht, die 'hip' sind.* ▲ *L'identité et la signalétique de ce restaurant se marient, d'une part, au style des vieilles maisons en briques du quartier et sont adaptées, d'autre part, au goût de la clientèle, qui se compose principalement de jeunes gens actifs et branchés.*

PAGE 99; #273-278 DESIGNERS: *Mark Popich, Robert Brogan, Jim Harper* DESIGN FIRMS: *The Leonhardt Group, Corbin Design* CLIENT: *Recreational Equipment Inc.* ■ *The directive was to use the client's traditional logo in mate-*

rials such as metal, wood, and stone to reflect its commitment to quality and the environment. ● *Das traditionelle Logo des Auftraggebers sollte in Metall, Holz und Stein verarbeitet werden, um sein Engagement für Qualität und für die Umwelt zum Ausdruck zu bringen.* ▲ *L'ancien logo de la société a été retravaillé avec des matériaux comme le métal, le bois et la pierre pour témoigner de l'importance que le client attache à la qualité et de son engagement en faveur de l'environnement.*

PAGE 100; #279-282 ART DIRECTORS: *Scott Paramski, Sean Patrick* DESIGNER: *Scott Paramski* DESIGN FIRM: *Impact Group Inc.* CLIENT: *Maroon Creek Club, Tom Fabio* ■ *This signage system was designed to blend with the natural environment.* ● *Dieses Beschilderungssystem wurde der natürlichen Umgebung angepasst.* ▲ *Ce système de signalétique a été adapté à son environnement naturel.*

PAGE 101; #283-286 ART DIRECTOR: *Garry Emery* DESIGN FIRM: *Emery Vincent Design* CLIENT: *Royal Alexandra Children's Hospital* ■ *The signage was developed to provide a link between the architecture and its inhabitants by means of landmarks and elements of surprise.* ● *Das Beschilderungssystem für ein Kinderspital stellt mit Hilfe von Steinskulpturen und †berraschungselementen eine Verbindung zwischen der Architektur und den Patienten her.* ▲ *Conçu pour une clinique pédiatrique, ce système de signalétique établit une relation entre l'architecture et les enfants par le biais de sculptures en pierre et d'éléments-surprise.*

PAGE 102; #287, 288 ART DIRECTORS: *Scott Paramski, Sean Patrick* DESIGNER: *Scott Paramski* DESIGN FIRM: *Impact Group Inc.* PHOTOGRAPHER: *Robert Millman* COPYWRITER: *Sean Patrick* CLIENT: *Heitman Financial/Snowmass Land Co.* ■ *The photographs with poems were mailed every other month to clients who had purchased property and were meant to capture the mood and spirit of the land.* ● *Geschenk für die Käufer von Bauland. Jeden zweiten Monat werden Photos mit Gedichten verschickt, die der Stimmung und dem Geist der Landschaft entsprechen.* ▲ *Destiné aux acheteurs de terrain et envoyé tous les deux mois, ce cadeau se présente sous forme de photographies et de poèmes qui rendent l'atmosphère du paysage.*

PAGE 103; #289 DESIGN FIRM: *Gruppe Mayländer Werbeagentur* DESIGNER: *Michaela Mayländer* CLIENT: *Horst Wanschura*

PAGE 104; #290, 291 ART DIRECTOR/DESIGNER/CLIENT: *Heinz Wild* DESIGN FIRM: *Wild & Frey* ■ *Announcement of change of address.* ● *Ankündigung einer Adressänderung.* ▲ *Annonce d'un changement d'adresse.*

PAGE 104; #292 ART DIRECTOR/DESIGNER: *Garrett Burke* DESIGN FIRM: *Willoughby Design* PHOTOGRAPHER/ILLUSTRATOR: *Mike Bryan* COPYWRITER: *Garrett Burke* PRINTER: *Westcoast Graphics* ■ *A memorable design for the birth announcement for the designer's daughter.* ● *Anzeige der Geburt einer Tochter des Designers.* ▲ *Faire-part annonçant la naissance de la fille du designer.*

PAGE 105; #293 ART DIRECTOR/DESIGNER: *Grant Jorgensen* DESIGN FIRM: *Grant Jorgensen Graphic Design* CLIENT: *Design Institute of Australia* PRINTER: *Finsbury Press* ■ *The three fold-out windows represent interior design by allowing the viewer to look inside and through the piece and cast shadows onto the printed "shadows" to represent controlled lighting. The internal colours and window shapes are from the Design Institute of Australia symbol.* ● *Innenarchitektur und Lichtgestaltung sind das Thema dieser Promotion des Design Institute of Australia. Die drei ausklappbaren Fenster gewähren dem Betrachter Einblick ins Innere, wobei die Farben im Inneren und die Formen der Fenster dem Symbol des Instituts entsprechen.* ▲ *Les thèmes sélectionnés pour promouvoir le Design Institute of Australia étaient l'architecture d'intérieur et l'éclairage. Les trois fenêtres rabattables permettent de regarder à l'intérieur et de découvrir des couleurs qui reprennent celles du symbole de l'institut. Les formes des fenêtres sont également calquées sur ce symbole.*

PAGE 106; #294 ART DIRECTOR: *Joe Duffy* DESIGNER: *KOBE* DESIGN FIRM: *Duffy Design* CLIENTS: *Fallon McElligott, Duffy Design* ■ *Commemmorative* item for the Fallon McElligott and Duffy Design 1996 creative retreat. ● Souvenir an eine kreative Klausur von Fallon McElligott, einer Werbeagentur, und Duffy Design im Jahre 1996. ▲ Souvenir d'une épreuve créative de l'agence Fallon McElligott et de Duffy Design en 1996.

PAGE 106; #295 DESIGNER: Kerry Kreps DESIGN FIRM: Sietsema Engel COPYWRITER: Suzanne Copsey CLIENT: Self-promotional Christmas greeting ■ A watch with a Christmas greeting which can be worn all year long. ● Eine Uhr als Werbegeschenk zum Weihnachtsfest, die das ganze Jahr über getragen werden kann. ▲ Montre offerte en cadeau de Noël et pouvant être portée toute l'année.

PAGE 106; #296, 297 ART DIRECTOR: Debbie Feasey DESIGNERS: Debbie Feasey, Ivan Angell DESIGN FIRM: DesignWorks (in-house) ILLUSTRATOR: Ross Bennett COPYWRITER: Lloyd Jones PRINTER: Timeworld ■ This watch, from a series entitled "Sign of the Times" promotes awareness of nuclear testing in the Pacific. ● Diese Uhr aus einer Serie mit dem Titel "Sign of the Times" macht auf die Atomtests im Pazifik aufmerksam. ▲ Cette montre de la série "Sign of the Times" attire l'attention sur les tests nucléaires effectués dans le Pacifique.

PAGE 107; #298 ART DIRECTOR/DESIGNER: Hugo Puttaert DESIGN FIRM: Vision & Factory PHOTOGRAPHER: Paul Gillard COPYWRITERS: Eric Albert, Johan Jacobs ■ This Christmas gift takes the recipient through a typical emotional day at the design firm and is both humorous and functional. ● Der Empfänger dieses humorvollen Weihnachtsgeschenks erlebt einen typischen Tag in einem Graphik-Studio. ▲ Le bénéficiaire de ce cadeau de Noël humoristique et fonctionnel est invité à passer une journée typique dans une agence de graphisme.

PAGE 108; #299-304 DESIGNER: Willard Whitson DESIGN FIRM: American Museum of Natural History (Exhibition Department) COPYWRITER: Dr. Craig Morris ■ Communicates information about the "unknown" Leonardo with a balance of reverence for original documents and didactic interpretation. ● Der "unbekannte" Leonardo da Vinci ist das Thema, wobei die Informationen aus Originaldokumenten und didaktischen Interpretationen bestehen. ▲ Léonard de Vinci, cet "inconnu", tel est le thème traité ici. Les informations proviennent de documents originaux et d'interprétations didactiques.

PAGE 109; #305-308 ART DIRECTORS: Chris Beatty, Jeff Laramore, Mark Bradley, Matt Lockett CREATIVE DIRECTORS: David Young, Jeff Laramore DESIGN FIRM/CLIENT: 2nd Globe SCULPTOR: David Kirby Bellamy COPYWRITER: David Hope ■ This exhibition booth reflects the firm's philosophy of turning everyday transactions into memorable experiences. ● Diese Ausstellungskoje demonstriert, wie aus alltäglichen Transaktionen unvergessliche Erfahrungen werden. ▲ Cet espace de l'exposition reflète la philosophie de la société qui consiste à transformer des transactions quotidiennes en expériences inoubliables.

PAGE 110; #309 ARCHITECT/PARTNER: James Biber ARCHITECT/ASSOCIATE: Michael Zweck Bronner DESIGN FIRM: Pentagram Design Inc. CLIENT: DuPont Company ■ Sculptural sign-walls, reproduced furniture, surface manipulations and a new color palette demonstrate the untapped design potential of the material. ● Anhand von diversen Anwendungsmöglichkeiten wird hier das Design-Potential eines synthetischen Materials von DuPont demonstriert. ▲ Démonstration du potentiel de ce produit synthétique de DuPont exemplifié par différentes applications.

PAGE 110; #310, 311 ARCHITECT/PARTNER: James Biber ARCHITECT/ASSOCIATE: Michael Zweck Bronner DESIGN FIRM: Pentagram Design Inc. CLIENT: Bausch & Lomb ■ Themes from Bausch & Lomb's history depicted in window vignettes at every elevator landing with quotations etched in dichroic glass, a Bausch & Lomb product. ● Themen aus der Geschichte von Bausch und Lomb sind bei jedem Fahrstuhlstopp in Fenstern sichtbar, begleitet von Zitaten, die in das spezielle Glas, ein Produkt der Firma, geätzt sind. ▲ A chaque arrêt de l'ascenseur, on peut voir des fragments de l'histoire de Bausch & Lomb présentés dans des vitrines et complétés par des citations gravées à l'eau forte sur un verre spécial, un produit de la maison.

PAGE 111; #312, 313 ART DIRECTOR: Mark Artus ENVIRONMENTAL DESIGNERS: Christian Davies, Jon Baines GRAPHIC DESIGNERS: Jackie Richmond, Paul Lechleiter GRAPHIC IMPLEMENTATION COORDINATOR: Kathleen Goode IMPLEMENTATION DRAWINGS: Randy Miller DESIGN FIRM: Fitch Inc. PHOTOGRAPHER: Mark Steele CLIENT: Chrysler Corporation ■ This 15,000 square foot showcase, located in the Mall of America features Chrysler's latest concept and production vehicles as well as hands-on displays and links to the World Wide Web. The intent of the showroom is to strengthen Chrysler's brand image. ● In diesem Ausstellungsraum im grössten Shopping Mall Amerikas in Minneapolis werden das neuste Konzept von Chrysler, die neuesten Fahrzeuge sowie Display-Material und die Verbindungen zum World Wide Web vorgestellt. Es geht dabei um die Stärkung des Marken-Image. ▲ Située dans le plus grand centre commercial des Etats-Unis à Minneapolis, cette salle d'exposition présente le dernier concept Chrysler, les nouveaux véhicules, le matériel promotionnel et les connexions avec le World Wide Web. L'objectif visé consiste à renforcer l'image de marque.

PAGE 112; #314-317 CREATIVE DIRECTOR: John Hoke DESIGN TEAM: Mike Tiedy, John Trotter, Toki Wolf, Derek Welch, Mike Ely, Stanley Hainsworth DESIGN FIRM: Nike Image Design PHOTOGRAPHER: Timothy Hursley

PAGE 113; #318-321 ART DIRECTOR: Jeff Weithman DESIGNERS: Jeff Weithman, Darrell Frier DESIGN FIRM: Nike Image Design PRINTER: Transworld Market-ing ■ This point-of-purchase package was designed to launch Nike into the eyewear business. The design inspiration was the oval Nike logo and the aerodynamic technical look of the product. ● Diese Ladenpromotion dient der Lancierung von Nike-Brillen. Das ovale Nike-Logo und der aerodynamische Stil der Brillen war bestimmend für den Stil des Display-Materials. ▲ Design réalisé dans le cadre du lancement des lunettes Nike dans différents points de vente. Le logo ovale Nike et le style aérodynamique des lunettes ont largement influencé les présentoirs.

PAGE 114; #322, 323 ART DIRECTOR: David Turner DESIGNER: Jeff Fassnacht DESIGN FIRM: Turner Duckworth PRINTER: Thomas Swan Sign Co. ■ The agency sought to design point-of-purchase items which intrigue the consumer and explain the service. ● Laden-Promotionsmaterial, das das Interesse der Kunden wecken und sie über den Service informieren soll. ▲ Matériel promotionnel destiné aux points de vente. Objectif: susciter l'intérêt du client et lui fournir des informations sur le service.

PAGE 114; #324 ART DIRECTORS: Dennis Crowe CREATIVE DIRECTOR: Brian Collins DESIGNER: Dennis Crowe DESIGN FIRM: Zimmermann Crowe Design CLIENT: Levi Strauss & Co. ■ A beacon display fixture designed to highlight feature jeans and entice customers into The Levi's in-store shop area. ● Mit dieser leuchtenden Ladeninstallation sollen die Kunden auf die speziellen Angebote bzw. die Levi's-Shops in den Läden aufmerksam gemacht werden. ▲ Cette installation de magasin lumineuse vise à rendre les clients attentifs aux espaces réservés à la vente d'articles Levi's et aux promotions spéciales.

PAGE 114; #325 ART DIRECTOR: Neal Zimmermann DESIGNERS: Neal Zimmermann, Eric F. Heiman PROJECT MANAGER: Joanne Lew Riley DESIGN FIRM: Zimmermann Crowe Design CLIENT: Levi Strauss & Co. PRINTER: Mobius ■ This retail program was designed for Western retailers who respond to Levi's traditional western image. Cost containment on production was an issue. ● Dieses Material wurde für den Einzelhandel konzipiert, der auf das traditionelle Western-Image von Levi's anspricht. Die Produktionskosten waren an einen bestimmten Rahmen gebunden. ▲ Conçu pour les points de vente, ce matériel promotionnel évoque l'image western de la marque. Les coûts de production étaient un facteur déterminant de ce programme promotionnel.

PAGE 115; #326 ART DIRECTOR: Dennis Crowe DESIGNERS: Dennis Crowe, Angie Wang, Roger Wong DESIGN FIRM: Zimmermann Crowe Design CLIENT: Levi Strauss & Co. ■ The "Americana" campaign was created for stores in the Atlanta area to promote Levi's jeans during the summer Olympics. An earth-toned palette was created to contrast the red, white and blue product offering. ● Die "Americana"-Kampagne wurde für Läden in der Gegend von Atlanta entworfen, um Levi's Jeans während der Sommerolympiade zu bewerben. Die

Palette von Erdfarben sollte einen Konstrast zum rot-weiss-blauen Produktangebot bilden. ▲ *Campagne "Americana" conçue pour la promotion des jeans Levi's dans la région d'Atlanta durant les Jeux Olympiques d'été. La palette des tons terre contraste avec l'offre du produit bleu-blanc-rouge.*

PAGE 115; #327 ART DIRECTORS: *Neal Zimmermann* PROJECT MANAGER: *Joanne Lew Riley* DESIGNERS: *Neal Zimmermann, Eric F. Heiman* DESIGN FIRM: *Zimmermann Crowe Design* CLIENT: *Levi Strauss & Co.* ■ *This retail program was designed for Western retailers who respond to Levi's traditional western image. Cost containment on production was an issue.* ● *Dieses Material wurde für den Einzelhandel konzipiert, der auf das traditionelle Western-Image von Levi's anspricht. Die Produktionskosten waren an einen bestimmten Rahmen gebunden.* ▲ *Conçu pour les points de vente, ce matériel promotionnel évoque l'image western de la marque. Les coûts de production étaient un facteur déterminant de ce programme promotionnel.*

PAGE 115; #328 ART DIRECTORS: *Neal Zimmermann* PROJECT MANAGER: *Joanne Lew Riley* DESIGNERS: *Neal Zimmermann, Claudia Mejia* DESIGN FIRM: *Zimmermann Crowe Design* CLIENT: *Levi Strauss & Co.* ■ *The design of this shop leverages the client's history with weathered, hand-worn signs which were shot with a .357 Magnum.* ● *Die Gestaltung dieses Ladens nimmt mit den verwitterten, abgenutzten Schildern mit Einschusslö chern einer .357-Magnum die Geschichte von Levi's auf.* ▲ *Usés et érodés par le temps, ces panneaux de magasin, troués au préalable par les balles d'un magnum .357, s'intègrent parfaitement à la légende Levi's.*

PAGE 115; #329 ART DIRECTOR: *Dennis Crowe* DESIGNERS: *Dennis Crowe, Angie Wang, Roger Wong* DESIGN FIRM: *Zimmermann Crowe Design* CLIENT: *Levi Strauss & Co* ■ *The "Americana" campaign was created for stores in the Atlanta area to promote Levi's jeans during the summer Olympics. An earth-toned palette was created to contrast the red, white and blue product offering.* ● *Die "Americana"-Kampagne wurde für Läden in der Gegend von Atlanta entworfen, um Levi's Jeans während der Sommerolympiade zu bewerben. Die Palette von Erdfarben sollte einen Konstrast zum rot-weiss-blauen Produktangebot bilden.* ▲ *Campagne "Americana" conçue pour la promotion des jeans Levi's dans la région d'Atlanta durant les Jeux Olympiques d'été. La palette des tons terre contraste avec l'offre du produit bleu-blanc-rouge.*

PAGE 115; #330, 331 ART DIRECTORS: *Neal Zimmermann* PROJECT MANAGER: *Joanne Lew Riley* DESIGNERS: *Neal Zimmermann, Claudia Mejia* DESIGN FIRM: *Zimmermann Crowe Design* CLIENT: *Levi Strauss & Co.* ■ *The design of this shop leverages the client's history with weathered, hand-worn signs which were shot with a .357 Magnum.* ● *Die Gestaltung dieses Ladens nimmt mit den verwitterten, abgenutzten Schildern mit Einschusslö chern einer .357 Magnum die Geschichte von Levi's auf.* ▲ *Usés et érodés par le temps, ces panneaux de magasin, troués au préalable par les balles d'un magnum .357, s'intègrent parfaitement à la légende Levi's.*

PAGES 116, 117; #332-336 ART DIRECTOR: *Sally Morrow* PRODUCER: *Brad Berman, Brad Berman Project Management/Creative Services* DESIGNERS: *Sally Morrow, Donjiro Ban* DESIGN FIRM: *Sandstrom Design* COPYWRITER: *Leslee Dillon* CLIENT: *Reebok* ■ *Graphic design, signage and applications for Reebok's supershow booth created under the "Planet Reebok" theme and featuring Reebok's corps of international athletes.* ● *Graphik-Design, Schilder und Ausstattung einer Ausstellungs-Koje für Reebok unter dem "Planet Reebok"-Thema, wobei die internationalen Reebok-Athleten die Stars sind.* ▲ *Design graphique, signalétique et installations pour l'espace d'exposition "Planet Reebok", présentant les athlètes internationaux qui portent la marque.*

PAGE 118; #337 DESIGN FIRM: *Jackhammer/The Richards Group* ART DIRECTOR: *Terence Reynolds* PHOTOGRAPHER: *Richard Reens* COPYWRITER: *Todd Tilford* CLIENT: *GT Interactive Software*

PAGE 119; #338 ART DIRECTOR: *Alberto Garcia-Izquierdo* ILLUSTRATOR: *Peter Krämer* CLIENT: *Deutsche Lufthansa AG* PRINTER: *Mondruck* ■ *Digital illustration published in Lufthansa Bordbuch, the inflight magazine of Lufthansa. The article it accompanied informs passengers about modern aircraft technology.* ● *Digitale Illustration für das Lufthansa Bordbuch, das Passagiermagazin der Lufthansa. In dem Artikel geht es um moderne Flugzeugtechnologie.* ▲ *Illustration numérique pour le Lufthansa Bordbuch, le magazine des passagers de la compagnie aérienne. Cet article traite de la technologie aéronautique.*

PAGE 120; #339 ART DIRECTOR: *Fred Woodward* DESIGNER: *Geraldine Hessler* ILLUSTRATOR: *Ralph Steadman* CLIENT/PUBLISHER: *Rolling Stone Magazine*

PAGE 121; #340 ART DIRECTOR/ILLUSTRATOR: *Milton Glaser* DESIGN FIRM: *Milton Glaser Inc.* CLIENT: *The New York Times Book Review*

PAGE 122; #341, 342 ART DIRECTOR: *Ingrid Hensinger* DESIGN FIRM/ILLUSTRATOR: *Siegmar Münk* CLIENT: *Fischer Taschenbücher* ■ *These computer illustrations entitled, "Born in Africa," and "The Handsomest Men in Town" were created for book covers.* ● *Computer-Illustrationen für Buchumschläge.* ▲ *Ilustrations numériques pour des jaquettes.*

PAGE 122; #343 ART DIRECTOR/ILLUSTRATOR/COPYWRITER: *Brad Holland* DESIGNERS: *Brad Holland, Roxanne Slimak* DESIGN FIRM: *D.K. Holland* CLIENT: *Rockport Allworth* ■ *These illustrations were drawn to accompany a magazine article. Their style is direct and funny and they were intended to hang "on the article like ornaments on a Christmas tree.* ● *Illustrationen für einen Magazinbeitrag. Ihr Stil ist direkt und witzig — sie sollten "wie Weihnachtsbaumschmuck" am Artikel hängen.* ▲ *Illustrations accompagnant un article de magazine. Leur style est direct et drôle, et elles devaient décorer l'article "comme des boules de Noël décorent un sapin".*

PAGE 122; #344 ART DIRECTOR/ILLUSTRATOR: *Greg Tucker*

PAGE 123; #345 ILLUSTRATOR: *Reinhard Herold* MEDIUM: *Airbrush Illustration*

PAGE 124; #346 ART DIRECTOR/ILLUSTRATOR: *Sandra Hendler* DESIGNER: *Nora Ridolfi* DESIGN FIRM: *CB Communications* COPYWRITER: *Rik Boyd* CLIENT: *Garnett Inc.* ■ *This image is for a story about a young black woman taken from Africa to live in Europe.* ● *Illustration für die Geschichte einer jungen Afrikanerin, die mit dem Leben in Europa zurechtkommen muss.* ▲ *Illustration pour l'histoire d'une jeune Africaine déracinée, contrainte de vivre en Europe.*

PAGE 124; #347 ART DIRECTOR/DESIGNER/ILLUSTRATOR: *Sandra Hendler (self-promotion)* ■ *This lighthearted look at anxiety at the end of the century has Humpty Dumpty symbolizing the fragile nature of people.* ● *Die Ängste, die sich mit der bevorstehenden Jahrtausendwende bemerkbar machen, werden hier mit Hilfe von Humpty Dumpty, einer Figur aus einem Kinderlied, auf leichte Art behandelt. Humpty Dumpty, der in dem Lied von der Mauer fällt, lässt sich nicht mehr zusammensetzen - hier symbolisiert er die fragile Natur der Menschen.* ▲ *Les angoisses qui commencent à se faire sentir à l'approche du troisième millénaire sont traitées ici avec une certaine légèreté grâce à Humpty Dumpty, le héros d'une chanson d'enfants. Dans la chanson, Humpty Dumpty tombe d'un mur, et il est impossible ensuite "d'en recoller les morceaux" — une allusion à la nature fragile de l'être humain.*

PAGE 125; #348 DESIGN FIRM: *Brey Graphics* ILLUSTRATOR: *Manfred Brey* CLIENT: *Rolling Stone Germany* ■ *Soccer as a social game.* ● *Fussball als Gesellschaftsspiel.* ▲ *Le football, un jeu de société.*

PAGE 126; #349 ART DIRECTOR/ILLUSTRATOR: *Greg Tucker*

PAGE 126; #350 ART DIRECTOR/DESIGNER: *John Ball* DESIGN FIRM: *Mires Design* ILLUSTRATOR: *Tracy Sabin* COPYWRITER: *Sarah Chan* CLIENT: *Harcourt Brace & Co.* ■ *Illustration for a textbook.* ● *Illustration für ein Schulbuch.* ▲ *Illustration pour un manuel scolaire.*

PAGE 127; #351 ART DIRECTORS: *Enrico Sempi, Antonella Trevisan* DESIGNER: *Antonella Trevisan* DESIGN FIRM: *Tangram Strategic Design* ILLUSTRATORS: *Antonella Trevisan, Guido Rosa, Sergio Quaranta* CLIENT: *Banca Popolare di Novara*

PAGE 127; #352 ART DIRECTOR: *Peter Iannerelli* DESIGN FIRM: *Ammirati Puris Lintas* PHOTOGRAPHER: *Hans Neleman* CLIENT: *Seiko Epson*

PAGE 127; #353 DESIGN FIRM: *Mara Kurtz Studio (in-house)* PRINTER: *Darby* ■ Holiday card for a design company using a familiar computer icon to symbolize starting over with the new year. ● Neujahrsgrüsse eines Designstudios, das eine vertraute Computer-Ikone als Symbol für den neuen Start einsetzte. ▲ Vlux de bonne année d'une agence de design, qui a utilisé une icône d'ordinateur familière pour symboliser un nouveau départ.

PAGE 128; #354 ART DIRECTOR: *Mike Grinley* ILLUSTRATOR: *Jeff Koegel* CLIENT: *Walking Magazine* ■ Illustration for a feature story, "Heart Health," about the frequency of heart attacks in women. ● Illustration für einen Magazinbeitrag, der sich mit den auch bei Frauen immer häufiger auftretenden Herzinfarkten befasst. ▲ Illustration d'un article de magazine consacré à l'infarctus chez la femme, un phénomène de plus en plus fréquent.

PAGE 128; #355 ART DIRECTOR: *Renee Gattone* PHOTOGRAPHER: *Jeff Koegel* CLIENT: *Packaging World Magazine* ■ This poster image announces a packaging machine exposition. ● Illustration für ein Plakat, das eine Ausstellung von Verpackungsmaschinen ankündigt. ▲ Illustration pour une affiche annonçant une exposition consacrée à des machines d'emballage.

PAGE 128; #356 ART DIRECTOR: *Susan Dazzo* ILLUSTRATOR: *Cathleen Toelke* CLIENT: *GQ* ■ This pastel illustration aims to convey the phantoms in the mind of a long-distance night swimmer. ● Diese Pastell-Illustration zeigt, was im Kopf eines Langstrecken-Nachtschwimmers vor sich gehen mag. ▲ Cette illustration pastel reflète ce qui se passe dans la tête d'un nageur de grand fond, la nuit.

PAGE 128; #357 ART DIRECTOR: *Jackie Seon* ILLUSTRATOR: *Cathleen Toelke* CLIENT: *Simon & Schuster* ■ The illustration from "The Secrets of the Bulls," by José Bernard is meant to evoke the exotic and romantic world of early 20th century Cuba. ● Die Illustration aus "Die Geheimnisse der Stiere" von José Bernard soll das exotische, romantische Kuba des frühen 20. Jahrhunderts heraufbeschwö ren. ▲ Cette illustration extraite de "Les Secrets des Taureaux" de José Bernard évoque le monde exotique et romantique de Cuba au début du siècle.

PAGE 129; #358 DESIGN FIRM: *Union Design* CLIENT: *Hennie Onstad Art Center* ■ Design program for an exhibition about art in digital media. ● Design-Programm für eine Ausstellung über digitale Kunst. ▲ Programme de design pour une exposition consacrée à l'art numérique.

PAGES 130, 131; #359-362 ART DIRECTOR/DESIGNER: *Steve Sandstrom* DESIGN FIRM: *Sandstrom Design* COPYWRITERS: *Austin Howe, Amy Rosenthal, Jean Rhode, Peter Wegner* PRINTER: *Image Graphics* ■ This design overcomes the difficulty of designing for yourself with intelligence, a sense of humor, and an image unlike any other design firm. ● Eigenwerbung für ein Design-Studio, die sich durch Intelligenz und Humor auszeichnet. ▲ Autopromotion d'une agence de design, qui se caractérise par son intelligence et son humour.

PAGE 132; #363 ART DIRECTOR/DESIGNER: *Nancy Skolos* CLIENT/DESIGN FIRM: *Skolos/Wedell* PHOTOGRAPHER: *Thomas Wedell* PRINTER: *Reynolds Dewalt* ■ The agency sought to create a design to reflect seamless photography and typography. ● Hier ging es um die Demonstration des Einsatzes von Photographie und Typographie. ▲ Il s'agissait de démontrer comment photographie et typographie sont associées et combinées.

PAGE 133; #364 ART DIRECTOR: *Toshihiro Onimaru* DESIGNER: *Do.* DESIGN FIRM: *Graphics & Designing Inc.* ILLUSTRATOR: *Toshihiro Onimaru* COPYWRITER: *Nil* CLIENT: *G & D Management Inc.*

PAGE 134; #365 ART DIRECTORS: *Lisa Ledgerwood, Mark Ledgerwood* DESIGNER/ILLUSTRATOR: *Mark Ledgerwood* DESIGN FIRM: *L3 Creative* CLIENT: *The Dial Corp* ■ This mark was intended to inspire leadership for an internal management group during a volatile time in the client's history. Thus, the two strong central figures standing steady amidst the rolling sea. ● Dieses Zeichen sollte die Stärke einer internen Management-Gruppe des Kunden in unbeständigen Zeiten darstellen: die beiden zentralen Figuren stehen stark und fest inmitten der tobenden See. ▲ Cet emblème reflète la force d'un groupe managérial appartenant à la société sur une période variable: les deux figures centrales, fortes et vigoureuses, résistent aux assauts d'une mer démontée.

PAGE 134; #366 ART DIRECTOR: *Mike Salisbury* DESIGNER: *Mary Evelyn McGough* DESIGN FIRM: *Mike Salisbury Communcations Inc.* ILLUSTRATOR: *Mary Evelyn McGough* CLIENT: *Rage Magazine* ■ This slick design for a new magazine targets Generation X men. ● Dieses Magazin soll Männer der Generation X ansprechen. ▲ Magazine destiné aux hommes de la génération X.

PAGE 134; #367 ART DIRECTORS/DESIGNERS: *Dean Butler, David Ansett* DESIGN FIRM: *Storm Design & Advertising* PHOTOGRAPHER: *Paul West* CLIENT: *Paul West Photography* ■ The focus of the design is the reputation and authority of the West family name, and the three-dimensional object reinforces the services they offer. ● Thema dieses Designs ist der Ruf und die Bedeutung des Namens West. Das dreidimensionale Objekt ist ein Hinweis auf die angebotenen Dienstleistungen. ▲ Thème de ce design: la réputation et la signification du nom West. L'objet tridimensionnel fait allusion aux prestations de services proposées.

PAGE 134; #368 DESIGNER: *Johann Terrettaz* DESIGN FIRM: *Tinguely Concept* CLIENT: *Nidecker Snowboards* ■ The logo is for a snowboard model designed for surfers who also snowboard, so the style was inspired by Hawaiian longboards. ● Logo für ein Snowboard, das Surfer ansprechen soll, die beide Sportarten ausüben. Ein 'Hawaiian Longboard' (typisches Surfboard aus der Anfangszeit dieser Sportart) diente dabei als Vorbild. ▲ Logo pour un snowboard destiné aux surfers qui pratiquent les deux disciplines. Un longboard hawa•en (planche typique des débuts de ce sport) a servi de modèle.

PAGE 134; #369 ART DIRECTOR: *Winnie Hart* DESIGNERS: *Winnie Hart, T. J. Todd* DESIGN FIRM: *Farnet Hart Design Studio* CLIENT: *Audubon Exploration* PRINTER: *Pel Hughes Printing* ■ The wing shape which completes the cross bar of the "A" is expressive of company name "Audubon" & indicative of their environmental sensitivities. ● Der Flügel im A für Audubon Exploration symbolisiert das Umweltengagement des Auftraggebers. ▲ L'aile qui complète le A pour Audubon Exploration symbolise l'engagement du client en faveur de l'environnement.

PAGE 134; #370 ART DIRECTOR/DESIGNER/ILLUSTRATOR: *Troy M. Litten* DESIGN FIRM: *Troy M. Litten Design* CLIENT: *Self-promotional logo*

PAGE 134; #371 ART DIRECTOR: *Jack Anderson* DESIGNERS: *Jack Anderson, Larry Anderson, Bruce Branson-Meyer* DESIGN FIRM: *Hornall Anderson Design Works* PHOTOGRAPHER/ILLUSTRATOR: *Mark Summers* CLIENT: *Rhino Chasers* ■ Rhino Chasers is a reference to experienced surfers of the 1950's who surfed the large waves known as "Rhinos." The identity is meant to reflect a free-spirited, "no fear" attitude. ● Rhino Chasers ist eine Anspielung auf die geübten Surfer der 50er Jahre: die grossen Wellen wurden "Rhinos" genannt. Das Zeichen soll den freien, furchtlosen Geist der Sportler reflektieren. ▲ Rhino Chasers est une allusion aux surfers expérimentés des années 50: les grandes vagues étaient appelées "rhinos". L'identité reflète l'esprit libre et téméraire des sportifs.

PAGE 134; #372 ART DIRECTOR/ILLUSTRATOR: *Jack Gernsheimer* DESIGNER: *Justin Wister* DESIGN FIRM: *Partners Design Inc.* CLIENT: *Canal Street Pub & Restaurant* ■ The firm sought to combine traditional treatment with a contemporary quality, reflect local history, and retain a degree of ambiguity and mystique. ● Hier ging es um eine zeitgemässe Darstellung von Tradition, wobei die lokale Geschichte und eine gewisse geheimnisvolle Stimmung zum Ausdruck kommen sollten. ▲ L'objectif était de présenter le thème de la tradition de façon contemporaine tout en intégrant l'histoire locale dans une atmosphère empreinte de mystère.

PAGE 134; #373 ART DIRECTOR: *Cliff Sloan* DESIGNER: *Janette Eusebio* DESIGN FIRM: *The Sloan Group* CLIENT: *Cafe Concepts* ■ The design promotes the restaurant's bi-coastal cuisine and lively late-night atmosphere as well as conveying a sense of warmth and accessibility. ● Die Küche des Restaurants, die Gerichte von beiden Küsten der USA bietet, die lebhafte nächtliche Aktivität sowie ein Gefühl von Wärme und Offenheit sollten in diesem Design zum Ausdruck kommen. ▲ Le design évoque la cuisine du restaurant qui propose des plats typiques des deux côtes des Etats-Unis, sa grande activité nocturne ainsi que l'atmosphère chaleureuse et conviviale qui le caractérise.

PAGE 135; #374 ART DIRECTOR/DESIGNER: *Steve Sandstrom* DESIGN FIRM: *Sandstrom Design* PRINTER: *Stout Marketing* ■ This signage program flexibly adapts to accommodate different retail needs. ● Diese Levi's-Schilder eignen sich für verschiedene Bedürfnisse der Einzelhändler. ▲ Le programme signalétique s'adapte aux différents points de vente Levi's.

PAGE 135; #375 ART DIRECTOR: *Dennis Crowe* DESIGNERS: *Dennis Crowe, Angie Wang, Roger Wong* DESIGN FIRM: *Zimmermann Crowe Design* CLIENT: *Levi Strauss & Co.* ■ This logo was designed for Western retailers who respond to Levi's traditional western image. ● Das Logo wurde für Western-Geschäfte entworfen, denen des traditionelle Western-Image von Levi's entgegenkommt. ▲ Ce logo a été conçu pour les points de vente de l'ouest des Etats-Unis, qui véhiculent la traditionnelle image western de Levi's.

PAGE 135; #376 ART DIRECTOR/DESIGNER *Steve Sandstrom* DESIGN FIRM: *Sandstrom Design* PRINTER: *Stout Marketing*

PAGE 136; #377 ART DIRECTORS/DESIGNERS: *Jeff Weithman, Dan Richards* DESIGN FIRM: *Richards/Weithman* CLIENT: *The Baby Jogger Company* ■ This mark tells the product story in a fun and interesting way. ● Dieses Zeichen informiert auf lustige, interessante Art über das Produkt. ▲ Ce signe évoque l'histoire du produit de façon amusante et intéressante.

PAGE 136; #378 ART DIRECTORS: *Diana Bidwill, Grenville Main* DESIGNER: *Diana Bidwill* DESIGN FIRM: *BNA Design Ltd.* ILLUSTRATOR: *Dean Grey* CLIENT: *U. U. Anchor Ltd.* ■ This logo for an airport cafe depicts the cafe owner's plane. ● Das Flugzeug des Besitzers wurde zum Thema des Logos für ein Flughafen-Café. ▲ Logo créé pour un café d'aéroport, illustrant l'avion de son propriétaire.

PAGE 136; #379 ART DIRECTOR: *Joseph Rattan* DESIGNER: *Brandon Murphy* DESIGN FIRM: *Joseph Rattan Design* ILLUSTRATORS: *Brandon Murphy, Diana McKnight* CLIENT: *Prime Retail* ■ The toucan, a bird indigenous to the area, is used as a symbol for this outlet mall in Puerto Rico. ● Der Tucan, der in dieser Gegend heimisch ist, wurde als Symbol für ein kleines Geschäft in Puerto Rico gewählt. ▲ Le toucan, un oiseau vivant dans la région, a été choisi comme symbole pour un petit magasin de Puerto Rico.

PAGE 136; #380 ART DIRECTOR/DESIGNER/PHOTOGRAPHER: *Youri Chasoff* CLIENT: *Jrina Stelmach*

PAGE 136; #381 DESIGNER: *Grant Peterson* DESIGN FIRM: *Studio Archetype*

PAGE 136; #382 DESIGN FIRM: *Ron Kellum Inc.* CLIENT: *Hybrid Recordings* ■ The symmetry of the letter "H" allowed designers the opportunity to demonstrate the idea of a hybrid and at the same time suggest the range of music available on the label. ● Die Symmetrie des Buchstaben "H" eignete sich bestens als Symbol eines Hybriden, wobei gleichzeitig auf das musikalische Programm des Labels hingewiesen wird. ▲ Le designer a choisi la lettre "H", dont la symétrie évoque parfaitement l'idée d'hybridité. Ce symbole fait également allusion au choix musical proposé par ce label.

PAGE 136; #383 ART DIRECTORS: *Woody Pirtle, John Klotnia* DESIGNERS: *Seung Il Choi, John Klotnia* DESIGN FIRM: *Pentagram Design, Inc.* CLIENT: *Pointbreak Communications* ■ The designers felt that the client, a data storage and retrieval company handling large amounts of information was best represented by the rise and fall of the ocean. They incorporated a wave and the letterforms "P" and "B" in the logo design. ● Die Gezeiten des Meeres dienen hier als Symbol für Pointbreak Communications, eine Datenverarbeitungsfirma. ▲ Les marées de l'océan symbolisent la société Pointbreak Communications spécialisée dans le traitement de données.

PAGE 136; #384 ART DIRECTOR/DESIGNER: *Rex Peteet, Mark Brinkman*

PAGE 136; #385 DESIGN FIRM: *Sibley/Peteet Design Inc.* COPYWRITER: *John Davis* CLIENT: *Center for Marine Conservation* PRINTER: *Baker Press* ■ The design demonstrates the client's involvement in the preservation of ocean and marine life. ● Thema ist das Engagement des Kunden für den Schutz der Meere. ▲ Ce design témoigne de l'engagement du client en faveur de la protection de l'océan et de la vie marine.

PAGE 136; #385 DESIGNER: *Derek Welch* DESIGN FIRM: *Nike Image Design* ■ This mark immediately communicates "Ken Griffey, Jr." with a familiar silhouette. ● Die vertraute Silhouette von "Ken Griffey, Jr." wurde zum Markenzeichen. ▲ La silhouette familière de "Ken Griffey Jr." est devenue une identité de marque.

PAGE 137; #386 ART DIRECTOR: *Toshihiro Onimaru* DESIGNER: *Do* DESIGN FIRM: *Graphics & Designing Inc.* ILLUSTRATOR: *Toshihiro Onimaru* CLIENT: *G & D Management Inc.*

PAGE 138; #387 ART DIRECTOR/DESIGNER: *Art Lofgreen* DESIGN FIRM: *Smith Ghormley Lofgreen Design* CLIENT: *Mesa Arts Center* ■ The firm wanted to create a sculptural monument sign for the Mesa Arts Center using the logo they had previously designed for it. ● Das Logo für das Mesa Arts Center diente als Ausgangspunkt für dieses skulpturale Zeichen. ▲ Le logo du Mesa Arts Center a servi de base pour cet emblème sculptural.

PAGE 138; #388 ART DIRECTOR/DESIGNER: *Halasi Zolta'n* DESIGN FIRM: *Art Force Studio* PHOTOGRAPHER: *Bakcsy A'rpa'd* CLIENT: *Hungarian Academy of Crafts & Design*

PAGE 138; #389 ART DIRECTOR: *Doo Kim* DESIGN FIRM: *Doo Kim Design* DESIGNERS: *Dongil Lee, Seung Hee Lee* CLIENT: *Korea International Trade Association*

PAGE 139; #390 ART DIRECTOR/DESIGNER: *Péter Vajda* DESIGN FIRM: *Alternativ Studio (in-house)*

PAGE 139; #391 ART DIRECTOR/DESIGNER: *Art Lofgreen* DESIGN FIRM: *Smith Ghormley Lofgreen Design* CLIENT: *Trax Tech Inc.* ■ The firm sought to develop a logo for the client which would reflect the client's freight tracking and documentation services. ● Logo für den Frachtsuch- und Dokumentations-Service des Auftraggebers. ▲ Logo pour le service de recherche de fret et de documentation du client.

PAGE 139; #392 DESIGNER: *Steve Ditko* DESIGN FIRM: *CFD Design* PHOTOGRAPHER: *Bruce Racine* CLIENT: *Promiscuous Smoker* ■ This cigar club logo is interpretive of a cigar band and demonstrates sex appeal of the Promiscuous name. ● Das Logo für einen Zigarrenraucher-Club ist eine Anspielung auf die Bauchbinde und auf den Sex-Appeal des Club-Namens. ▲ Logo pour un club de fumeurs de cigares faisant allusion à la bague d'un cigare et au sex-appeal inhérent au nom du club.

PAGE 139; #393 ART DIRECTOR/DESIGNER/ILLUSTRATOR: *Bruce Holdeman* DESIGN FIRM: *601 Design Inc.* CLIENT: *Tandem Cycle Works of Colorado* ■ Logo dipicting a tandem bicycle using the letters "CWC." ● Logo für einen Hersteller von Tandem-Fahrrädern. ▲ Logo pour un fabricant de tandems.

PAGE 139; #394 ART DIRECTOR/DESIGNER: *Webb Blevins* DESIGN FIRM: *Nike Image Design* ILLUSTRATOR: *Webb Blevins* PRINTER: *Graphic Arts Center* ■ This logo graphically describes a new support/comfort technology used in Nike skates and footwear. ● Noch mehr Halt und Bequemlichkeit bei Nike-"Skates" und -Schuhen dank neuer Technik. ▲ Encore plus de maintien et de confort pour les skates et chaussures Nike grâce à une nouvelle technologie.

PAGE 140; #395-397 ART DIRECTOR/DESIGNER: *Kimmo Kivilahti* DESIGN FIRM: *Hasan & Partners* PHOTOGRAPHER: *Marjo Tokkari* CLIENT: *Vaakuna 10th Floor Restaurants* ■ These menus and drink lists were designed to both match the character of the restaurants and be so unique that people would want to steal them. ● Die Speise- und Getränkekarten sollten nicht nur die Atmosphäre des Restaurants widerspiegeln, sondern so einzigartig sein, dass *sie die Gäste zum Stehlen verführen.* ▲ *Les cartes des menus et des vins ne devaient pas uniquement refléter l'atmosphère du restaurant, mais être à ce point uniques qu'on ait envie de les voler.*

PAGE 141; #398-400 DESIGNERS: *Renata Melman, Margarete Takeda, Patricia Oliveira* DESIGN FIRM: *Des Design* CLIENT: *Club B.A.S.E.*

PAGE 142; #401 ART DIRECTOR/DESIGNER: *Chika Azuma* DESIGN FIRM: *Verve Records (in-house)* PHOTOGRAPHER: *Larry Sultan* ■ *The double-sided poster|trim combination was designed so that record stores can use it according to their store size. The bandage on the little boy's head ended up as a puffy sticker which was stuck on the CD case. It also appears any way the combination is used so that it maintains consistency and identity with the CD.* ● *Das beidseitig bedruckte Plakat kann von den Händlern ihrer Ladengrö sse entsprechend eingesetzt werden. Das Pflaster am Kopf des kleinen Jungen wurde zum Sticker, der auf die CD-Hülle geklebt wurde.* ▲ *L'affiche imprimée recto verso peut être utilisée en fonction de la taille du magasin. L'emplâtre que porte le petit garçon a été collé sur le CD.*

PAGE 142; #402 ART DIRECTORS: *Carol Chen, Graham Eliot* PHOTOGRAPHER/ILLUSTRATOR: *Graham Elliott* CLIENT: *Sony Music*

PAGE 142; #403 ART DIRECTOR/DESIGNER/PHOTOGRAPHER/SCULPTOR: *Allan Lawrence Harry* CLIENT: *Groope* PRINTER: *Sony DADC, Austria* ■ *The design for Groope's debut CD, "Hetero," seeks to capture the atmosphere of their music.* ● *Das Design für Groopes erste CD, "Hetero", sollte eine Interpretation der Musik sein.* ▲ *Le design du premier CD de Groope, "Hetero", livre une interprétation de la musique.*

PAGE 142; #404 ART DIRECTOR: *George Dare* DESIGNER: *George Dare* DESIGN FIRM: *Dare-Art* PHOTOGRAPHER/ILLUSTRATOR: *George Dare* COPYWRITER: *George Dare* CLIENT: *Eye Q Music* PRINTER/MANUFACTURER: *Warner Music Manufacturing Europe*

PAGE 143; #405 ART DIRECTOR/DESIGNER/COPYWRITER: *George Dare* DESIGN FIRM: *Dare-Art* ARTIST: *Ralf HildenBeutel* RECORD LABEL: *Harthouse* CLIENT: *Eye Q Music* PRINTER/MANUFACTURER: *Warner Music Manufacturing Europe.*

PAGE 144; #406, 407 ART DIRECTOR/DESIGNER: *Norman Moore* DESIGN FIRM: *Design Art, Inc.* PHOTOGRAPHERS: *Patrick Leonard, Marc Moreau, Jim Ponchard, Tim Leonard* COPYWRITER: *Patrick Leonard* CLIENT: *Unitone Records* ■ *This design recreates an old-fashioned leather bound journal account of a fly fishing trip.* ● *Ein altmodisches, ledergebundenes Tagebuch über einen Angelausflug diente hier als Thema.* ▲ *Un ancien journal intime relié en cuir et consacré à une journée de pêche a servi de thème.*

PAGE 144; #408, 409 ART DIRECTOR: *Stefan Sagmeister* DESIGNERS: *Stefan Sagmeister, Veronica Oh* DESIGN FIRM: *Sagmeister Inc.* PHOTOGRAPHER: *Timothy Greenfield Sanders* WRITER: *Lou Reed* CLIENT: *Warner Brothers Music* ■ *The objective was to show the metamorphosis described in the lyrics through a dark blue tinted jewel box.* ● *Die dunkelblaue Hülle der CD ist eine Anspielung auf die Metamorphose, die im Text beschrieben wird.* ▲ *Le packaging bleu foncé du CD fait allusion à la métamorphose décrite dans le texte.*

PAGE 144; #410, 411 ART DIRECTOR/DESIGNER: *Joel Zimmerman* DESIGN FIRM: *Sony Music (in-house)* PHOTOGRAPHER: *David Gahr*

PAGE 144; #412, 413 ART DIRECTOR/DESIGNER: *Mark Burdett* DESIGN FIRM: *Sony Music (in-house)* PHOTOGRAPHER: *Frank W. Ockenfels III*

PAGE 145; #414 ART DIRECTOR: *Brad Ghormley* DESIGNER: *Rodd Whitney* DESIGN FIRM: *Smith Ghormley Lofgreen Design* CLIENT: *Piranha Interactive Publishing* PRINTER: *Pierce Arrow* ■ *The agency wanted to create a fun, travel-oriented package based on souvenirs from around the country.* ● *Souvenirs aus dem ganzen Land wurden zum Thema für dieses amüsante, Reise-orientierte Paket.* ▲ *L'agence a choisi de créer un paquet amusant consacré aux voyages et rempli de souvenirs du pays tout entier.*

PAGE 146; #415-417 ART DIRECTOR/DESIGNER: *Elizabeth Kairys* DESIGN FIRM/PUBLISHER: *Salon Magazine (in-house)* ■ *Salon HTML pages are optimized for 14-inch monitors and are designed to have a total weight of 30-40 kilobytes for easy downloading, with an attractive opening screen to engage the reader.* ● *Die Seiten des digitalen Magazins Salon sind auf 14î-Computerbildschirme ausgerichtet. Die Erö ffnungsseite soll dank besonderer Attraktivität zum Lesen des Magazins einladen.* ▲ *Les pages du magazine numérique Salon sont destinées à des écrans d'ordinateur de 14 pouces. La page d'introduction doit inviter le lecteur à consulter le magazine.*

PAGE 146; #418, 419 ART DIRECTOR/DESIGNER: *Mignon Khargie* DESIGN FIRM/PUBLISHER: *Salon Magazine (in-house)*

PAGE 146; #420 ART DIRECTOR/DESIGNER: *Elizabeth Kairys* DESIGN FIRM/PUBLISHER: *Salon Magazine (in-house)* ■ *Salon HTML pages are optimized for 14-inch monitors and are designed to have a total weight of 30-40 kilobytes for easy downloading, with an attractive opening screen to engage the reader.* ● *Die Seiten des digitalen Magazins Salon sind auf 14î-Computerbildschirme ausgerichtet. Die attraktive Erö ffnungsseite soll zum Lesen des Magazins einladen.* ▲ *Les pages du magazine numérique Salon sont destinées à des écrans d'ordinateur de 14 pouces. La page d'introduction doit inviter le lecteur à consulter le magazine.*

PAGE 147; #421-424 ART DIRECTOR: *Joe Duffy* DESIGNERS: *Todd Bartz, Dan Olson* DESIGN FIRM: *Duffy Design* COPYWRITERS: *Chuck Carlson, Steve Chavez* CLIENT: *Nikon Inc.* ■ *The challenge in building a website for Nikon Inc. was to unify its diverse product divisions under a single brand identity. The strong Nikon yellow and black colors, in addition to thin rules, reminiscent of a lens or viewfinder marks were used to communicate the precision and innovation of the Nikon brand.* ● *Beim Entwurf der Website für Nikon Inc. ging es vor allem darum, die diversen Produktbereiche unter einem Markenauftritt zusammenzufassen. Die Nikon Farben, ein kräftiges Gelb und Schwarz, in Kombination mit den feinen Linien, die an die Objektive bzw. Sucher erinnern, stehen für die Präzision und Innovation der Nikon-Produkte.* ▲ *Lors de la conception du site Web de Nikon Inc., il s'agissait avant tout de réunir les différents domaines de produits sous une seule identité de marque. Les couleurs Nikon, un jaune franc et le noir, combinées à de fines lignes évoquent la précision et l'aspect novateur des produits de la marque.*

PAGE 148; #425-429 ART DIRECTOR/DESIGNER: *Jill Taffet* DESIGN FIRM: *CBO Multimedia* DIGITAL ARTISTS: *Sabrina Soriano, Robert Vega* CLIENT: *Warner Bros., Denise Bradley* ■ *This interactive kiosk reflects the kinetic blend of animation and live action found in the movie it promotes— "Space Jam."* ● *Dieser interaktive Kiosk reflektiert die kinetische Mischung von Animation und Life-Action, die "Space Jam" auszeichnet, den Film, für den hier geworben wird.* ▲ *Ce kiosque interactif reflète la combinaison cinétique entre dessin animé et action live qui caractérise le film "Space Jam" promu ici.*

PAGE 149; #430-434 ART DIRECTOR/DESIGNER: *Jill Taffet* DESIGN FIRM: *CBO Multimedia* DIGITAL ARTISTS: *Luke Davis, Sabrina Soriano, Kaz Matsume* CLIENT: *Twentieth Century Fox, Scott Zimbler* ■ *This website simulates the cockpit of a B-3 stealth bomber and allows users to play an interactive game as well as access "secret information" about the B-3 stealth bomber and the movie the site promotes.* ● *Diese Website ist eine Simulation des Cockpits eines B-3 Bombenflugzeugs und ermö glicht dem Benutzer, ein interaktives Online-Spiel zu spielen sowie auch "geheimen Informationen" über den Bomber und den Film, für den geworben wird, auf die Spur zu kommen.* ▲ *Ce site web est une simulation du cockpit d'un bombardier B-3. L'utilisateur peut jouer à un jeu interactif on-line et accéder à des "informations secrètes" sur l'avion et le film présenté.*

PAGE 150; #435-440 ART DIRECTOR: *Andrew Sather* DESIGNERS: *Bernie Dechant, Andrew Sather Matia Wagabaza* DESIGN FIRM: *Adjacency: brand new media* PHOTOGRAPHERS: *Kenneth Greer, Michael Voorhees, Mike Medby* COPYWRITER: *Andrew Sather* CLIENT: *Rollerblade, Inc.* ■ *Since the client's corporate identity was in transition, the design needed to be flexible and relevant regardless of where the transition led to. The website set out to capture the dynamism of the sport of in-line skating itself.* ● *Da der Auftraggeber sich* im Umbruch befand, musste das Design flexibel und relevant sein, unabhängig davon, wie die Firma in Zukunft aussehen würde. Zum Thema der Website wurde deshalb die Dynamik des Inline-Skating gewählt. ▲ L'identité visuelle du client se trouvant dans une phase de transition, le design devait être à la fois facilement adaptable et pertinent, indépendamment de la future image de marque. Le site web met en avant le dynamisme du in-line skating.

PAGE 151; #441 ART DIRECTORS: *Dana Arnett, Chris Schreiber* DESIGNERS: *Ken Fox, Michael A. Peterson, Ron Spohn, Geoff Mark* DESIGN FIRM: *VSA Partners, Inc.* COPYWRITER: *Jack Sichterman* CLIENT: *Harley-Davidson, Inc.* ■ The design goal was to develop an official online presence that embodies the feel and culture that is uniquely Harley-Davidson. A digital platform for enthusiasts and new seekers alike offers a chance to explore various components of the Harley-Davidson experience. ● Das einzigartige Image und die Kultur von Harley-Davidson sollten in dieser Website zum Ausdruck kommen. Es wird eine digitale Plattform für Harley-Fans und auch neue Interessenten geboten, die hier die Mö glichkeit haben, diverse Komponenten der Harley-Davidson-Erfahrung zu erkunden. ▲ Ce site web devait illustrer l'image unique et la culture Harley-Davidson. Il propose également une plate-forme numérique aux fans de Harley et aux néophytes qui ont ainsi la possibilité de découvrir le monde de Harley-Davidson.

PAGE 151; #442 ART DIRECTOR/DESIGNER: *Jeffrey Jones* DESIGN FIRM: *Elemental Interactive Design & Development* ILLUSTRATORS: *John Baker, Bill Plympton, Doug Ross* CLIENT: *IBM Corporation* ■ The objective was to present IBM's financial data in interactive form while showcasing IBM's Network-Centric Computing strategy and how it could work for businesses and individuals. ● Hier ging es darum, die Finanzdaten von IBM in interaktiver Form zu präsentieren und dabei zu demonstrieren, was die Network-Centric Cumputing-Strategie (NCC) von IBM für Unternehmen oder Einzelpersonen zu leisten vermag. ▲ L'objectif était de présenter les résultats financiers d'IBM sous une forme interactive et de montrer ce que la stratégie Network-Centric Computing d'IBM peut faire pour les entreprises et les utilisateurs privés.

PAGE 152; #443-448 ART DIRECTORS: *Mark Wronski* CREATIVE DIRECTORS: *Rich Conklin, Tim Meraz* DISKETTE PROGRAM DESIGNERS: *David Tanimoto, Christopher Hoffman* INTERACTIVE DEVELOPER: *Genex Media* PACKAGING DESIGNER: *Trish Butters* DESIGN FIRM: *The Designory, Inc.* COPYWRITER: *Christopher Hoffman* CLIENT: *Mercedes-Benz of North America* ■ Users explore a virtual Mercedes automobile at their own pace and on their own path, anywhere from the outermost layer of paint to the innermost workings of the drivetrain. ● Interessenten haben hier Gelegenheit, einen virtuellen Mercedes in ihrem eigenen Tempo und nach eigenem Gutdünken zu untersuchen, ob es sich um Äusserlichkeiten wie den Lack oder um die Motorentechnik handelt. ▲ L'utilisateur a la possibilité d'examiner une Mercedes virtuelle à son rythme et sous toutes les coutures, de la carrosserie au moteur.

PAGE 153; #449-454 ART DIRECTOR: *Judy Kirpich* DESIGNER: *Johnny Vitorovich* DESIGN FIRM: *Grafik Communications, Ltd.* PRIMARY PHOTOGRAPHER: *Pam Soorenko* SUPPORT PHOTOGRAPHY: *Pat Crowe, Debbie Fox, Oi Veerasaran, Johnny Vitorovich, Susan Osborn, stock* COPYWRITERS: *Beth Biedronski, Linda Burchfield, Kate Pullen, Eugene Guilaran, Vanessa Hartman, Lewis Temple, Halle Wachsmuth, Stephanie Wizen, Tiffany Witt* CLIENT: *Alexandria & Arlington Animal Shelter* ■ The goal was to correct the misconception that one finds only old, sick and abused animals at shelters, so the site featured photographs of many of the beautiful animals available for adoption. ● Hier ging es darum, die weit verbreitete Annahme, man finde in Tierheimen nur alte, kranke und misshandelte Tiere, zu widerlegen. Die Web-Site präsentierte deshalb Bilder der vielen schö nen, gesunden Tiere, die das Tierheim abzugeben hat. ▲ L'objectif était de réfuter l'opinion très répandue qui veut que l'on ne trouve que des animaux vieux, malades et maltraités dans les refuges pour animaux. Ce site web présente des photos de plusieurs superbes bêtes à adopter.

PAGE 154; #455, 457 ART DIRECTORS: *Tim Hale, Stephen Zhang* DESIGNERS: *Stephen Zhang, David Eden* DESIGN FIRM: *Fossil Design Studio (in-house)* ILLUSTRATORS: *Mark Ross, Stephen Zhang* PRINTER: *Supergraphics* ■ The wrapped bus, with gauche painted faces peering

down on all passers-by, translates Fossil's powerful classic brand image of America's awakening and optimistic attitude of the late forties and fifties. ● Der eingewickelte Bus mit den unbeholfen gemalten Gesichtern, die auf die Passanten herunterschauen, erinnert an das starke, klassische Markenzeichen von Fossil aus den optimistischen Aufbruchjahren der USA in den späten 40ern und in den 50ern. ▲ Le bus emballé et les visages gauchement peints qui regardent les passants de haut rappellent l'image rétro de Fossil durant l'âge d'or aux Etats-Unis dans les années 50.

PAGE 154; #456 ART DIRECTOR: *Dave Curtis* DESIGNERS: *Matt Sullivan, Stephanie Wade* DESIGN FIRM: *Curtis Design* PHOTOGRAPHER/ILLUSTRATOR: *Justin Carroll* CLIENT: *Christopher Ranch* ■ The design directive was to develop an identity for an agribusiness company which would translates well from stationery to packaging to truck graphics. ● Es ging um die Entwicklung eines Firmenzeichens für ein Unternehmen, das im Agrarbereich tätig ist. Es sollte sich für alle Bereiche, von Briefpapier über Verpackungen bis zur Kennzeichnung der Lastwagen eignen. ▲ Création d'une identité visuelle pour une société de l'agroalimentaire, du papier à lettres aux emballages en passant par l'habillage des camions.

PAGE 155; #458 CREATIVE DIRECTORS: *Anthony Goldschmidt, Mark Crawford* ART DIRECTOR: *Brad Johnson* DESIGN FIRM: *Intralink Film Graphic Design* COPYWRITER: *Marie Moneysmith* CLIENT: *Warner Bros., Joel Wayne* ■ This billboard for the movie Twister shockingly portrays the damage left in the tornado's wake, and lets the viewers imagine what force could have caused such damage. Designing it as a three dimensional piece helped to heighten the level of realism. ● Dieses Billboard für den Film Twister zeigt die entsetzlichen Verwüstungen, die der Tornado angerichtet hat, und gibt dem Betrachter eine Vorstellung davon, mit welcher Kraft er gewütet haben muss. Das dreidimensionale Design unterstützte die realistische Wirkung. ▲ Ce panneau pour le film Twister montre les ravages occasionnés par une tornade et permet d'imaginer la force du cataclysme. Le design tridimensionnel renforce l'impact du panneau.

PAGE 156; #459 ART DIRECTOR/CREATIVE DIRECTOR: *Jose Serrano* DESIGNERS: *Jose Serrano, Miguel Perez* DESIGN FIRM: *Mires Design* PHOTOGRAPHER: *Carl VanderSchuit* CLIENT: *Voit Sports* ■ The use of corrugated cardboard reflects environmental consciousness, while the metallic silver inks attract the rugged, thrill-seeking audience most likely to buy the brand. ● Der Einsatz von Wellkarton reflektiert das Umweltbewusstsein, während die silbrigen Druckfarben das etwas wilde, abenteuerlustige Publikum anziehen soll, das auf die Marke anspricht. ▲ L'utilisation de carton ondulé reflète le souci du respect de l'environnement tandis que les couleurs argentées et métallisées visent à séduire le public cible, amateur de sensations fortes.

PAGE 157; #460 ART DIRECTOR: *Claudio Novaes* DESIGNERS: *Claudio Novaes, Carla Anita Tanaka* DESIGN FIRM: *Claudio Novaes Graphic Design* CLIENT: *Marabá Filmes*

PAGE 158; #461, 462 ART DIRECTORS: *Heather Cooley, Jack Coverdale* DESIGNER: *Heather Cooley* DESIGN FIRM: *Parachute* ADVERTISING AGENCY: *Clarity Coverdale Fury* PHOTOGRAPHER: *Mark Hauser, Ripsaw* ILLUSTRATOR: *Stan Watts* COPYWRITER: *Jerry Fury* CLIENT: *Millennium Import Company* ■ This box is for the direct mail promotion of a luxury vodka. ● Box für eine Direct Mail Aktion, in der ein Wodka der Luxus-Klasse beworben wird. ▲ Boîte réalisée pour la promotion par publipostage d'une vodka de qualité supérieure.

PAGE 158; #463 ART DIRECTOR/DESIGNER/COPYWRITER: *Mark Oliver* DESIGN FIRM: *Mark Oliver, Inc.* PHOTOGRAPHERS/ILLUSTRATORS: *Carey Austin, Liz Wheaton* CLIENT: *Firestone Vineyard* PRINTER: *SY Valley Printing* ■ The bottle and label tie wines to dramatic vistas of the land and winery. ● Thema der Flaschen und Etiketten eines Weinguts ist die atemberaubende Landschaft, in der der Wein wächst. ▲ Bouteille et étiquettes *illustrent la beauté sauvage de la région où le vin est cultivé.*

PAGE 158; #464 ART DIRECTOR: *Jeremy Haines* DESIGNER: *Jeffrey Steventon* DESIGN FIRM: *Haines McGregor* CLIENT: *IDV*

PAGE 159; #465 ART DIRECTOR: *Glenn Tutssel* DESIGNERS: *Nick Hanson, Fiona Burnett* DESIGN FIRM: *Tutssels* CLIENT: *United Distillers* ■ *The design, based on a traditional Scottish brooch and pin, mixes stylish cosmopolitan modernity with traditional Celtic motifs.* ● *Das Design, das auf einer traditionellen schottischen Brosche basiert, verbindet weltoffene Modernität mit traditionellen keltischen Motiven.* ▲ *Inspiré d'une broche écossaise, le design marie style moderne cosmopolite et motifs celtes traditionnels.*

PAGE 160; #466 ART DIRECTOR: *Joe Duffy* DESIGNERS: *Alan Leusink, KOBE* DESIGN FIRM: *Duffy Design* ILLUSTRATOR: *Bret Meredith* CLIENT: *Jim Beam Brands*

PAGE 160; #467 ART DIRECTOR/DESIGNER: *Thomas Bond* DESIGN FIRM: *SBG Partners* CLIENT: *Brown Forman* ■ *A classically understated flask-style bottle in a shape unique to the bourbon category was combined with ACL graphics to emphasize timeless simplicity and a historic positioning for a new brand.* ● *Zeitlose Schlichtheit und Tradition kommen in dieser klassischen, zurückhaltenden Flasche in der typischen Bourbon-Form zum Ausdruck, die für die Einführung einer neuen Marke entworfen wurde.* ▲ *Bouteille de bourbon sobre et classique, créée pour le lancement d'une nouvelle marque.*

PAGE 161; #468-473 ART DIRECTOR/DESIGNER: *Gregg Boling* DESIGN FIRM: *Dye, Van Mol & Lawrence* ILLUSTRATOR: *Jim Hsehi* COPYWRITER: *Nelson Eddy* CLIENT: *Jack Daniels* PRINTER: *Lithographics* ■ *This sales kit for a new line of beers is made from oak and carries each of the line's beer flavors, some ingredients that go into the beers, and a brochure which explains the points of difference from other beers.* ● *Diese Mappe mit Verkaufsmaterial für eine neue Biermarke ist aus Eiche und zeigt alle Sorten der Marke sowie einige der Ingredienzen des Biers. Dazu gehört auch eine Broschüre, die den Unterschied gegenüber anderen Biermarken erklärt.* ▲ *Kit promotionnel en bois de chêne pour une nouvelle marque de bière. Toutes les bières de la gamme sont présentées ainsi que certains ingrédients rentrant dans leur composition. Une brochure explique en quoi ces bières sont différentes des autres marques.*

PAGE 162; #474 ART DIRECTOR: *Joe Duffy* DESIGNER: *Alan Leusink* DESIGN FIRM: *Duffy Design* PHOTOGRAPHER/ILLUSTRATOR: *Brett Meredith* CLIENT: *Molson Brewery*

PAGE 162; #475 ART DIRECTORS: *Miguel Angel Pellot, Loren Li Ortiz* DESIGNERS: *Miguel Angel Pellot, Enrique Renta* DESIGN FIRM: *EJE Sociedad Publicitaria* PHOTOGRAPHER: *Ernesto Robles* COPYWRITERS: *Miguel Angel Pellot, Enrique Renta* CLIENT: *Bacardi-Martini*

PAGE 162; #476 ART DIRECTORS: *Thomas Fairclough, John Marota* DESIGNERS: *Thomas Fairclough, Tom Anista, Jamey Wagner* DESIGN FIRM: *Antista Fairclough Design* CLIENT: *Anheuser-Busch, Inc.* ■ *The design uses rich and festive detail and beer cues to support the product's image as a premium brew with superior taste.* ● *Hier ging es darum, die hervorragende Qualität des Biers zum Ausdruck zu bringen.* ▲ *L'objectif était de souligner la qualité supérieure de cette bière.*

PAGE 162; #477 ART DIRECTOR/COPYWRITER: *Mark Oliver* DESIGNERS/ILLUSTRATORS: *Mark Oliver, Patty Devlin-Driskel* DESIGN FIRM: *Mark Oliver, Inc.* CLIENT: *Firestone Walker Brewing Co.* PRINTER: *Louis Roesch* ■ *The bottle design for a hand-crafted brew defines American heritage.* ● *Amerikanische Tradition ist das Thema dieser Flaschenausstattung für ein handgebrautes Bier.* ▲ *Cette bouteille de bière de fabrication artisanale devait refléter l'esprit de la tradition américaine.*

PAGE 163; #478, 479 ART DIRECTOR: *Bill Cahan* DESIGNER/ILLUSTRATOR: *Kevin Roberson* DESIGN FIRM: *Cahan & Associates* COPYWRITER: *Stefanie Marlis* CLIENT: *Boisset USA* ■ *This packaging attempts to capture the spirit of the historic Apollo mission. The blue bottle and simple graphics relate to the*

vastness of space. ● *Diese Verpackung steht ganz im Zeichen der Apollo-Mission. Die blaue Flasche und die schlichte Graphik beziehen sich auf die Weite des Weltraums.* ▲ *Packaging créé sur le thème de la mission Apollo. La bouteille bleue et le graphisme sobre évoquent l'immensité de l'espace.*

PAGE 164; #480 ART DIRECTOR: *Glenn Tutssel* DESIGNER: *Polly French* DESIGN FIRM: *Tutssels* CLIENT: *Boots the Chemist* PRINTER: *ACL Cartons Ltd.* ■ *The transparent pack and distinctive, sophisticated graphics create a strong identity for this range of haircare products.* ● *Die transparente Verpackung und die eigenwillige Graphik sorgen für einen starken Markenauftritt dieser Haarpflegeprodukte.* ▲ *L'emballage transparent et le graphisme original créent une image forte pour cette gamme de produits capillaires.*

PAGE 164; #481 ART DIRECTORS: *Karen Welman, Jonathan Ford* DESIGNER: *Lawrence Haggerty* DESIGN FIRM: *Pearlfisher (in-house)*

PAGE 165; #482 ART DIRECTOR: *Steve Sandstrom* DESIGNERS: *Steve Sandstrom, Janée Warren* DESIGN FIRM: *Sandstrom Design* COPYWRITER: *Steve Sandoz* CLIENT: *Tazo* ■ *This new product introduction within the Tazo Tea line continues the graphic look of the existing Tazo products. The text printed on the wooden sticks is revealed as one eats.* ● *Hier ging es um die Einführung eines neuen Produktes innerhalb der Tazo-Teelinie. Die graphische Gestaltung schliesst an die bereits vorhandenen Produkte an. Der Text auf den Holzstäbchen wird während des Essens sichtbar.* ▲ *Lancement d'un nouveau produit dans la gamme de thés Tazo. Le packaging s'inscrit dans la lignée des produits existants. Le texte des baguettes apparaît lorsqu'on s'en sert.*

PAGE 165; #483 ART DIRECTORS: *David Turner, Bruce Duckworth* DESIGNERS: *Jeff Fassnacht, Brian Cox* DESIGN FIRM: *Turner Duckworth* PRINTER: *Thomas Swan Sign Co.* ■ *Point-of-purchase items designed to intrigue the consumer and explain the service.* ● *Promotionsmaterial für den Einzelhandel, das die Kunden ansprechen und über den Service informieren soll.* ▲ *Matériel publicitaire pour les points de vente destiné à intriguer le client et à lui présenter les spécificités du service.*

PAGE 166; #484 ART DIRECTOR/DESIGNER: *David Lemley* DESIGN FIRM: *David Lemley Design* CLIENT: *Brown & Haley* PRINTER: *Metalcraft Orient* ■ *This packaging, which looks like it might be new or antique and uses a handlettered logo and a simple color palette, leverages the heritage of the brand while introducing a new product.* ● *Verpackung für ein neues Produkt. Die Handschrift des Logos und die schlichte Farbpalette unterstreichen die Tradition der Marke.* ▲ *Packaging d'un nouveau produit. L'écriture calligraphiée du logo et une palette de couleurs simple soulignent la longue tradition de la marque.*

PAGE 166; #485 ART DIRECTOR/DESIGNER: *Jeff Weithman* DESIGN FIRM: *Nike Image Design (in-house)* ILLUSTRATORS: *Darnell Freier, Webb Blevins* PRINTER: *Rose City Packaging* ■ *The packaging was designed as an integral component of a launch package introducing Nike into the eyewear business. The dot pattern was designed as an energetic reinterpretation of the outsole waffle pattern on early Nike shoes.* ● *Die Verpackung wurde als Bestandteil einer Einführungspromotion für Nike-Brillen konzipiert. Das Punktmuster ist eine Anspielung auf das Waffelmuster der Sohlen der ersten Nike-Sportschuhe.* ▲ *Packaging conçu dans le cadre d'une opération promotionnelle pour les lunettes Nike. Le motif à pois est un clin d'Ïil au profil gaufré des semelles des premières chaussures de sport Nike.*

PAGE 166; #486, 487 ART DIRECTORS: *Charles Anderson, Todd Piper-Hauswirth* DESIGNER: *Todd Piper-Hauswirth* DESIGN FIRM: *Charles S. Anderson Design Company* PHOTOGRAPHER: *Paul Irmiter* CLIENT: *K-Ration*

PAGE 167 #488 ART DIRECTOR/DESIGNER: *Kai Mui* DESIGN FIRM: *Kai Mui Group* COPYWRITER: *Ana Bornhofen* CLIENT: *AKI S.p.A. Italia* ■ *This underwear packaging is designed to stand out against Calvin Klein look-alike designs in the high-end and women's market in Italy. The metal motif is part of the store theme.* ● *Verpackung für italienische Damenunterwäsche der gehobenen Preisklasse, die einen Kontrast zu den Calvin-Klein-Imitationen bilden sollte.* ▲ *Packaging pour de la lingerie fine italienne visant à se démarquer des emballages imitant Calvin Klein.*

PAGE 168; #489 ART DIRECTOR: *Tim Hale* DESIGNER: *Bill Morgan* DESIGN FIRM: *Fossil Design Studio (in-house)* ■ This series of tins capture Fossil's existing retro image in a more contemporary style. The antique props were used in place of the retro illustrative art to reinforce the time period and the brand identity. ● Eine Reihe von Dosen als Uhrenverpackung, wobei das traditionelle Image von Fossil auf zeitgemässe Art zum Ausdruck kommt. ▲ Cette série de boîtes en métal pour les montres Fossil décline l'image rétro de la marque d'une manière plus moderne.

PAGE 169; #490-495 ART DIRECTOR: *Jaimie Alexander* DESIGNERS: *Mandy Putnam, Paul Westrick* DESIGN FIRM: *Fitch Inc.* PHOTOGRAPHER: *Mark Steele* CLIENT: *Wolverine World Wide* ■ Brand identity and packaging for Hush Puppies children's line. The program components included labels, hangtags, packaging, retail presentation and sales materials. The designers attempted to establish a link between the adult line of footware and the children's line of footwear and apparel. ● Marke und Verpackung für Kinderschuhe der Marke Hush Puppies. Das Design-Programm erstreckt sich auf Etiketten, Anhänger, Verpackung, Laden-Displays und Verkaufsmaterial. Dabei sollte zwischen der Produktlinie für Erwachsene und der Kinderlinie für Schuhe und Kleidung eine Verbindung hergestellt werden ▲ Identité visuelle et packaging conçus pour des chaussures d'enfants de la marque Hush Puppies. Le programme graphique comprenait également des étiquettes, des clips, différents packagings, des présentoirs et du matériel publicitaire. Il s'agissait aussi de créer un lien entre les gammes pour adultes et celles pour enfants.

PAGE 170; #496, 497 ART DIRECTOR: *David Poythress* DESIGNER/ILLUSTRATOR: *Gregory Ridge* DESIGN FIRM: *David Poythress Designs Ltd.* CLIENT: *Wrangler Inc.* ■ The designers developed a unified graphic image for all western licensee packaging that they felt looked as good printed flexographically as it does offset, without increasing costs. ● Hier ging es um die Vereinheitlichung der Verpackungen für alle Wrangler-Händler. Die Agentur fand, dass der Anilingummidruck ebensogut wie Offset sei, wobei die Kosten nicht höher waren. ▲ L'objectif était d'uniformiser les packagings de tous les revendeurs Wrangler. L'agence a opté pour une impression flexographique qui offre une qualité aussi bonne que l'offset sans augmenter les coûts.

PAGE 171; #498 ART DIRECTOR/COPYWRITER: *John Blackburn* DESIGNER: *Belinda Duggan* DESIGN FIRM: *Blackburn's Ltd.* ILLUSTRATOR: *Fred van Deelan* CLIENT: *Gleneagle Spring Waters Co Ltd.* ■ The design for this new mineral water bottle is meant to be "discreet, yet confident" and to "stand tall above the clarets and chardonnays." ● Die Gestaltung der Flasche dieses neuen Mineralwassers sollte "diskret, aber bestimmt" wirken und aus "den Bordeaux und Chardonnays herausragen". ▲ Le design de cette bouteille pour une nouvelle eau minérale devait être "discret, mais assuré" et "affirmer clairement sa supériorité sur les bouteilles de bordeaux et de chardonnay".

PAGE 171; #499 ART DIRECTORS/DESIGNERS: *Tom Antista, Thomas Fairclough* DESIGN FIRM: *Antista Fairclough Design* PHOTOGRAPHER/ILLUSTRATOR: *Kevin Newman* CLIENT: *Sutton Place Gourmet* ■ The strategy was to create an identity that conveyed a quality gourmet feel, and could be adapted to an array of branded products for the store. ● Hier ging es um ein anspruchsvolles Gourmet-Image, das sich auch auf eine Reihe von Markenprodukten des Ladens anwenden lassen sollte. ▲ Le client, une épicerie fine, souhaitait une identité visuelle haut de gamme à même d'être déclinée pour une série de produits de marque du magasin.

PAGE 172; #500 ART DIRECTOR: *Cheryl Heller* DESIGNERS: *Carole Freehauf, Veronica Oh* DESIGN FIRM: *Siegel & Gale* PHOTOGRAPHERS: *Christian Witkin, Philip-Lorca di Corcia, Judith Roy Ross, Francois Robert, Bill Phelps, Geof Kern, Dan Winters, Michael Lewis, Robbie McClaran, Lars Topelmann* COPYWRITER: *Cheryl Heller* CLIENT: *S. D. Warren Company* ■ The goal was to create excitement around the introduction of a bright blue-white paper targeting designers and premium printers. ● Ziel war es, Drucker und Graphiker für eine leuchtend blau-weisse Papierqualität zu begeistern. ▲ L'objectif était de séduire imprimeurs et graphistes lors du lancement d'un nouveau papier bleu-blanc éclatant.

PAGE 172; #501 ART DIRECTOR: *Bart Crosby* DESIGNER: *Angela Norwood*

DESIGN FIRM: *Crosby Associates Inc.* PHOTOGRAPHERS: *Wayne Calabrese (color photo), Photonica (B&W photo)* CLIENT: *Champion International Corporation* PRINTER: *AM Lithography* ■ The objective was to increase awareness of a variety of Champion's papers, and to offer ideas for using them creatively to enhance work. ● Die Aufgabe bestand darin, auf eine Auswahl von Champion-Papieren aufmerksam zu machen und zu demonstrieren, wie man sie auf kreative Art einsetzen kann. ▲ L'objectif était d'attirer l'attention sur une gamme de papiers Champion et de montrer comment les utiliser de façon créative.

PAGE 173; #502-504 ART DIRECTOR/DESIGNER: *Olaf Stein* FIRM: *Factor Design GmbH* CALLIGRAPHER: *Pia Lindner* COPYWRITER: *Hannah S. Friche* CLIENT: *Römerturm Feinstpapier* ■ Swatchbook system showing client's paper lines. ● Ein Musterbuch-System mit den Papiersorten des Kunden. ▲ Catalogue d'échantillons présentant les différentes gammes de papiers du client.

PAGE 174; #505-508 ART DIRECTOR: *Dana Arnett* DESIGNERS: *Ken Fox, Fletcher Martin* DESIGN FIRM: *VSA Partners, Inc.* PHOTOGRAPHER: *Scott Shigley* CLIENT: *Potlatch Corp.* PRINTER: *Wood Lithographics* ■ This parody on daily planners has the calendar year interspersed with Ben Day's accomplishments. Ben Day, the greatest designer in the world, is a fictional character invented by VSA Partners. In addition to providing day-to-day organization and humor, the calendar reminds people of Potlatch Paper, and the things that make design exciting. ● Eine Parodie auf Agenden - wobei die Leistungen von Ben Day, den für Potlatch erfundenen "besten Designer der Welt", im ganzen Kalenderjahr immer wieder vermerkt sind. Hier wird nicht nur eine humorvolle Agenda geboten, sondern die Leute werden auch an Ben Day, an Potlatch-Papier und dessen hervorragende Eigenschaften erinnert. ▲ Parodie d'un agenda dans lequel les réalisations de Ben Day sont indiquées tout au long de l'année (Ben Day est un personnage fictif créé par la société). Grâce à cet agenda pratique et plein d'humour, Ben Day et les papiers Potlatch restent présents à l'esprit de l'utilisateur.

PAGE 174; #509-512 ART DIRECTOR: *John Van Dyke* DESIGNERS: *John Van Dyke, Ann Kumasaka* DESIGN FIRM: *Van Dyke Company* PHOTOGRAPHERS: *Holly Stewart, others* COPYWRITER: *John Koval* CLIENT: *Simpson Coated Papers* ■ This promotion directed at printers and merchants is about the printability of the paper and makes the point with a lot of ink on paper. ● Diese Werbesendung richtet sich an Drucker und Händler. Anhand von Beispielen, bei denen extrem viel Druckfarbe verwendet wurde, wird die Druckqualität des Papiers demonstriert. ▲ Destinée aux imprimeurs et aux vendeurs, cette publicité illustre la qualité d'impression du papier même lors de l'utilisation d'une grande quantité d'encre.

PAGE 175; #513-516 ART DIRECTORS: *Woody Pirtle, Ivette Montes de Oca* DESIGNERS: *Ivette Montes de Oca, Seung Il Choi* DESIGN FIRM: *Pentagram Design Inc.* LETTERING: *Kenny Dugan* CLIENT: *Mohawk Paper Mills* ■ This promotion, organized as a journal of Arizona, shows off the paper's capabilities for bright color reproduction. ● Diese Papierwerbung in Gestalt eines Journals von Arizona präsentiert die Farbbrillanz der Reproduktionen auf dem Papier. ▲ Présentée sous la forme d'un journal de l'Arizona, cette publicité illustre la brillance des couleurs des reproductions sur ce papier.

PAGE 175; #517-520 ART DIRECTORS: *Michael McGinn* CREATIVE DIRECTOR: *James A. Sebastian* DESIGNER: *Sarah Kloman* DESIGN FIRM: *Designframe Inc.* ILLUSTRATORS:: *Coco Masuda, Ward Schumaker, Brian Cairns* PHOTOGRAPHERS: *David Arky, Illan Rubin, Geof Kern, James Wojcik, Neil Farris, Pierre-Yves Goavec* STOCK PHOTOGRAPHY: *Michael Lamonica (Graphistock), Ken Ross (FPG International)* COPYWRITER: *David Konigsberg* CLIENT: *Strathmore Papers* PRINTER: *Diversified Graphics* ■ Third in a series of informative books on color. Each book features a selection of Strathmore papers and demonstrates the papers' printability. This third volume focuses on the psychology of color perception and how it has been used in design and marketing. ● Das dritte einer Reihe von Büchern zum Thema Farbe. In jedem Band wird eine Auswahl von Strathmore-Papieren gezeigt und ihre Eignung für den Druck demonstriert. Im dritten Band geht es um die Wirkung der Farben auf die Psyche und um ihren gezielten Einsatz in der graphischen Gestaltung und im Marketing. ▲ Ce livre est le troisième d'une série sur le thème *de la couleur. Chaque volume présente une sélection de papiers Strathmore et illustre leurs qualités d'impression. Le troisième livre est consacré à l'influence des couleurs sur le psychisme et à leur utilisation ciblée dans les domaines de la conception graphique et du marketing.*

PAGE 176; #521 ART DIRECTOR/COPYWRITER: *Bob Seabert* DESIGNER: *Lesley MacLean* DESIGN FIRM: *Mangos Inc.* PHOTOGRAPHER: *J. Paul Simeone* CLIENT: *UK Paper North America* PRINTER: *Imperial Litho* ■ *This eye-catching swatchbook continuously promotes the product rather than simply being a reference tool.* ● *Dieses attraktive Musterbuch ist mehr als nur das - es wirbt konstant für die Produkte, statt sie nur zu präsentieren.* ▲ *Ce jeu d'échantillons séduisant va au-delà de sa fonction première; il fait une publicité constante pour les produits et ne se contente pas de les présenter.*

PAGE 176; #522 ART DIRECTOR/COPYWRITER: *Bob Seabert* DESIGNER: *Lesley MacLean* DESIGN FIRM: *Mangos Inc.* CLIENT: *UK Paper North America* ■ *The agency sought to make the swatchbook not just a product sample, but a promotional tool.* ● *Dieses Musterbuch sollte nicht nur Produktmuster zeigen, sondern der Firma auch als Werbemittel dienen.* ▲ *Ce jeu d'échantillons devait également servir de support publicitaire.*

PAGE 177; #523 ART DIRECTOR/DESIGNER: *Jason Schulte* DESIGN FIRM: *Charles S. Anderson Design Company* CLIENT: *French Paper Company*

PAGE 177; #524, 525 ART DIRECTOR: *Paul Wharton* DESIGNERS: *Mike Lizama, Tom Riddle* DESIGN FIRM: *Little & Company* PHOTOGRAPHER/ILLUSTRATOR: *Rodney Smith* COPYWRITER: *Sandra Bucholtz* CLIENT: *Fraser Papers* PRINTER: *Litho Watt/Paterson Inc.* ■ *The purpose of this portfolio is to demostrate a new palette of colors. It features several usable and useful items, each featuring a new color.* ● *Mit dieser Mappe soll eine neue Farbpalette vorgestellt werden. Sie zeigt verschiedene brauchbare und nützliche Dinge, die jeweils in einer neuen Farbe gezeigt werden.* ▲ *Portfolio présentant une nouvelle gamme de couleurs. Les divers objets utilisés à cette fin présentent chacun une couleur différente.*

PAGES 178, 179; #526-529 ART DIRECTOR: *Valerie Taylor Smith* DESIGNER: *Michael Hernandez* DESIGN FIRM: *Nike Image Design (in-house)*

PAGE 180; #530, 531 ART DIRECTOR/DESIGNER: *Jason Busa* DESIGN FIRM: *Big Bang Idea Engineering* COPYWRITER: *Bob Bagot* CLIENT: *The Kalakala Foundation*

PAGE 181; #532-534 ART DIRECTOR/DESIGNER: *Taku Satoh* DESIGN FIRM: *Taku Satoh Design Office Inc.* PHOTOGRAPHER: *Tamotsu Fujii* CLIENT: *Bang & Olufsen* ■ *These posters for a hi-fi audio systems manufacturer were printed with matte ink and finished so that the image quality would suggest the sound quality of the product.* ● *Der Mattdruck der Plakate für den Hersteller von Hi-fi-Audiosystemen sollte ein Gefühl von hoher Qualität zu erzeugen, vergleichbar mit der Tonqualität der Produkte.* ▲ *Affiches pour un fabricant de systèmes audio haute-fidélité. La qualité de l'impression mate suggère la qualité du son.*

PAGE 182; #535 ART DIRECTOR: *Andrea Rauch, Rauch Design* DESIGNER: *Milton Glaser* DESIGN FIRM: *Milton Glaser Inc.* CLIENT: *Vespa Scooters* ■ *This design commemorates the fiftieth anniversary of Vespa Piaggio Scooters.* ● *Plakat zum fünfzigjährigen Bestehen der Vespa Piaggio Scooters.* ▲ *Affiche réalisée pour le cinquantième anniversaire des scooters Vespa.*

PAGE 183; #536 ART DIRECTOR: *Neal Zimmermann* DESIGNERS: *Neal Zimmermann, Eric F. Heiman* DESIGN FIRM: *Zimmermann Crowe Design* CLIENT: *Levi Strauss & Co.* ■ *These posters are support point of sale items designed for retailers in non-urban regions of the U.S. who respond to a historical/traditional image of Levi Strauss & Co.* ● *Diese Plakate wurden für Läden in ländlichen Gegenden der USA entworfen, deren Publikum besonders auf das traditionelle Western-Image von Levi Strauss anspricht.* ▲ *Affiches spécialement conçues pour les points de vente des régions rurales des Etats-Unis où les gens sont attachés à l'image western classique de Levi Strauss.*

PAGE 184; #537, 538 ART DIRECTORS: *Frank Kofsuske, Sean Mullins*

DESIGNERS: *Frank Kofsuske, Mark Blaisdell* DESIGN FIRM: *Em Dash* PHOTOGRAPHER: *Daniel Proctor* COPYWRITER: *Sean Austin* CLIENT: *Pottery Barn*

PAGE 185; #539-541 ART DIRECTOR: *Arseni Mechtcheriakov* DESIGNER: *Chernogayev Dmitry* DESIGN FIRM: *Design Bureau Agey Tomesh* PHOTOGRAPHER/ILLUSTRATOR: *Kozyrev Denis* COPYWRITER: *Skenderov Dmitry* CLIENT: *Dial Electronics* PRINTER: *Panas-AERO* ■ *Posters themes are based on paradoxical usage of household appliances in unusual life situations. Idea of advertisement's headline springs from allusion to a widely used Russian phrase: "There is always room for heroism in life."* ● *Der Slogan dieser Plakate ist eine Anspielung auf ein russisches Sprichwort: "Es gibt im Leben immer Raum für Heldentum." Hier werden Haushaltsgegenstände in ungewö hnlichen Situationen gezeigt.* ▲ *Le slogan de cette affiche est un clin d'Til à un proverbe russe: "Dans la vie, il y a toujours de la place pour l'héroisme." Différents appareils ménagers sont présentés dans des situations inhabituelles.*

PAGE 186; #542 ART DIRECTOR/DESIGNER: *Eric Rindal* CREATIVE DIRECTOR: *George Chadwick* DESIGN FIRM: *FCB Promotion & Design* PHOTOGRAPHER/ILLUSTRATOR: *John Casado* CLIENT: *Levi Strauss & Co.*

PAGE 186; #543 ART DIRECTOR/DESIGNER: *Jon Simonsen* DESIGN FIRM: *Muller & Company* PHOTOGRAPHER: *Kenny Johnson* ILLUSTRATOR: *Jon Simonsen* CLIENT: *Westport Ballet Theatre* ■ *Poster created for an urban dance event located in the historical Westport section of Kansas City. The design firm wanted to create an image that would match the event's setting and mood.* ● *Plakat für eine Ballettaufführung in einem Theater im historischen Westport-Distrikt von Kansas City. Ort und Stimmung der Aufführung waren die Leitmotive für die Designer.* ▲ *Affiche pour un ballet donné dans un théâtre situé dans le quartier historique de Westport à Kansas City. Les designers ont choisi de mettre l'accent sur le lieu et l'atmosphère du spectacle.*

PAGE 187; #544 ART DIRECTOR/DESIGNER: *Taku Satoh* DESIGN FIRM: *Taku Satoh Design Office Inc.* PHOTOGRAPHER: *Taishi Hirokawa* CLIENT: *Taku Satoh Design Office Inc.* ■ *This poster, featuring an original two-meter 150kg barber pole created by the designer, demonstrates the idea that product design both influences and is influenced by the surrounding environment.* ● *Die bemalte Stange auf dem Plakat, die normalerweise als Geschäftszeichen für Frisö re dient, ist zwei Meter lang und 150 kg schwer. Sie wurde von dem Designer entworfen und soll verdeutlichen, dass Produktdesign die Umgebung beeinflusst und von ihr beeinflusst wird.* ▲ *La barre de l'affiche est une enseigne de coiffeurs. Cette barre de 250 kg et de deux mètres de long a été créée par le designer qui entendait montrer ainsi que le design de produits a une influence sur l'environnement et vice versa.*

PAGE 188; #545, 546 ART DIRECTOR/DESIGNER: *Eric Rindal* DESIGN FIRM: *Foote, Cone, & Belding* PHOTOGRAPHER/ILLUSTRATOR: *John Casado* CLIENT: *Levi Strauss & Co.* ■ *The design communicates the masculine strength and attitude of Levi's Guy's Fitting Jeans by taking industrial elements and manipulating them into the torso of a woman.* ● *Mit diesem Plakat für Levi's Jeans mit spezieller Passform für Männer, sollen männliche Eigenschaften und Stärke zum Ausdruck kommen.* ▲ *Affiche pour des jeans Levi's pour hommes jouant sur des attributs typiquement masculins et la virilité.*

PAGE 189; #547-549 ART DIRECTOR: *Petra Reichenbach* DESIGN FIRM: *Scholz & Friends Berlin* PHOTOGRAPHER: *Alfred Seiland* COPYWRITER: *Sebastian Turner* CLIENT: *Frankfurter Allgemeine Zeitung*

PAGE 190; #550 ART DIRECTOR/DESIGNER: *Rüdiger Goetz* DESIGN FIRM: *Simon & Goetz* CLIENT: *Adp. Engineering GmbH* ■ *This high-quality mountain bike reflects technical and engineering quality.* ● *Bei diesem hochklassigen Mountain Bike geht es um Technik.* ▲ *Un VTT haut de gamme avec une technique sophistiquée.*

PAGE 190; #551 DESIGNERS: *Fridolin Beisert, Michael Sans* DESIGN FIRM: *Art Center College of Design* PHOTOGRAPHER: *Steven Heller*

PAGE 191; #552 ART DIRECTOR/DESIGNER: *Péter Vajda* DESIGN FIRM: *Alternativ Studio* PHOTOGRAPHER: *Dániel Horváth*

PAGES 192, 193; #553-556 DESIGNER: *Dale Frommelt* DESIGN FIRM: *Dale Frommelt Design* PHOTOGRAPHER: *Kurtis Krackle*

PAGES 194, 195; #557-561 ART DIRECTOR/DESIGNER: *Jennifer Sterling* DESIGN FIRM: *Jennifer Sterling Design* CLIENT: *Sterling Design*

PAGE 196; #562 ART DIRECTOR/DESIGNER: *Jennifer Sterling* DESIGN FIRM: *Jennifer Sterling Design* ILLUSTRATORS: *Jonathon Rosen, Jennifer Sterling* COPYWRITER: *Robert Rollie* CLIENT: *Quickturn Design Systems Inc.* PRINTER: *Active Graphics* ■ *The cards were part of a promotion at DHC promoting the magic of emulation. Penn & Teller were hired for the event and the cards represent magic on one side and the magic of emulation on the other side.* ● *Die Karten sind Teil einer Promotion, deren Thema der Zauber von Nachahmungen ist. Penn & Teller, zwei aus dem Fernsehen bekannte Zauberer, wurden für den Anlass engagiert, und die Karten stehen einerseits für Zaubertricks, andererseits für den Zauber von Nach- ahmungen.* ▲ *Cartes conçues dans le cadre d'une promotion sur le thème de la magie des imitations. Les deux magiciens américains Penn et Teller ont été engagés pour l'occasion. Les cartes représentent d'une part la magie, de l'autre la magie des imitations.*

PAGE 197; #563 ART DIRECTOR/CREATIVE DIRECTOR: *Jose Serrano* DESIGNERS: *Jose Serrano, Miguel Perez* DESIGN FIRM: *Mires Design* ILLUSTRATOR: *Tracy Sabin* CLIENT: *Bordeaux Printers* ■ *This promotion for a printer who wanted to communicate the image of high-end printing uses labels and hang-tags signed by representatives and production people to reassure clients that the printed samples had been carefully inspected.* ● *Diese Werbung für eine Druckerei besteht aus Etiketten und Anhängern, die von Vertretern und Produktionsmitarbeitern abgezeichnet wurden, um den Kunden zu verdeut- lichen, dass die Andrucke sorgfältig geprüft werden.* ▲ *Publicité pour une imprimerie composée d'étiquettes simples et d'étiquettes à ficelle visées par les représentants et les collaborateurs de la production afin de montrer au client que les épreuves ont été soigneusement contrôlées.*

PAGE 197; #564 ART DIRECTOR/CREATIVE DIRECTOR: *John Ball* DESIGNERS: *John Ball, Miguel Perez* DESIGN FIRM: *Mires Design* PHOTOGRAPHER: *Marshall Harrington* COPYWRITER: *Brian Woolsey* CLIENT: *Equifax Business Geometrics* ■ *This ad for an information research service simplifies a complex product into a dramatic "yes or no" proposition.* ● *Diese Anzeige für einen Informationsdienst vereinfacht ein komplexes Arbeitsgebiet derart, dass mit Ja oder Nein geantwortet werden kann.* ▲ *Cette annonce pour un service d'infor- mation simplifie un produit complexe à un tel point qu'il suffit de répondre par oui ou par non.*

PAGE 197; #565, 566 ART DIRECTOR/DESIGNER/COPYWRITER: *Robert Wong* DESIGN FIRM: *CKS Partners, Inc.* ■ *This goal of this design was to be eye-catch- ing, to the point, and inexpensive.* ● *Hier ging es um die Schaffung eines attrak- tiven, zielgerichteten und kostengünstigen Designs.* ▲ *Création d'un design séduisant, ciblé et peu onéreux.*

PAGE 198; #567 ART DIRECTOR/DESIGNER: *James Victore* DESIGN FIRM: *Victore Design Works* CLIENT: *Portfolio Center*

PAGE 199; #568 ART DIRECTORS: *Hans Neleman, Keith Seward* DESIGNERS/ANIMATORS: *Keith Seward, Necro Enema Amalgamated* ANIMATORS: *Caroline Mouris, Frank Mouris (Animation of Life "Demo")* DESIGN FIRM: *Neleman Studio (self-promotion)* PHOTOGRAPHER: *Hans Neleman* ■ *This CD-ROM is designed to promote Hans Neleman's still life, personal, and portrait photography as well as his work in the medium of film. It includes clips from television commercials and music videos, lists of clients and awards, and biographical information.* ● *CD-ROM als Werbung für die Arbeit von Hans Neleman im Bereich der Photographie und des Films. Es werden u.a. Clips aus TV-Spots und Musik-Videos gezeigt, sowie eine Liste der Kunden und Auszeichnungen und biographische Daten.* ▲ *Ce CD-ROM publicitaire présente le travail de Hans Neleman dans les domaines de la photographie et du film. Il inclut notamment des clips de spots télévisés, des vidéos musicales, une liste des clients et des distinctions ainsi que des détails biographiques.*

PAGE 199; #569 ART DIRECTOR: *Michael Tobin* DESIGNERS: *Sheila Smith, MaryEllen Vander Brink* DESIGN FIRM: *Ritta & Associates* PHOTOGRAPHERS: *Bill Cash, Guy Spangenberg* COPYWRITERS: *Catherine Armstrong, Vicki List* CLIENT: *BMW of North America, Inc.* PRINTER: *Mid-Atlantic Graphics* ■ *This design introduces the BMW roadster 2.8 — and builds on its celebrity status in "Golden Eye" and the VH1 Fashion Awards Show.* ● *Hier wird der BMW- Roadster 2.8 im Rahmen einer Modeschau des TV-Senders VH1 vorgestellt, unter Anspielung auf den James-Bond-Film Golden Eye .* ▲ *Présentation du roadster 2.8 BMW — le bolide de James Bond dans Golden Eye et la vedette d'un grand défilé de mode diffusé sur la chaîne américaine VH1.*

PAGE 200; #570 ART DIRECTOR: *Norbert Möller* DESIGN FIRM: *Peter Schmidt Studios* CLIENT: *H.F. & Ph. Remtsma GmbH & Co.*

PAGE 201; #571 ART DIRECTOR: *Robert Achten* DESIGNER: *Katherine Taylor* DESIGN FIRM: *Origin Design Company Ltd. (in-house)* PHOTOGRAPHER/ ILLUSTRATOR: *Ian Robertson* CLIENT: *Origin Design*

PAGE 202; #572 ART DIRECTOR: *Steven Sikora* DESIGNERS: *Richard Boynton, Steven Sikora* DESIGN FIRM: *Design Guys* CLIENT: *Marshall Fields* ■ *The objective was to capture the essence of Utah's Sundance ski resort and make sense of it in an urban retail setting.* ● *Hier ging es darum, die Atmosphäre eines Ski-Ortes auf die Ladengestaltung in einem städtischen Umfeld zu über- tragen.* ▲ *L'objectif était de capturer l'atmosphère d'un domaine skiable dans l'Utah pour un magasin implanté en milieu urbain.*

PAGE 202; #573 ART DIRECTOR: *Valerie Taylor-Smith* DESIGNER: *Clint Gorthy* DESIGN FIRM: *Nike Image Design* ■ *A new line of packaging announcing the new streamlined face of Niketown.* ● *Eine neue Verpackungslinie für das neue, modernisierte Image von Niketown.* ▲ *Nouvelle ligne de packagings pour l'im- age revisitée de Niketown.*

PAGE 202; #574 ART DIRECTOR/DESIGNER: *Yasuo Tanaka* DESIGN FIRM: *Package Land Co., Ltd. (in-house)*

PAGE 202; #575 ART DIRECTOR: *Dean Lubensky* DESIGNER: *Lori Ann Reinig* DESIGN FIRM: *Parham Santana Inc.* CLIENT: *VH1* ■ *An upscale icon-like look was conceived to house the energy of the VH1 sales presentation.* ● *Tragtasche für den amerikanischen TV-Sender VH1.* ▲ *Sacs à provisions créés pour la chaîne de télévision américaine VH1.*

PAGE 203; #576 ART DIRECTOR/DESIGNER: *Kohko Nabatame* DESIGN FIRM: *Nabatame Design Office* COPYWRITER: *Chiyoko Kamura* CLIENT/PRINTER: *Nagaoka Kojimaya Co. Ltd.*

PAGE 204; #577 ART DIRECTORS: *Peter Scott, Glenda Rissman* DESIGNER: *Darrell Corriveau* DESIGN FIRM: *Q30 Design Inc.* CLIENT: *Canada Post Corporation*

PAGE 204; #578 ART DIRECTOR: *Malcolm Waddell* DESIGNER: *Gary Mansbridge* DESIGN FIRM: *Eskind Waddell* PHOTOGRAPHER: *Sherman Hines* CLIENT: *Canada Post Corporation* ■ *These Arctic stamps have been designed as a continuous strip to depict a general history of the far North. The white space, a common denominator among the disparate images, conveys the vastness of the Arctic and links all facets of northern life, past and present, into one panoramic whole.* ● *Diese Briefmarken mit arktischen Motiven gehö ren zu einer Reihe der kanadischen Post über den Norden. Die weissen Flächen, die den verschiedenen Motiven gemeinsam sind, symbolisieren die Weite der Arktis und das Lebens im Polarkreis.* ▲ *Série de timbres sur le thème de l'Arctique réalisée pour les postes canadiennes. Les espaces blancs, récurrents sur tous les timbres, symbolisent l'immensité de l'Arctique et la vie dans le Grand Nord.*

PAGE 204; #579 ART DIRECTOR/DESIGNER: *Nancy Skolos* DESIGN FIRM: *Skolos/Wedell* ILLUSTRATOR: *Thomas Wedell* CLIENT: *United States Postal Service* ■ *This stamp commemorates the fifty year history of the computer as an extension of the human mind.* ● *Briefmarke als Erinnerung an die Erfindung des Computers vor fünfzig Jahren, der eine Erweiterung des menschlichen*

Verstandes bedeutete. ▲ *L'ordinateur, un prolongement du cerveau humain. Timbre-poste célébrant l'invention de l'ordinateur il y a cinquante ans.*

PAGE 204; #580 DESIGN FIRM: *B. J. Robinson* CLIENT: *Royal Mail National* PRINTER: *The House of Questa*

PAGE 205; #581 ART DIRECTOR/DESIGNER: *Glenn Tutssel* DESIGN FIRM: *Tutssels* CLIENT: *Royal Mail*

PAGE 205; #582 DESIGNER: *Michael Wolff* CLIENT: *Royal Mail National* PRINTER: *Walsall Security Printers Ltd.* ■ *Postage stamps for senders of greeting cards with the joint theme of humour and communications.* ● *Speziell für Grusskarten entworfene Briefmarken, bei denen es um Humor und Kommunikation geht.* ▲ *Timbres-poste sur le thème de l'humour et de la communication, spécialement créés pour l'envoi de cartes de vŒux.*

PAGE 205; #583 ART DIRECTORS: *Barry Robinson, Jane Ryan* DESIGN DIRECTOR: *John Larkin* DESIGNER: *Peter Rae* DESIGN FIRM: *Design House* PHOTOGRAPHER: *Nick Knight* CLIENT: *Royal Mail National* PRINTER: *The House of Questa* ■ *This design is part of an on-going special stamp programme.* ● *Diese Entwürfe gehö ren zu einer speziellen Briefmarkenedition.* ▲ *Projet réalisé dans le cadre d'une série de timbres limitée.*

PAGE 205; #584 ART DIRECTORS: *Barry Robinson, Jane Ryan* DESIGNER: *Stephanie Nash* DESIGN FIRM: *Michael Nash Associates* CLIENT: *Royal Mail National* PRINTER: *Harrison & Sons Ltd.*

PAGE 205; #585 ART DIRECTORS: *Barry Robinson, Jane Ryan* DESIGNER/PHOTOGRAPHER: *Simon Clay* CLIENT: *Royal Mail National* PRINTER: *Harrison & Sons Ltd.*

PAGE 205; #586 ART DIRECTORS: *Barry Robinson, Jane Ryan* DESIGNER: *Moseley Webb* ILLUSTRATOR: *Charles Tunnicliffe* CLIENT: *Royal Mail National* PRINTER: *Harrison & Sons Ltd.*

PAGE 206; #587 ART DIRECTOR/CREATIVE DIRECTOR/DESIGNER: *José A. Serrano* DESIGN FIRM: *Mires Design* ILLUSTRATOR: *Tracy Sabin* CLIENT: *Hot Rod Hell* ■ *This promotional T-shirt for a hot rod and custom car shop reflects the influences of the 1950s car craze on the hobbyists who patronize the shop.* ● *Das T-Shirt für eine Werkstatt, die sich auf frisierte und handgemachte Autos*

spezialisiert hat, reflektiert die Autobesessenheit der 50er Jahre, die auf die Betreiber der Werkstatt abgefärbt hat. ▲ *Ce tee-shirt pour un garage spécialisé dans les véhicules trafiqués et customisés illustre la passion des voitures dans les années 50 dont ont hérité les gérants du garage.*

PAGE 206; #588 ART DIRECTOR/CREATIVE DIRECTOR: *Scott Mires* DESIGNERS: *Scott Mires, Deborah Horn* DESIGN FIRM: *Mires Design* ILLUSTRATOR: *Tracy Sabin* CLIENT: *Harcourt Brace Co.* ■ *This T-shirt was created to commemorate the completion of a year-long project, and was given to everyone who was involved.* ● *Das T-Shirt wurde allen Beteiligten zum Abschluss eines Projektes überreicht, das ein Jahr gedauert hatte.* ▲ *Tee-shirt "commémoratif" offert aux participants d'un projet achevé au terme d'un an.*

PAGE 206; #589 ART DIRECTOR/DESIGNER: *Todd Nickel*

PAGE 206; #590 DESIGNER/COPYWRITER: *David Betz* DESIGN FIRM: *D. Betz Design* PHOTOGRAPHER: *Barney Grök* CLIENT: *Virtual Telemetrix* ■ *To err is human, to broadcast it is divine. For the imperfect, underachieving, second-place finisher in all of us.* ● *Irren ist menschlich, und das zu verbreiten ist gö ttlich. Für alle von uns, die nicht perfekt sind, die Erwartungen nicht erfüllen und ständig den Zweiten machen.* ▲ *L'erreur est humaine, la propager est divin. Pour tous ceux d'entre nous qui ne sont pas parfaits et finissent toujours seconds.*

PAGE 207; #591, 592 ART DIRECTOR: *Derik Meinköhn* DESIGNER: *Kirsten Ritschel (Graphics)* DESIGN FIRM: *Grabarz & Partner Werbeagentur* COPYWRITER: *Ralf Heuel* CLIENT: *Grabarz & Partner Werbeagentur* ■ *These T-shirts, which the agency's staff was "forced" to wear at parties and events, were designed to recruit copywriters.* ● *Diese T-Shirts, die alle Mitarbeiter der Agentur bei Parties und Anlässen tragen 'mussten', dienten der Anwerbung von Textern.* ▲ *Ce tee-shirt, que tous les collaborateurs de l'agence étaient tenus de porter lors de manifestations spéciales, a été créé pour recruter des rédacteurs.*

PAGE 208; #593, 594 ART DIRECTOR/DESIGNER: *Shinnoske Sugisaki* DESIGN FIRM: *Shinnoske Inc.* PHOTOGRAPHER: *Yasunori Saito* COPYWRITER: *Shiho Sugisaki* CLIENT: *Morisawa & Co. Ltd.* ■ *Complicated and precise images are intended to show the possibilities of digital fonts.* ● *Komplizierte, präzise Bilder sollten die Mö glichkeiten digitaler Schriften demonstrieren.* ▲ *Images compliquées et précises illustrant les applications des écritures numériques.*

INDEX

VERZEICHNISSE

INDEX

CREATIVE DIRECTORS · ART DIRECTORS · DESIGNERS

ACHTEN, ROBERT WELLINGTON, NEW ZEALAND 64 4 499 3241 .... 24, 64, 201
ADAM, HUBERTUS BIELFELD, GERMANY 49 521 131547 68
ALEXANDER, JAIMIE WORTHINGTON, OH 6174393400 169
ANDERSON, CHARLES MINNEAPOLIS, MN 612 339 5181 166
ANDERSON, JACK SEATTLE, WA 206 467 5800 .... 72, 134
ANDERSON, LARRY SEATTLE, WA 206 467 5800 134
ANGELL, IVAN WELLINGTON, NEW ZEALAND 644 384 6164 106
ANSETT, DAVID MELBOURNE, AUSTRALIA 61 395103222 134
ANTISTA, TOM ATLANTA, GA 404 816 3201 .... 96, 162, 171
ARDEN, CHRISTINE WELLINGTON, NEW ZEALAND 644 499 0828 57
ARNETT, DANA CHICAGO, IL 312 427 6413 .... 24, 151, 174
ARTUS, MARK WORTHINGTON, OH 617 439 3400 111
ASHBY, NEAL WASHINGTON, DC 202 775 0101 24
ATTILA, SIMON BUDAPEST, HUNGARY 361 140 8114 .... 82, 83
AZUMA, CHIKA NEW YORK, NY 212 333 8198 142

BACON, MARTIN LONDON, ENGLAND 44 181 651 3368 49
BAINES, JON WORTHINGTON, OH 617 439 3400 111
BAKER, RICHARD NEW YORK, NY 212 484 1788 79
BALL, JOHN SAN DIEGO, CA 619 234 6631 .... 126, 197
BAN, DONJIRO PORTLAND, OR 503 248 9466 .... 116, 117
BARTZ, TODD MINNEAPOLIS, MN 612 321 2333 147
BATES, DAVID SEATTLE, WA 206 467 5800 72
BEARSON, LEE NEW YORK, NY 212 484 1655 79
BEATTY, CHRIS INDIANAPOLIS, IN 317 264 8010 109
BEISERT, FRIDOLIN GLENDALE, CA 818 240 8879 190
BENTKOWSKI, TOM NEW YORK, NY 212 522 4817 88
BERMAN, BRAD PORTLAND, OR 503 248 9466 .... 116, 117
BETZ, DAVID SEATTLE, WA 206 728 8804 206
BIBER, JAMES NEW YORK, NY 212 683 7000 110
BIDWILL, DIANA WELLINGTON, NEW ZEALAND, 64 4 499 0828 136
BIERUT, MICHAEL NEW YORK, NY 212 683 7000 .... 31, 39, 89
BLACK, PAUL DALLAS, TX 214 939 9194 98
BLACKBURN, JOHN LONDON, ENGLAND 44 171 734 7646 171
BLAISDELL, MARK SAN FRANCISCO, CA 415 285 9060 184
BLEVINS, WEBB BEAVERTON, OR 503 532 0119 .... 57, 139
BOLING, GREGG NASHVILLE, TN 615 244 1818 161
BOND, THOMAS SAN FRANCISCO, CA 415 391 9070 160
BOYNTON, RICHARD MINNEAPOLIS, MN 612 338 4462 202
BRADLEY, MARK INDIANAPOLIS, IN 317 264 8010 109
BRADY, JOHN PITTSBURGH, PA 412 288 9300 25
BRALEY, MICHAEL SAN FRANCISCO, CA 415 834 0300 .... 52, 53
BRANSON-MEYER, BRUCE SEATTLE, WA 206 467 5800 134
BREEZE, JENNIFER SAN FRANCISCO, CA 415 834 0300 .... 52, 53
BRENGMAN, ROBERT SEATTLE, WA 206 624 0551 99
BRIDAVSKY, ESTHER NEW YORK, NY 212 683 7000 .... 31, 39
BRIGHT, TIM WELLINGTON, NEW ZEALAND 64 4 499 3241 64
BRINKMAN, MARK AUSTIN, TX 512 302 0734 136
BROCK, MICHAEL LOS ANGELES, CA 213 932 0283 49
BROWN, HOWARD PHILADELPHIA, PA 215 557 4759 24
BRYAN, NICOLE MUNICH, GERMANY 89 95720172 58
BUCKLEY, PAUL NEW YORK, NY 212 366 2171 .... 30, 35
BUG, BEA FRANKFURT, GERMANY 697950080 89
BURDETT, MARK NEW YORK, NY 212 833 5186 144
BURKE, GARRETT LOS ANGELES, CA 310 289 3250 104
BURNETT, FIONA LONDON, ENGLAND 44 171 753 8466 159
BUSA, JASON SEATTLE, WA 206 728 0202 180
BUTLER, DEAN MELBOURNE, AUSTRALIA 61 395103222 134
BUTTERS, TRISH LONG BEACH, CA 310 432 5707 152
BYUNG-GEOL, MIN SEOUL, KOREA 822 743 8065 66

CAHAN, BILL SAN FRANCISCO, CA 415 621 0915 .... 46, 163
CALKINS, MIKE PHILADELPHIA, PA 215 557 4759 24
CARAIN, FRANCO CASTELFRANCO, ITALY 523595836 54
CASH, MAGGI TORONTO, CANADA 416 504 6075 38
CHADWICK, GEORGE SAN FRANCISCO, CA 415 772 8101 186
CHAN, MEI LEE HONG KONG, CHINA 852 2810 6640 61
CHASOFF, YOURI ESTONIA, RUSSIA 3722 472541 136
CHEN, CAROL NEW YORK, NY 212 833 5186 142
CHIOUTUCTO, EDWARD NEW YORK, NY 212 683 7000 73
CHOI, SEUNG IL NEW YORK, NY 212 683 7000 .... 20, 136, 175
CHUMACEIRO, EDUARDO CARACAS, VENEZUELA 37
CHWAST, SEYMOUR NEW YORK, NY 212 255 6456 65
CLAY, SIMON LONDON, ENGLAND 44171 614 7201 205
COLLINS, BRIAN SAN FRANCISCO, CA 415 777 5560 114
CONKLIN, RICH LONG BEACH, CA 310 432 5707 152
COOLEY, HEATHER MINNEAPOLIS, MN 612 359 4388 158
CORRIVEAU, DARRELL TORONTO, CANADA 416 603 0126 204

COVERDALE, JACK MINNEAPOLIS, MN 612 359 4388 158
CRAWFORD, MARK LOS ANGELES, CA 310 859 7001 155
CREASY, CHUCK NASHVILLE, TN 615 244 1818 28
CRISTELLO, JULIE SAN FRANCISCO, CA 415 834 0300 .... 52, 53
CROSBY, BART CHICAGO, IL 312 951 2800 172
CROWE, DENNIS SAN FRANCISCO, CA 415 777 5560 .... 114, 115, 135
CURTIN, PAUL SAN FRANCISCO, CA 415 296 1788 47
CURTIS, DAVE SAN FRANCISCO, CA 415 567 4402 154
CUYLER, JOEL NEW YORK, NY 212 5561798 88

DARE, GEORGE OFFENBACH, GERMANY 0658003245 142
DAVIES, CHRISTIAN WORTHINGTON, OH 617 439 3400 111
DAZZO, SUSAN NEW YORK, NY 212 880 8800 128
DE ABREU, GABY SUNNINGHILL, SOUTH AFRICA 27 11 803 5815 .... 74, 75
DECHANT, BERNIE MADISON, WI 608 284 9170 150
DEKANT, CHRISTIAN FRANKFURT, GERMANY 69 9688550 63
DEVLIN-DRISKEL, PATTY SANTA BARBARA, CA 805 963 0734 162
DIECKERT, KURT GEORGE HAMBURG, GERMANY 40 35603 0 55
DINETZ, BOB SAN FRANCISCO, CA 415 621 0915 46
DITKO, STEVE PHOENIX, AZ 602 955 2707 139
DMITRY, CHERNOGAYEV MOSCOW, RUSSIA 7 095 200 0903 185
DO. TOKYO, JAPAN 813 3449 0651 .... 97, 133, 137
DUCKWORTH, BRUCE SAN FRANCISCO, CA 415 495 8691 .... 40, 41, 67, 166
DUFFY, JOE MINNEAPOLIS, MN 612 321 2333 .... 34, 106, 147, 160
DUGGAN, BELINDA LONDON, ENGLAND 44 171 734 7646 171
DUMAS, RON BEAVERTON, OR 503 532 0119 48

EDEN, DAVID RICHARDSON, TX 972 699 6807 154
ELIOT, GRAHAM NEW YORK, NY 212 833 5186 142
ELY, MIKE BEAVERTON, OR 503 671 6453 112
EMERY, GARRY MELBOURNE, AUSTRALIA 613 9699 3822 .... 45, 96, 101
EUSEBIO, JANETTE NEW YORK, NY 212 366 5094 134

FAHLEN, EDEN SAN FRANCISCO, CA 415 495 8691 67
FAIRCLOUGH, THOMAS ATLANTA, GA 404 816 3201 .... 96, 162, 171
FALKENTHAL, ACHIM BIELEFELD, GERMANY 49 521131547 68
FASSNACHT, JEFF SAN FRANCISCO, CA 415 495 8691 .... 40, 41, 67, 114, 166
FEASEY, DEBBIE WELLINGTON, NEW ZEALAND 64438461 106
FORD, JONATHAN LONDON, ENGLAND 44 1716038666 164
FOX, KEN CHICAGO, IL 312 427 6413 .... 151, 174
FREEHAUF, CAROLE NEW YORK, NY 212 707 3878 172
FRENCH, POLLY LONDON, ENGLAND 44 171 753 8466 164
FRIER, DARRELL BEAVERTON, OR 503 532 0119 113
FROELICH, JANET NEW YORK, NY 212 556 1798 88

GANGI, CHRISTIN NEW YORK, NY 212 334 1212 80
GARCIA-IZQUIERDO, ALBERTO DÜSSELDORF, GERMANY 211 2108087 119
GATTONE, RENEE HUNTINGTON BEACH, CA 714 969 1775 128
GERICKE, MICHAEL NEW YORK, NY 212 683 7000 73
GERNSHEIMER, JACK BERNVILLE, PA 610 488 7611 134
GHORMLEY, BRAD PHOENIX, AZ 602 381 0304 145
GILMORE-BARNES, CATHERINE NEW YORK, NY 212 556 1798 88
GIRIANO, FANON CASTELFRANCO, SPAIN 523595836 54
GLASER, MILTON NEW YORK, NY 212 889 3161 .... 58, 121, 182
GLUTH, AL HOUSTON, TX 713 784 4141 44
GOETZ, RÜDIGER FRANKFURT, GERMANY 69 9688550 .... 63, 190
GOLDBERGER, SUSAN NEW YORK, NY 212 334 1212 80
GOLDSCHMIDT, ANTHONY LOS ANGELES, CA 310 859 7001 155
GONZALES, SAMUEL BARCELONA, SPAIN 484 66 00 29
GOODE, KATHLEEN WORTHINGTON, OH, 617 439 3400 111
GORTHY, CLINT BEAVERTON, OR 503 671 6453 202
GRETTER, GARY NEW YORK, NY 212 649 4006 80
GRINLEY, MIKE HUNTINGTON BEACH, CA 714 969 1775 128
GROSSMAN, MICHAEL NEW YORK, NY 212 334 1212 80
GUNSELMAN, MICHAEL WILMINGTON, DE 302 655 7077 23

HAGGERTY, LAWRENCE LONDON, ENGLAND 44 171 603 8666 164
HAINES, JEREMY LONDON, ENGLAND 44 171 1352 8322 158
HAINSWORTH, STANLEY BEAVERTON, OR 503 671 6453 112
HALE, TIM RICHARDSON, TX 972 699 6807 .... 27, 154, 168
HANKINSON, STEVEN NEW YORK, NY 212 219 8400 37
HANSON, J. GRAHAM NEW YORK, NY 212 675 1332 .... 94, 95
HANSON, NICK LONDON, ENGLAND 44 171 753 8466 159
HARPER, JIM SEATTLE, WA 206 624 0551 99
HARRY, ALLAN LAWRENCE LUCERNE, SWITZERLAND 41 41 2401369 143
HART, WINNIE NEW ORLEANS, LA 504 522 6300 134
HAYES, EMILY NEW YORK, NY 212 683 7000 231
HEBE, REINER LEONBERG, GERMANY 715243036 47

234

· ·

PHOTOGRAPHERS · ILLUSTRATORS · ARTISTS

· ·

. . . .

DESIGN FIRMS · ADVERTISING AGENCIES

. . . .

GRAPHIS PUBLICATIONS

GRAPHIS PUBLIKATIONEN

PUBLICATIONS GRAPHIS

GRAPHIS ADVERTISING

DVERTISING

98

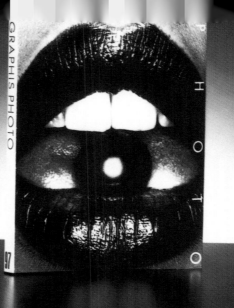

GRAPHIS PHOTO

PHOTO

97

POSTER

BOTTLE
DESIGN

DIAGRAM

Typogr

JOHNNY

MAGAZINE

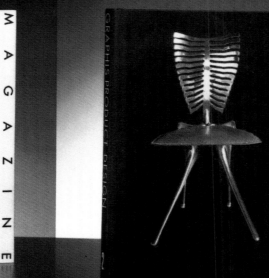

GRAPHIS PRODUCT DESIGN

PRODUCT DESIGN

GRAPHIS STUDENT DESIGN

STUDENT DESIGN

G R A P H I S   B O O K S

BOOKS   **ALL REGIONS**

☐ APPLE DESIGN: THE WORK OF THE APPLE INDUSTRIAL DESIGN GROUP US$ 44.95
☐ GRAPHIS ADVERTISING 98   US$ 69.95
☐ GRAPHIS AMATEUR PHOTOGRAPHY 1   US$ 39.95
☐ GRAPHIS ANNUAL REPORTS 5   US$ 69.95
☐ GRAPHIS BOOK DESIGN 1   US$ 75.95
☐ GRAPHIS BOTTLE DESIGN   US$ 39.95
☐ GRAPHIS BROCHURES 2   US$ 75.95
☐ GRAPHIS DESIGN 98   US$ 69.95
☐ GRAPHIS DIAGRAM 2   US$ 69.95
☐ GRAPHIS FINE ART PHOTOGRAPHY 2   US$ 85.95
☐ GRAPHIS MAGAZINE DESIGN 1   US$ 69.95
☐ GRAPHIS MUSIC CDS 1   US$ 75.95
☐ GRAPHIS NUDES 2   US$ 50.00
☐ GRAPHIS PAPER PROMOTIONS 1   US$ 69.95
☐ **GRAPHIS PAPER SPECIFIER SYSTEM (GPS)**   US$ 395.00**
☐ GRAPHIS PHOTO 97   US$ 69.95
☐ GRAPHIS POSTER 97   US$ 69.95
☐ GRAPHIS PRODUCTS BY DESIGN 2   US$ 69.95
☐ GRAPHIS STUDENT DESIGN 97   US$ 44.95
☐ GRAPHIS T-SHIRTS 2 (AVAILABLE SPRING '98)   US$ 49.95
☐ GRAPHIS TYPOGRAPHY 2   US$ 69.95
☐ THE HUMAN CONDITION: PHOTOJOURNALISM 97   US$ 49.95
☐ PASSION & LINE   US$ 50.00
☐ SHORELINE: THE CAMERA AT WATER'S EDGE   US$ 85.00
☐ WEB DESIGN NOW   US$ 69.95
☐ WORLD TRADEMARKS 100 YRS. (2 VOL. SET)   US$ 250.00

** SHIPPING/HANDLING FOR GPS: ADD $30 (IN USA) OR $100 (OUTSIDE USA).

SHIPPING IN USA: ADD $4.00 FOR THE FIRST BOOK AND $3.00 FOR EACH

ADDITIONAL BOOK. SHIPPING OUTSIDE USA: ADD $10.00 PER BOOK.

NOTE! NY RESIDENTS ADD 8.25% SALES TAX

☐ CHECK ENCLOSED (PAYABLE TO GRAPHIS)
  (US$ ONLY, DRAWN ON A BANK IN THE USA)

USE CREDIT CARDS (DEBITED IN US DOLLARS)

☐ AMERICAN EXPRESS   ☐ MASTERCARD   ☐ VISA

CARD NO.   EXP. DATE

CARDHOLDER NAME

SIGNATURE

(PLEASE PRINT)

NAME

COMPANY

ADDRESS

CITY

STATE/PROVINCE   ZIP CODE

COUNTRY

TELEPHONE

SEND ORDER FORM AND MAKE CHECK PAYABLE TO:
GRAPHIS INC.,
141 LEXINGTON AVENUE, NEW YORK, NY 10016-8193, USA

G R A P H I S   M A G A Z I N E

MAGAZINE	USA	CANADA	CENTRAL/ SOUTH AMERICA/ ASIA/PACIFIC
☐ ONE YEAR (6 ISSUES)	US$ 89.00	US$ 99.00	US$ 125.00
☐ TWO YEARS (12 ISSUES)	US$ 159.00	US$ 179.00	US$ 235.00
☐ AIRMAIL SURCHARGE (6 ISSUES)	US$ 59.00	US$ 59.00	US$ 59.00
☐ REGISTERED MAIL SURCHARGE (6 ISSUES)	N/A	N/A	US$ 15.00

☐ ONE YEAR (6 ISSUES)   US$ 59.00
   FOR STUDENTS WITH COPY OF VALID STUDENT ID AND
   PAYMENT WITH ORDER

☐ CHECK ENCLOSED   ☐ PLEASE BILL ME

USE CREDIT CARDS (DEBITED IN US DOLLARS)

☐ AMERICAN EXPRESS

☐ MASTERCARD

☐ VISA

CARD NO.   EXP. DATE

CARDHOLDER NAME

SIGNATURE

(PLEASE PRINT)

NAME

COMPANY

ADDRESS

CITY

STATE/PROVINCE   ZIP CODE

COUNTRY

TELEPHONE

SERVICE BEGINS WITH ISSUE THAT IS CURRENT WHEN
ORDER IS PROCESSED.

SEND ORDER FORM AND MAKE CHECK PAYABLE TO:
GRAPHIS INC.,
141 LEXINGTON AVENUE, NEW YORK, NY 10016-8193, USA

(C9B0A)

C A L L

F O R

E N T R I E S

GRAPHIS **PRODUCTS BY DESIGN**
ENTRY DEADLINE: DECEMBER 15, 1998

GRAPHIS **ADVERTISING**
ENTRY DEADLINE: OCTOBER 31, 1998

GRAPHIS **DESIGN**
ENTRY DEADLINE: NOVEMBER 15, 1998

Graphis Products by Design (Entry Deadline: December 15, 1998)
■ All products designed or launched since January, 1997 are eligible. Cameras, electronics, exhibition displays, fashion, furniture, games, home, industrial, lighting, luggage, medical, office, sports, transportation, varia. ● Zugelassen sind alle Produkte, die nach Januar 1997 auf den Markt gekommen sind bzw. entworfen wurden: Kameras, elektronische Geräte, Ausstellungs-Displays, Uhren und Schmuck, Mode-Accessoires, Möbel und Einrichtungsgegenstände, Spiele, Werkzeuge, Leuchten, Gepäck, Medizinalgeräte, Büro- und Sportartikel, Fahrzeuge. ▲ Sont susceptibles d'être sélectionnés tous les produits créés ou lancés sur le marché après janvier 1997 qui entrent dans les catégories suivantes: appareils-photo, électronique, présentoirs d'exposition, horlogerie-bijouterie et accessoires de mode, meubles, jeux, maison et décoration, outillage, luminaires, bagages, appareils médicaux, articles de sport et de bureau, véhicules.

Graphis Advertising (Entry Deadline: October 31, 1998)
■ Eligibility: All work produced between December 1997 and October 1998. Automotive, bank, beverages, broadcast, camera/film, computer/electronics, credit cards, delivery service, education, events, fashion, food, insurance, outdoor, paper company, printer, products, promotion, publishing, retail, social, sports, travel. ● In Frage kommen: Arbeiten, die zwischen Dezember 1997 und Oktober 1998 entstanden sind. Automobile, Banken, Getränke, Rundfunk/Fernsehen, Kameras/Film, Computer/Elektronik, Kreditkarten, Kurierdienste, Ausbildung, Veranstaltungen, Mode, Nahrungsmittel, Versicherungen, Aussenwerbung, Papierhersteller, Druckereien, Produkte, Promotionen, Verlage, Einzelhandel, soziale Anliegen, Sport, Reisen. ▲ Seront admis: les travaux réalisés entre décembre 1997 et octobre 1998. Automobiles, banques, boissons, radiodiffusion/télévision, appareils, photo/film, ordinateurs/électronique, cartes de crédit, courriers rapides, formation, manifestations, mode, alimentation, assurances, publicité extérieure, fabricants de papier, imprimeurs, produits, promotions, éditions, commerce de détail, social, sports, voyage.

Graphis Design (Entry Deadline: November 15, 1998)
■ Eligibility: All work produced between December 1997 and November 1998. Annual reports, books, brochures, calendars, corporate identity/signage, currency, diagrams, editorial, ephemera, games, illustration, letterhead, logos, menus, music, new media, packaging, paper companies, posters, products, promotion, shopping bags, stamps, t-shirts, typography. ● In Frage kommen: Arbeiten, die zwischen Dezember 1997 und November 1998 entstanden sind. Jahresberichte, Bücher, Broschüren, Kalender, Corporate Identity/Beschilderungen, Geldnoten, Münzen, Diagramme, redaktionelles Design, Ephemera (kurzlebige Graphik), Spiele, Illustrationen, Briefschaften, Logos, Menus, CD Design, neue Medien, Packungen, Promotionen für Papierhersteller, Plakate, Produktdesign, Promotionsmateriel, Tragtaschen, Briefmarken, T-Shirts, Typographie. ▲ Seront admis: les travaux réalisés entre décembre 1997 et novembre 1998. Rapports annuels, livres, brochures, calendriers, identité institutionnelle, billets de banque, monnaies, diagrammes, design rédactionnel, graphisme éphémère, jeux, illustrations, lettres, logos, menus, musique, nouveau médias, promotions des fabricants de papier, affiches, design de produits, matériel promotionnel, sacs, timbres, T-Shirts, typographie.

■ **What to send:** Reproduction-quality duplicate transparencies (4"x5" or 35mm), printed piece, or both. Transparencies are required for large, bulky or valuable pieces. ALL 35MM SLIDES MUST BE CARDBOARD-MOUNTED. NO GLASS SLIDE MOUNTS! *All transparencies must be clearly marked with the name of the agency (entrant) and client.* If you send printed pieces, they should be unmounted. WE REGRET THAT ENTRIES CANNOT BE RETURNED. ● **Was einsenden:** Wenn immer möglich, schicken Sie uns bitte reproduktionsfähige Duplikatdias. *Bitte Dias mit Ihrem Namen versehen.* Bitte schicken Sie auf keinen Fall Originaldias. KLEINBILDDIAS BITTE IM KARTONRAHMEN, KEIN GLAS! Falls Sie uns das gedruckte Beispiel schicken, bitten wir Sie, dieses gut geschützt aber nicht aufgezogen zu senden. WIR BEDAUERN, DASS EINSENDUNGEN NICHT ZURÜCKGESCHICKT WERDEN KÖNNEN. ▲ **Que nous envoyer:** Nous vous recommandons de nous faire parvenir de préférence des duplicata de diapositives 4x5" ou 35mm. N'oubliez pas d'inscrire votre nom dessus). NE PAS ENVOYER DE DIAPOSITIVES SOUS VERRE! Si vous désirez envoyer des travaux imprimés, protégez-les, mais ne les montez pas sur carton. NOUS VOUS SIGNALONS QUE LES ENVOIS QUE VOUS NOUS AUREZ FAIT PARVENIR NE POURRONT VOUS ÊTRE RETOURNÉS.

■ **How to package your entry:** Please tape (do not glue) the completed entry form (or a copy) to the back of each printed piece. For transparencies, enclose forms loose and make sure transparencies are labelled. Also enclose an extra photocopy of the entry form with each entry. Do not send anything by air freight. Write "No Commercial Value" on the package, and label it "Art for Contest." ● Wie und wohin senden: Bitte befestigen Sie das ausgefüllte Einsendeetikett (oder eine Kopie davon) mit Klebstreifen auf jeder Arbeit und legen Sie noch ein Doppel davon lose bei. Bitte auf keinen Fall per Luftfracht senden. Deklarieren Sie «Ohne jeden Handelswert» und «Arbeitsproben für Wettbewerb». ▲Comment préparer votre envoi: Veuillez scotcher (ne pas coller) au dos de chaque spécimen les étiquettes dûment remplies. Nous vous prions également de faire un double de chaque étiquette, que vous joindrez à votre envoi, mais sans le coller ou le fixer. Ne nous expédiez rien en fret aérien. Indiquez «Sans aucune valeur commerciale» et «Echantillons pour concours».

■ **Entry fees:** Make check or money order payable to Graphis Inc. If you are submitting three entries or fewer, the fee per entry is: US$ 25, £ 15, DM 43, FF 146, SFr 36. If you are submitting four or more entries, the fee per entry is: $20, £ 13, DM 35, FF 117, SFr 29. To pay by Visa, Mastercard or American Express, include your card number, expiration date, and signature of approval; the entry fee will be debited in US$. ● **Einsendegebühren:** Bis zu drei Arbeiten (pro Arbeit): US$ 25, £ 15, DM 43, FF 146, SFr 36.-. Bei vier oder mehr Arbeiten (pro Arbeit): $20, £ 13, DM 35, FF 117, SFr 29.-. Für die Bezahlung mit Visa, Mastercard oder American Express fügen Sie die Kartennummer, das Verfalldatum sowie Ihre Unterschrift als Zeichen der Genehmigung hinzu; die Einsendegebühr wird Ihrer Karte in US-Dollar belastet. ▲ **Droits d'admission:** Jusqu'à troix travaux (par travail): US$ 25, £ 15, DM 43, FF 146, SFr 36. Quatre travaux et plus (par travail): $20, £ 13, DM 35, FF 117, SFr 29. Pour régler par carte Visa, Mastercard ou American Express, veuillez inclure le numéro de votre carte, sa date d'expiration et votre signature d'approbation. Le droit d'inscription sera débité en dollars US.

COMPLETE FORM, TAPE IT TO ENTRY, ENCLOSE A PHOTOCOPY AND PAYMENT. SEND TO CLOSEST ADDRESS:
GRAPHIS BOOK CONTEST, C/O AMERICAN BOOK CENTER, BROOKLYN NAVY YARD, BLDG. #3, BROOKLYN, NY 11205 USA
GRAPHIS BOOK CONTEST, C/O CRONAT, PARC 3, F-68870 BARTENHEIM FRANCE

ENTRY FORM

GRAPHIS **PRODUCTS BY DESIGN**
ENTRY DEADLINE: DECEMBER 15, 1998

GRAPHIS **ADVERTISING**
ENTRY DEADLINE: OCTOBER 31, 1998

GRAPHIS **DESIGN**
ENTRY DEADLINE: NOVEMBER 15, 1998

☐ **GRAPHIS PRODUCTS BY DESIGN**
(DECEMBER 15, 1998)
CATEGORY CODES
☐ PR1 CONSUMER PRODUCTS
☐ PR2 COMMERCIAL PRODUCTS
☐ PR3 ELECTRONICS
☐ PR4 FURNITURE
☐ PR5 VARIA

☐ **ADVERTISING**
(OCTOBER 31, 1998)
CATEGORY CODES
☐ AD1 AUTOMOTIVE
☐ AD2 BANK
☐ AD3 BEVERAGES
☐ AD4 BROADCAST
☐ AD5 CAMERA/FILM
☐ AD6 COMPUTER/ELECT.
☐ AD7 CREDIT CARDS
☐ AD8 DELIVERY SERVICE
☐ AD9 EDUCATION
☐ AD10 EVENTS
☐ AD11 FASHION
☐ AD12 FOOD
☐ AD13 INSURANCE
☐ AD14 OUTDOOR
☐ AD15 PAPER COMPANY
☐ AD16 PRINTER
☐ AD17 PRODUCTS
☐ AD18 PROMOTION
☐ AD19 PUBLISHING
☐ AD20 RETAIL
☐ AD21 SOCIAL
☐ AD22 SPORTS
☐ AD23 TRAVEL

☐ **GRAPHIS DESIGN**
(NOVEMBER 15, 1998)
CATEGORY CODES
☐ DE1 ANNUAL REPORTS
☐ DE2 BOOKS
☐ DE3 BROCHURES
☐ DE4 CALENDARS
☐ DE5 CORP. ID
☐ DE6 CURRENCY/STAMPS
☐ DE7 DIAGRAMS
☐ DE8 EDITORIAL
☐ DE9 EPHEMERA
☐ DE10 GAMES
☐ DE11 ILLUSTRATION
☐ DE12 LETTERHEAD
☐ DE13 LOGOS
☐ DE14 MENUS
☐ DE15 MUSIC (CD DESIGN)
☐ DE16 NEW MEDIA
☐ DE17 PACKAGING
☐ DE18 PAPER COMPANIES
☐ DE19 POSTERS
☐ DE20 PRODUCTS
☐ DE21 PROMOTION
☐ DE22 SHOPPING BAGS
☐ DE24 T-SHIRTS

CONTACT NAME _____ ENTRY NAME _____

TELEPHONE _____ FAX _____

COMPANY _____

STREET ADDRESS _____

CITY/STATE _____ ZIP/COUNTRY _____

ART DIRECTOR _____

MAILING ADDRESS _____ E-MAIL ADDRESS _____

CITY/STATE _____ ZIP/COUNTRY _____

TELEPHONE _____

DESIGNER _____

MAILING ADDRESS _____ E-MAIL ADDRESS _____

CITY/STATE _____ ZIP/COUNTRY _____

TELEPHONE _____

ILLUSTRATOR _____ MEDIUM _____

MAILING ADDRESS _____

CITY/STATE _____ ZIP/COUNTRY _____

TELEPHONE _____

PHOTOGRAPHER /PRODUCT PHOTOGRAPHER / AGENCY (PLEASE CIRCLE)

MAILING ADDRESS _____

CITY/STATE _____ ZIP/COUNTRY _____

TELEPHONE _____

AUTHOR / COPYWRITER /EDITOR (PLEASE CIRCLE)

MAILING ADDRESS _____

CITY/STATE _____ ZIP/COUNTRY _____

TELEPHONE _____ FAX _____

PRINTER/MANUFACTURER _____

PAPER _____ TYPEFACE _____

CLIENT/PUBLISHER _____ CITY/STATE/COUNTRY _____

PROVIDE A BRIEF DESCRIPTION (100 WORDS OR LESS) OF THE DESIGN OR ADVERTISING STRATEGY:

SIGNATURE _____ DATE _____

COMPLETE FORM, TAPE IT TO ENTRY, ENCLOSE A PHOTOCOPY AND PAYMENT. SEND TO CLOSEST ADDRESS:

☐ PAYMENT ENCLOSED   ☐ PAYMENT BY CREDIT CARD # _____ AMOUNT $ _____ EXP. DATE _____

GRAPHIS BOOK CONTEST, C/O AMERICAN BOOK CENTER, BROOKLYN NAVY YARD, BLDG. #3, BROOKLYN, NY 11205 USA

GRAPHIS BOOK CONTEST, C/O CRONAT, PARC 3, F-68870 BARTENHEIM FRANCE